On the Contrary

On the Contrary
Critical Essays, 1987–1997

Paul M. Churchland and Patricia S. Churchland

A Bradford Book
The MIT Press
Cambridge, Massachusetts
London, England

This book was set in Sabon on the Monotype "Prism Plus" PostScript Imagesetter by Asco Trade Typesetting Ltd., Hong Kong, and was printed and bound in the United States of America.

Library of Congress Cataloging-in-Publication Data

Churchland, Paul M., 1942–
  On the contrary: critical essays, 1987–1997 / Paul M. Churchland
  and Patricia S. Churchland.
    p. cm.
  "A Bradford book."
  Includes bibliographical references and index.
  ISBN 0-262-03254-6 (hardcover : alk. paper)
  1. Philosophy of mind. 2. Science—Philosophy. I. Churchland,
Patricia Smith. II. Title.
BD418.3.C473   1998
128'.2—dc21   97-40386
                                                      CIP

For Harry Stanton,

who stands now as Plato's ideal Form, to which lesser publishers may only approximate. He had the wisdom and the character to launch book after book in search of truth instead of profit. A half-dozen disciplines and an entire generation of authors mourn his passing. Thank you, Harry, from all of us.

Contents

Preface

A book-length treatise has its own rightful gravity, no doubt, but the most useful and revealing of anyone's writings are often those much shorter essays penned in conflict with or criticism of one's professional colleagues. There one is compelled to confront the opposition without the elaborate staging that a larger treatise permits, and without the benefit of premises that may be alien to a broad audience.

The eighteen short essays here collected were all written as critical responses to a variety of philosophical positions advanced by some two dozen distinguished philosophical theorists. Almost all of these theorists are still living, and all of them, without exception, are held by us in high regard. The many scholars here addressed are our academic colleagues first, and our intellectual adversaries second. Without the sorts of novel theories and broadly based intellectual discussions that their own work has generated, there would be no critical tradition worthy of addressing, and there could be no intellectual progress worthy of the name. We are sensible that the best we can hope for in our own essays is to be a useful part of that collective discussion and perhaps to move it a few notches forward.

These modesties safely in place, it must also be said that we have our own axes to grind and our own theories to defend. The reader of these essays will not be long in discerning a family of positive theoretical and methodological recommendations that unites almost all of their diverse concerns. Still, that is not the principle on which these essays have here been assembled: it is their critical and reactive functions that here are primary. We mean to give our colleagues—or rather, their various philosophical positions—as rough a time as we can responsibly manage.

Criticism is the focal theme, and, less centrally, evoked response to the many interesting criticisms leveled at our own work.

Most of the essays here collected were originally commissioned, so to speak, as occasion pieces and over a period of a decade, for some irresistible symposium, review, or collection. The result was a highly scattered set of publications, many of them in slightly out-of-the-way forums, or in forums outside of philosophy entirely. As well, our best and most considered responses to many of our favorite adversaries were hobbled by their mutual isolation. This book presumes to redress that situation, and to provide a coherent set of critical essays with a single accessible home.

We were not alone in constructing some of these critiques. Several of our colleagues at the University of California, San Diego (UCSD), and several of our present and former graduate students, made profound contributions to the substance of several of the essays. Our thanks to all of them for their wisdom, and especially to V.S. Ramachandran and Rick Grush for allowing us to include the two essays with shared authorship. Thanks finally to three anonymous referees, whose suggestions helped make this a more coherent and accessible volume.

Paul M. Churchland and Patricia S. Churchland

Acknowledgments

We are grateful to the original publishers for permission to reprint material from the following essays: "Folk psychology," in *Companion to the Mind*, ed. S. Guttenplan (Oxford: Blackwells, 1996); "Theory, taxonomy, and methodology," in *Proceedings of the Aristotlean Society* (1988): 313–19; "Evaluating our self-conception," *Mind and Language* (1993): 211–22; "Activation vectors vs. propositional attitudes: How the brain represents reality," *Philosophy and Phenomenological Research* (1992); "Could a machine think?' *Scientific American* (1990): 26–31; "Intertheoretic reduction: A neuroscientist's field guide," *Seminars in the Neurosciences* (1990): 249–56; "Conceptual similarity across sensory and structural diversity: The Lepore/Fodor challenge answered" *Journal of Philosophy* (1998): 5–32; "Betty Crocker's theory of consciousness: A review of John Searle's *The Rediscovery of the Mind*," *London Review of Books* (1994); "The rediscovery of light," *Journal of Philosophy* (1996): 211–28; "Knowing qualia: A reply to Jackson" in *A Neuro-computational Perspective*, P. M. Churchland (Cambridge, MA: MIT Press, 1989): 67–76; "Recent work on consciousness: Philosophical, theoretical, and empirical" *Seminars in Neurology* (1997): 101–8; "Filling in: Why Dennett is wrong," in *Dennett and His Critics*, ed. B. Dahlbom (Oxford: Blackwells, 1993); "Gaps in Penrose's toiling," *Journal of Consciousness Studies* (1995): 10–29; "Feeling reasons" in *The Neurobiology of Decision-Making*, eds. A. R. Damasio et al. (Berlin: Spring-Verlag, 1996); "A deeper unity: Some Feyerabendian themes in neurocomputational form," in *Beyond Reason*, ed. G. Munevar (Netherlands: Kluwer, 1991); 'Reply to Glymour," in *Cognitive Models of Science*, vol. 15 of *Minnestoa Studies in the Philsophy of Science*, ed.

R. Giere (Minneapolis: University of Minnesota Press, 1992); "To transform the phenomena: Feyerabend, proliferation, and recurrent neural nets," *Philosophy of Science* 1(suppl) (1997); "How parapsychology could become a science," *Inquiry* (1987): 27–39.

I

Folk Psychology and Eliminative Materialism

1

Folk Psychology

Paul M. Churchland

"Folk psychology" denotes the prescientific, commonsense conceptual framework that all normally socialized humans deploy in order to comprehend, predict, explain, and manipulate the behavior of humans and the higher animals. This framework includes concepts such as *belief, desire, pain, pleasure, love, hate, joy, fear, suspicion, memory, recognition, anger, sympathy, intention*, and so forth. It embodies our baseline understanding of the cognitive, affective, and purposive nature of people. Considered as a whole, it constitutes our conception of what a person is.

The term "folk psychology" is also intended to portray a parallel with what might be called "folk physics," "folk chemistry," "folk biology," and so forth. The term involves the deliberate implication that there is something *theory*-like about our commonsense understanding in all of these domains. The implication is that the relevant framework is speculative, systematic, and corrigible, that it embodies generalized information, and that it permits explanation and prediction in the fashion of any theoretical framework.

There is little disagreement about the existence of this shared conceptual framework, but there are important disagreements about its nature, its functions, its epistemology, and its future. In particular, the claim that our commonsense conception of human nature is like an empirical *theory* has been strongly contested by a number of writers, as has the related claim that it might be empirically false. These issues are best addressed by rehearsing the history of this notion.

I. Origins of the Idea

The first explicit portrayal of our collective self-conception as importantly theory-like appears in a landmark paper by Wilfrid Sellars (1956). Sellars describes an imaginary stage of human prehistory in which people have acquired the use of language, but have not yet developed the vocabulary for, nor even any conception of, the complex mental states and processes routinely recognized by modern humans. Their explanatory resources for explaining human behavior are limited to a few purely dispositional terms, all of which can be operationally defined (like "is soluble") in terms of some observable circumstance (such as being put in water) that is sufficient for an observable behavior (such as dissolving). For this reason, Sellars refers to these people, pejoratively, as "our Rylean ancestors." They can explain some human behaviors, but only very few. Being limited to a set of operationally defined dispositional concepts, they have no conception of the complex dance of occurrent internal states driving human behavior, no conception of the internal economy that is just waiting to be characterized by a full-blown *theory* of human nature.

As Sellars develops the story, this deficit is repaired by a visionary theorist named, to signify Everyman, "Jones." Taking as his model the overt declarative utterances already current in his society, Jones postulates the existence, within all humans, of covert, utterance-like events called "thoughts." These internal events are postulated to have the same semantic and logical properties as their overt counterparts, and to play an internal role comparable to the ongoing discursive and argumentative role often performed by overt speech. A suitable sequence of such internal events—some rough chain of practical reasoning, for example—is thus fit to explain certain human behaviors as the natural outcome of hidden speechlike antecedents, despite the absence of any overtly voiced practical reasonings preceding the behavior on that occasion.

A further postulation by Jones, this time exploiting the model of external perceptual objects, brings the range of qualitatively distinct *sensations* into the picture. These are said to be internal perceivables, covert objects that can provoke appropriate cognition and action even in the absence of their external public counterparts. Related postulations bring *intentions* onto the scene, and also *beliefs* and *desires* as relatively lasting states of any individual (they are dispositions to have occurrent thoughts and intentions, respectively). In sum, Jones postulates the basic ontology of our current folk psychology, and assigns to its elements their now familiar causal roles, much to the explanatory and predictive advantage of everyone who gains a command of its concepts.

Once learned by everyone, Jones's theory gets a final boost when it turns out that each adept can further learn to make spontaneous *first-person* ascriptions of the new concepts, ascriptions which are strongly consistent with the ascriptions made by others on purely explanatory or third-person criteria.

Jones's society has now reached the same conceptual level that we moderns enjoy. And what has raised them to this position, on Sellars's account, is their acquisition of a novel explanatory framework with a novel internal ontology. Sellars's lesson is that our modern folk psychology has precisely the same epistemological status, logical functions, and modeling ancestry as the framework postulated by Jones in the heroic myth. It is, in short, an empirical theory.

II. Development of the Idea

linked to language

Sellars made much of the fact that our conception of the semantic properties of thoughts is derivative upon an antecedent conception of the semantic properties of overt declarative utterances. Our accounts of semantic properties in general, therefore, should not take the semantic features of thoughts as explanatory primitives fit for illuminating the semantics of overt speech, as is the common impulse (cf. Grice 1957, Searle 1983). Instead, Sellars proposed a conceptual/inferential role account that would provide an independent but parallel explanation for semantics in both domains.

A more salient development of Sellars's account is the novel solution it provides to an old skeptical problem: the problem of other minds. The behaviorist attempt to forge a "logical" connection between inner states and overt behavior, and the argument from analogy's attempt to forge an inductive connection between them, can both be put aside in favour of the quite different *hypothetico-deductive* connection implied by Sellars's account. Third-person ascriptions of mental states are typically *singular explanatory hypotheses* from which we can draw, in the context of folk psychology as a whole, consequences concerning the subject's observable behavior. As with explanatory hypotheses in general, these mentalistic hypotheses are believable exactly to the degree that they are successful in allowing us to explain and to anticipate behavior. In the main, the ascription of mental states to others is explanatorily and predictively successful. So it is reasonable to believe that other humans have mental states. Indeed, on this account the same hypothesis would be similarly reasonable as applied to any creature, human or nonhuman, so long as its behavior yielded to the same explanatory strategy.

If folk psychology (hereinafter FP) is a theory, then its concepts must be embedded in a framework of laws, laws at least tacitly appreciated by those adept in its use. In the '60s and '70s, this inference was imposed on everyone by the unquestioned logical empiricist assumption that any theory is a set of sentences or propositions, typically universal in their logical form. Accordingly, some writers set about to "recover" the laws of FP from our common explanatory practices—from the factors ordinarily appealed to in explanations of human behavior, and from the ways in which they are occasionally subjected to criticism and defense (P. M. Churchland 1970, 1979).

Any search of this kind quickly turns up hundreds of putative laws, all of which have the familiar ring of the obvious. These range from the very simple to the quite complex. For example:

1. People who suffer bodily damage generally feel pain.
2. People who are angry are generally impatient.
3. People who fear that P generally hope that not-P.
4. People who desire that P, and believe that Q is a means to P, and have no overriding desires or preferred strategies, will generally try to bring it about that Q.

These "laws," and thousands more like them, were claimed to sustain commonsense explanations and predictions in the standard deductive-nomological or "covering-law" fashion. And the specific content of those laws was claimed to account for the relevance of the explanatory factors standardly appealed to in our daily practice. Examination of the fine logical structure of the many FP laws involving the propositional attitudes also revealed deep parallels with the logical structure of laws in the various mathematical sciences (P. M. Churchland 1979, 1981). Further, the portrait of FP as a network of causal laws dovetailed neatly with the emerging philosophy of mind called functionalism (Putnam 1960; Fodor 1968; Lewis 1972).

Critics often objected that such "causal laws" are either, strictly speaking, false, or else only vacuously true by reason of sheer analyticity or implicit *ceteris paribus* clauses (Wilkes 1981, 1984; Haldane 1988). But defenders replied that folk-theoretic laws should not be expected to be anything more than rough-and-ready truths, and that theoretical laws in every science are to some degree qualified by *ceteris paribus* clauses, or restricted in their application to standard or to idealized situations. All told, the developing case for FP's theoretical status was compelling.

III. Consequences of the Idea

These proved alarming, at least to the idea's many critics. First, Sellars's account yields a modern version of the Kantian claim that one can know oneself, in consciousness, only as one represents oneself with one's own concepts. On Sellars's view, one represents oneself with the concepts of FP, a speculative empirical theory. Introspective knowledge is thus denied any special epistemological status: one's spontaneous first-person psychological judgments are no better (and no worse) than one's spontaneous observation judgments generally. They are all hostage to the quality of the background conceptual scheme in which they are framed. This contingency did not trouble Sellars. He was entirely confident that FP was empirically true. But it does trouble some others who are less willing to roll the dice against future experience.

A second consequence is that the traditional mind-body problem emerges as a straightforward scientific question—as a question of how the theoretical framework of FP will turn out to be related to whatever neuropsychological theory might emerge to replace it. If FP reduces smoothly to a materialist successor theory, then the identity theory will be vindicated. If it proves disjunctively so "reducible," then functionalism will be vindicated. If it proves irreducible by reason of finding no adequate materialist successor at all, then some form of dualism will be vindicated. And if it proves irreducible by reason of failing utterly to map onto its successful materialist successor theory, then a position called eliminative materialism will be vindicated. The successor theory will then displace Jones's antique theory in our social and explanatory practices, and the ontology of FP will go the way of phlogiston, caloric fluid, and the crystal spheres of ancient astronomy.

This eliminative possibility was urged as real fairly early in the discussion (Feyerabend 1963b; Rorty 1965). Later it was defended as empirically the most likely outcome (P. M. Churchland 1981). The bare possibility of a wholesale rejection of FP is of course a simple consequence of FP's speculative theoretical status. The positive likelihood of its rejection requires more substantial empirical premises. To this end, Churchland cited three major empirical failings of FP.

First, FP fails utterly to explain a considerable variety of central psychological phenomena: mental illness, sleep, creativity, memory, intelligence differences, and the many forms of learning, to cite just a few. A true theory should not have such yawning explanatory gaps. Second, FP has not progressed significantly in at least 2500 years. The Greeks appear to have used essentially the same framework that we deploy. If anything, FP has been in steady retreat during this period, as intentional explanations have been withdrawn from yet one domain after another—from the heavenly bodies, from the wind and the sea, from a plethora of minor gods and spirits, from the visitation of disease, and so forth. FP has not shown the expansion and developmental fertility one expects from a true theory. Last, FP shows no sign of being smoothly integrable with the emerging synthesis of the several physical, chemical, biological, physiological, and neurocomputational sciences. Since active coherence with the rest of what we presume to know is a central measure of credibility for any theory, FP's emerging wallflower status bodes ill for its future.

That FP is fated to be judged empirically false is the most intriguing and alarming of the three major consequences of Sellars's original idea, but clearly it is not a direct consequence of that idea alone. It requires additional premises about the empirical failings of FP. These additional premises can and have been hotly contested (Kitcher 1984a; Dennett 1981; Horgan and Woodward 1985). Most of these authors are quite prepared to accept or even to urge the theoretical nature of FP, but they are unanimous in their defense of its empirical integrity and rough truth.

As these authors see it, FP is simply not responsible for explaining most of the puzzling phenomena listed two paragraphs ago. Those problems are set aside as the burden of some other theory. To the second complaint, it is replied that folk psychology has indeed changed somewhat over the centuries, although its approximate truth has never required of it more than minor adjustments. And to the third complaint there are voiced a number of *tertiam quids*—proposed alternatives to the stark choice, "Either reduce FP, or eliminate it." Here the varieties of nonreductive materialism—functionalism and anomalous monism, for example—play a prominent role (see especially Fodor 1975; Dennett 1981; Davidson 1970; and Clark 1989).

A more radical and purely a priori response to eliminative materialism dismisses it as simply incoherent, on grounds that in embracing or stating its case it must presuppose the integrity of the very framework it proposes to eliminate (Baker 1987; Beghossian 1990). Consider, for example, the evident conflict between the eliminativist's apparent *belief* that FP is false, and his simultaneous claim that there *are no* beliefs.

A straightforward response concedes the real existence of this and many other conflicts, but denies that they signal anything wrong with the idea that FP might someday be replaced. Such conflicts signal only the depth and far-reaching nature of the conceptual change being proposed. Insofar, they are only to be expected, and they do nothing to mark FP as unreplaceable. Even if current FP were to permit no coherent denial of itself within its own theoretical vocabulary, a new psychological framework need have no such limitation where the denial of FP is concerned. So long as a coherent, comprehensive alternative to FP can be articulated and explored, then no argument a priori can rightly single out FP as uniquely true of cognitive creatures.

In this connection it is worth noting that a similar "incoherence argument" could be deployed to permit the uncritically conservative defense of any framework for understanding cognition, no matter how inadequate it might be, so long as it happened to enjoy the irrelevant distinction of being currently in use by the people attempting to criticize it. In short, the incoherence argument covertly begs the question in favor of current FP, the very framework being called into question (P. M. Churchland 1981; Devitt 1990).

This response returns us to the empirical issues raised two paragraphs ago. Whether FP is false and whether it will fail to reduce are empirical issues whose decisive settlement must flow from experimental research and theoretical development, not from any arguments a priori. The empirical jury is still out and there is ample room for reasonable people to disagree.

However, it must be noted that, according to the most fertile theoretical accounts currently under exploration in computational neuroscience (Anderson and Rosenfeld 1988; P. S. Churchland and Sejnowski 1992), the basic unit of occurrent cognition is apparently not the sentence-like state, but rather the high-dimensional neuronal activation vector (that is, a pattern of excitation levels across a large population of neurons). And the basic unit of cognitive processing is apparently not the inference from sentence to sentence, but rather the synapse-induced transformation of large activation vectors into other such vectors. It is not certain that such accounts of cognition are true, nor even if they are, that FP will fail to find some reduction thereto. But recent science already suggests that Jones's linguaformal theory—folk psychology—fails utterly to capture the *basic* kinematics and dynamics of human and animal cognition.

IV. Criticism and Defense of the Idea

Many philosophers resist entanglement in these empirical issues and reject the possibility of FP's demise by rejecting the idea that FP is an empirical theory in the first place. Some play down the predictive and explanatory role of FP, and focus attention instead on the many social activities conducted with its vocabulary, such as promising, greeting, joking, threatening, congratulating, insulting, reassuring, inviting, provoking, sympathizing, questioning, demanding, cajoling, sniping, offering, advising, directing, confiding, and so forth (Wilkes 1981, 1984). On this view, FP is less an empirical theory than an intricate social *practice*, one in which all normal humans learn to participate (see also Putnam 1988). A supporting consideration is the clearly *normative* character of many of the so-called laws of FP, a feature at odds with the presumably descriptive character of any empirical theory. And if FP is not a theory, then there is no danger that it might be false and hence no question of its being eliminated.

There is much to said for the positive half of this portrayal of FP, and it is surely counterproductive to resist it. But its negative half betrays a shallow understanding of what theories are and what the command of one typically involves. Since Thomas Kuhn's 1962 book, *The Structure of Scientific Revolutions*, it has been evident that learning the theories peculiar to any discipline is not solely or even primarily a matter of learning a set of laws and principles: it is a matter of learning a complex social practice, of entering a specialized community with shared values and expectations, both of the world and of each other. One slowly acquires the right skills of recognition and categorization, the right skills of instrumental and symbolic manipulation, the right sorts of expectations, and the right standards of communication and evaluation.

[handwritten margin note: OK! Entrance into a culture!]

Moreover, during normal science the exemplars of achieved understanding play a strongly normative role, both in setting the standards for further understanding, and even in imposing a standard on nature itself. Such peripheral phenomena as may fail to conform to the current paradigm are regularly counted as deviant, abnormal, pathological, or at least nonideal. And so it is with humans whose cognitive and social behavior fails to live up to the baseline expectations embodied in FP.

The contrast drawn between a "theory" and a "practice" is therefore a false and misleading one. Theories typically sustain a complex family of practices in their proprietary domain, and practices are typically rooted in a shared and systematic understanding of the domain in which they are conducted. Part of the point of drawing out the specific theoretical commitments of FP was to *explain* the details of our actual social practices, especially where the anticipation, comprehension, and manipulation of human behavior is concerned (Churchland 1970).

The "criticism from practice" may be easily turned aside, but a different line of criticism cuts more deeply against the original claim of theoretical status for FP. This complaint focuses attention on the large number of laws that presumably must be stored in any FP adept, and on the psychological unreality of the idea that one's running comprehension and anticipation of one's ongoing social situation involves the continual application of appropriate general sentences somehow retrieved from memory, and the repeated performance of complex deductions from these and other premises in order to achieve the desired comprehension and anticipation (Gordon 1986; P. M. Churchland 1988a; Goldman 1992). People are generally unable to articulate the "laws" on which their running comprehension is alleged to rest, and it is in any case mysterious how they could perform such prodigious feats of retrieval and deductive processing in the mere twinklings of time typically involved in our ongoing social commerce.

This wholly genuine difficulty moves Gordon and Goldman to defend a refurbished version of the argument from analogy, called the "simulation theory," as an account of our knowledge of other minds. The problems with this venerable approach are familiar. The capacity for knowledge of one's own mind may already presuppose the general knowledge that FP embodies (Strawson 1958), and a generalization from one's own case may be both logically too feeble and explanatorily too narrow in its scope to account for the full range and robustness of one's general knowledge of human nature (Churchland 1984). But there is an alternative response to our difficulty about knowing and deploying lawlike sentences, one that strikes at the legacy of logical empiricism itself.

The difficulties in claiming FP as an explanatory theory stem not from that claim itself, but rather from the logical empiricist's crudely linguaformal conception of theories as sets of sentences, and his correlative conception of explanation as the deduction of the explanandum from such sentences. The psychological unreality of this picture, noted above in connection with FP explanations, is in fact a chronic defect of the logical empiricist's account in *every* theoretical domain in which cognitive agents are adepts, including the established sciences. This defect, and others, provide compelling grounds for rejecting entirely the classical picture of what theoretical knowledge is and how it is deployed on specific occasions for recognition, explanation, or prediction (Van Fraassen 1980; P. M. Churchland 1989b, 1989c). This critical assessment coheres with the already existing positive epistemological traditions established by Kuhn in America, by Heidegger on the Continent, and more recently by the connectionists in the field of artificial intelligence and cognitive neurobiology. FP can thus continue to be counted an explanatory theory, but the claim that it has this status needs to be reformulated within a new and independently motivated story of what theoretical knowledge, explanatory understanding, and pragmatic skills really are.

V. Transformation of the Idea

As sketched at the close of section III, the emerging account of how brains embody information has nothing to do with sentences, or with states that are even remotely sentence-like. A familiar analogy may help introduce this alternative account.

A television screen embodies a sequence of representations which are nonsentential in nature, in their syntax as well as their semantics. A specific TV representation has no logical structure: rather, it is a specific pattern of activation or brightness levels across a large population of tiny screen pixels. A human retina embodies a representation in much the same sense: what matters is the *pattern of activations* across the photoreceptors. These two examples are overtly pictorial in their "semantics," but this is an incidental feature of the examples chosen. Tastes are also coded as a pattern of activations across the several types of gustatory neurons on the tongue, sounds are coded as a pattern of activations across the auditory neurons in the cochlea, and smells are coded as a pattern of activations across the olfactory neurons, but none of these representations is "pictorial" in the familar two-dimensional spatial sense. And yet such pattern coding—or *vector* coding, as it is commonly called—is extremely powerful. Since each vectorial representation is one permutation of the possible values of its elements, the number of distinct things representable explodes as a power function of the number of available elements. Think how many distinct pictures a TV screen can display, using only 200,000 pixels, and think how many more the retina can embody, using fully 100 million pixels.

The suggestion of the preceding is that the brain's basic mode of occurrent representation is the activation vector across a proprietary population of neurons—retinal neurons, olfactory neurons, auditory neurons, and so forth. Such activation vectors have a virtue beyond their combinatorially explosive powers of representation. They are ideally suited to participate in a powerful mode of *computation*, namely, vector-to-vector *transformation*. An activation pattern across one neural population (e.g., at the retina) can be transformed into a distinct activation pattern (e.g., at the visual cortex) by way of the axonal fibers projecting from the first population to the second, and by way of the millions of carefully tuned synaptic connections that those fibers make with the neurons at the second or target population.

That second population of neurons can project to a third, and those to a fourth, and so on. In this way, a sensory activation pattern can undergo many principled transformations before it finally finds itself, profoundly transformed by the many intervening synaptic encounters, reincarnated as a vector of activations in a population of *motor* neurons, neurons whose immediate effect is to direct the symphony of muscles that produce coherent bodily behavior appropriate to the original input vector at the sensory periphery. The animal dodges a seen snowball, freezes at the sound of a predator, or moves forward at the smell of food, all as a result of its well-tuned synaptic connections and their repeated transformation of its representational vectors.

Those synaptic connections constitute a second domain of stored information in the brain, a domain beyond the occurrent domain of fleeting neuronal activations. The well-tuned synaptic connections embody all of the creature's general knowledge and *skills*: of interpretation, of recognition, of anticipation, and of coherent, interactive behavior. Here also is where *learning* enters the picture. Learning is not a matter of assembling a vast mass of sentences, as on the classical account. Instead, learning is a matter of configuring the trillions of synaptic connections between neurons so that incoming sensory vectors are automatically and almost instantaneously transformed into appropriate "prototype" vectors at the higher populations of cortical neurons. Such prototype vectors constitute the brain's learned perceptual and explanatory categories. These prototypes typically involve more information than is strictly present in the sensory input on any given occasion, and they thus constitute ampliative interpretations of that input, interpretations that place the input into an antecedently prepared context and fund expectations of features so far unperceived.

Further transformations produce further activation vectors or vector sequences in downstream neuronal populations, and these lead quite quickly to appropriate motor responses, since activation vectors are also an ideal means of directing and coordinating large populations of muscles. All of this happens in milliseconds because the relevant transformations are achieved by massively parallel processing: the many elements in any input pattern go through the matrix of synaptic connections simultaneously.

This brief sketch indicates how neurocomputational ideas suggest a unified account of perceptual recognition, explanatory understanding, prediction, and motor control—an account untroubled by problems of retrieval or speed of processing. The motivation for this account derives primarily from its apparent success in accounting for the functional significance of the brain's microstructure, and the striking cognitive behaviors displayed by artificial neural networks. A secondary motive derives from the illumination it brings to traditional issues in epistemology and the philosophy of science. To learn a theoretical framework is to configure one's synaptic connections in such a fashion as to partition the space of possible neuronal activation patterns into a system or hierarchy of prototypes. And to achieve explanatory understanding of an event is to have activated an appropriate prototype vector from the waiting hierarchy (P. M. Churchland 1989c).

Finally, a much smaller motive derives from the relief this view provides to our earlier difficulty with the theoretical status of FP. No longer need FP labor under its archaic portrayal as a set of universally quantified sentences, and no longer need its functions be falsely cast in terms of laborious deductions. The claim that FP is a corrigible theory need not be hobbled by its initial logical positivist dress. Instead, we can claim that FP, like any other theory, is a family of learned vectorial prototypes, prototypes that sustain recognition of current reality, anticipation of future reality, and manipulation of ongoing reality.

As the heroic myth of Jones underscores, FP does indeed portray human cognition in terms of overtly sentential prototypes, viz., in terms of the many propositional attitudes. But there is no reason why it must be *correct* in so representing our cognition, nor in representing itself in particular. Perhaps the internal kinematics and dynamics of human and animal cognition is not at all like the sentential dance portrayed in FP. This recalls the position of eliminative materialism discussed earlier. Perhaps we harbor instead a kinematics of activation patterns and a dynamics of vector-to-vector transformations driven by learned configurations of synaptic connections. Evidently it is not inconceivable that FP might someday be challenged by a better account of human nature. Evidently the process is already underway. Jones would surely approve.

2

Theory, Taxonomy, and Methodology: A Reply to Haldane's "Understanding Folk"

Paul M. Churchland

I must begin by thanking John Haldane for his very thorough and careful reading of my work (1988), and for the intelligence and fairness of his critical comments (Haldane 1988). I shall try to live up to the standard of critical exchange he has set.

I

The issue at stake between Haldane and me is whether the commonsense conceptual framework that we use to understand persons has the epistemological status and the functional character of those conceptual frameworks we call *theories*. To support a negative answer to this question, one might try to find some feature that is characteristic of theories, but is missing in the case of "folk psychology." Haldane lays the groundwork for such a strategy on p. 231, where he says:

What, then, is a *theory*? For present purposes the following characterization will serve. *An empirical theory is an abstract structure containing a set of predicates P, and a set of law-like generalizations G in which the elements of P occur essentially. The members of G include both inner principles, covering the behavior of postulated unobservables; and bridge principles, relating the latter to observable phenomena. The terms in P are largely, or wholly, defined by their roles in the principles of G.* [Italics his.]

This definition of a *theory* is drawn from the logical empiricist tradition, and it is importantly flawed in its implication that theories are always or typically about *un*observable things, things that always or typically need to be related, by bridge laws, to a level of observable phenomena that antedates and is conceptually independent of the entities postulated by the theory. The implication is that it is these antecedently conceived observable phenomena that form the explanatory target for any aspirant theory, and the explanatory bull's eye for any successful theory.

This positivistic conception of theories has been subjected to severe criticism during the last twenty-five years (see Hanson 1958; Feyerabend 1962, 1963b; Kuhn 1962; P. M. Churchland 1979, 1988b). It is flawed in many respects, but most relevantly in its failure to appreciate that new theories often *bring with them* a novel and proprietary vocabulary for describing the observable world, a vocabulary that can augment or occasionally even displace the old observational vocabulary. A dramatic example of this is Einstein's special theory of relativity (STR), which reconfigures all of the basic *observational* concepts of mechanics: spatial length, temporal duration, mass, and every other notion whose definition depends on them (force, energy, wavelength, frequency, and so on). These are all one-place predicates within the classical conception. But they are all replaced by two-place predicates within STR, predicates that apply to objects only relative to an inertial frame of reference. In the end, STR is not required to explain the observational data as antecedently conceived. It properly explains the data only as newly conceived and described within STR itself.

This flaw is of central importance in the context of the present issue, because Haldane subsequently raises the objection that typical descriptions of human behavior are not purely kinematical, but make systematic use of concepts that strongly imply personhood already (pp. 234–7, 250). That is to say, the descriptions of human behavior relevant to folk psychological explanations are typically not conceptually independent of the concepts of folk psychology. Rather, they use concepts that are a proper part of folk psychology.

This is entirely true, but it is no objection to the thesis that folk psychology is a theory, and no indication that its explanatory profile is in any way atypical. On the contrary, our theoretical convictions regularly configure, and reconfigure, the way we describe the data-to-be-explained. STR provides one example, as we saw, and modern chemistry provides a second. It is a rare chemist who does not use the taxonomy of the periodic table and the combinatorial lexicon of chemical compounds to describe both the observable facts and their theoretical underpinnings alike. For starters, one can just smell hydrogen sulfide, taste sodium chloride, feel any base, and identify copper, aluminum, iron, and gold by sight. And this theory is barely two hundred years old. Given the great age of folk psychology, a systematic conceptual invasion of the explanandum domain is exactly what one should expect to find.

Haldane briefly considers this general construal of the situation (p. 235, lines 20–5), but immediately says, "This interpretation is unhappy, however, since if observable behavior is included within the domain of conscious intelligence then nothing non-psychological remains as the phenomena for which the hypothesis would serve as an explanation." This objection simply repeats the false conception criticized above. As well insist that STR is not an explanatory theory on grounds that, if observable masses- and frequencies- and lengths-relative-to-our-inertial-frame are all included within the domain of relativistic phenomena (as they are), then there remains nothing *non*relativistic for which STR might serve as an explanation.

II

A second major issue between us concerns the theory-ladenness of our perceptual and introspective discriminations generally. Haldane suggests that the range of perceptual concepts possible for us may be very narrowly constrained by the specific sensitivity of the transducers that activate them. Such concepts, he concludes, might be free of potentially indictable theory, since all they need do is "reproduce" one's natural preconceptual discriminations.

This, I believe, is a vain hope. Those peripheral, transductional discriminations are real, but they radically underdetermine such concepts as they may eventually come to activate. Mary Hesse gave a compelling argument for this some twenty years ago (Hesse 1970, pp. 35–77). Her argument began with the fact that "is similar to" is not a transitive relation. Accordingly, the boundaries that divide one perceptual category from another, and from various fakes and illusions, will be sensorily indeterminate and must be marked off by factors beyond those found in considerations of phenomenological similarity alone. They must be marked off by *systematic* factors: by the speculative imposition of a rich network of lawlike relations, relations that connect the proper limits of each category to the objective occurrence of other categories, and to conditions "normal" for its reliable perceptual application. Such speculative and systematic—that is, such *theoretical*—constraints must of course answer to the global character of one's ongoing experience, but it is a familiar fact that overarching theory is epistemically underdetermined by finite experience. Accordingly, there is in principle always *room* for dramatic changes in the observational taxonomy one embraces. It is never fixed by the bare and ambiguous "sensory manifold" alone.

Current research in cognitive neurobiology sustains and amplifies Hesse's analytical insight, in ways I shall now explain. We can specify the relevant "space" of possible preconceptual visual input states, for example, by assigning a unique axis to each rod and cone in the retina, an axis that measures the level of activation of its proprietary cell. The resulting abstract hyperspace will have roughly 10^8 dimensions (since that is the number of light-sensitive cells in each retina), and at least 10^{10^8} functionally distinct points in it (since each cell admits of at least 10 distinct activation levels). Each point in that space will represent a distinct global state of the retina, a particular global pattern or "vector" of cellular activation levels.

A priori, there are indefinitely many ways in which this vast and continuous space might be partitioned into similarity classes, that is, into a cognitive taxonomy. There are so ridiculously *many* dimensions of potentially relevant similarity and difference that some ruthless selection is required. A posteriori, the job is in fact done at the next population of neurons to which the peripheral cells project, and at subsequent populations in the processing hierarchy. It is these subsequent layers of cells that dictate which incoming vectors will be processed as importantly similar, and which as distinct. What determines the categorial groupings is the specific configuration of the myriad *synaptic weights* that connect the input population to the next population. It is the weight configuration that does the selective processing (see P. M. Churchland 1989b for a summary of how neural networks do this).

But that weight configuration is not directly fixed by the character of the peripheral transducers themselves. On the contrary, synaptic weights are known to be plastic, and they are shaped by long-term learning. Research into the behavior of artificial neural networks, at least, shows an enormous range and dramatic variability in the perceptual taxonomies that can be developed in any neuronal layer downstream from the input layer. It all depends on the specific profile of the ongoing experience fed to the network, and most important, on the specific schedule of reinforcement to which it is subjected. Here, too, exactly which observational taxonomy emerges is dictated by long-term experience and considerations of global coherence.

Conceivably we are not so plastic as the artificial networks; conceivably our weight configurations, like our peripheral transducers, are genetically fixed in some way. This would change the epistemological situation very little. Plasticity aside, any configuration of weights constitutes a speculative *theory* in its own right, since it imposes one taxonomy upon the inputs at the expense of trillions of other taxonomies that might have been imposed instead. On the neurocomputational view here being sketched, a conceptual framework or theory can usefully be seen as identical to a specific configuration of synaptic weights (for an extended discussion of this view, see P. M. Churchland 1989a, chapters 9 and 11). And since no cognition/computation takes place except by passing activation vectors through banks of synapses weighted in some specific configuration, no cognition/computation can take place in the absence of a specific theory, one out of trillions of possible alternative theories none of which is dictated by the peripheral stimulations themselves. Accordingly, even in the unlikely event that all our weights were genetically fixed, "hardwired" as it were, our perceptual discriminations would still be theory-laden. A hard-wired theory is still a theory.

In sum, our preconceptual discriminations do not provide a natural or pretheoretical taxonomy of classes, to which our cognitive activity must cleave. On the contrary, their transductional behavior radically underdetermines the categories we use. This is so whether we view things phenomenologically (as in Hesse's argument), or neurocomputationally (as in mine). And it is so whether the categories are about the external world, or about our own inner states.

III

Haldane objects to the parallel that I draw between the predicate-forming functors of folk psychology ("believes that *p*") and mathematical physics ("has a mass$_{kg}$ of n"), a parallel aimed at defusing certain prima facie contrasts between folk psychology and paradigmatic theories. The prima facie contrast concerns the existence of the abstract *logical* relation "is rational in the light of" that holds between explanans and explanandum in the case of action explanations, but which is absent in physical explanations. My response was to point out the existence of the abstract *mathematical* relation "is the quotient of" (and many others) that holds between explanans and explanandum in the case of certain electrical explanations (and in many others). Abstract relations thus being commonplace and various in theoretical explanations, folk psychology therefore earns no atheoretical distinction by boasting one.

Haldane's objection here is somewhat opaque to me, and I am not entirely sure I will do it justice. He insists that the proposition p is essential to identifying the belief-that-p, but seems to think that the number V is not essential to identifying the voltage-of-V. Beliefs, according to him, are intrinsically propositional, while voltages are not intrinsically numerical (p. 246, bottom paragraph).

I am unable to see the difference here implied. Numbers are indeed essential to specific voltages (or masses, or velocities, or temperatures), exactly as propositions are essential to specific beliefs (or desires, or preferences). The former case involves neither more nor less contingency than does the latter. I reaffirm the parallel and remain confident it will bear scrutiny. Folk psychology, if seen as a system of rough laws, shares profound structural similarities with theories in mathematical physics.

IV

Haldane defends the ideology of folk psychology (pp. 251–2) by arguing that it is unreasonable to criticize it for explanatory and predictive failures beyond the sphere of common observation, or beyond the purposes it was intended to serve.

This is an unfortunate defense, as can be seen from other uses of the same strategy. One can defend Ptolemy's ragtag astronomy (as Ptolemy *did*) by insisting that it was never supposed to address the real physics, or the actual causes, or the complete story of astronomical behavior, and by insisting that it properly serves only the narrow interest of predicting the angular positions of the planets as seen from Earth. One can defend any hangdog theory by this strategy, so long as it has some paltry success for some benighted purpose within some sheltered domain. Folk psychology deserves, and requires, a more discriminating defense than this.

Haldane's defense is also *logically* insupportable. Any theory whatsoever has an infinitely large class of logical consequences, and if a single one of them is false, then the theory itself must be false, however far beyond common experience or domestic concern its falsifying consequence may lie.

Lastly, it is an inappropriate defense, because many of folk psychology's explanatory failures lie right at home. Think of sleep, mental illness, perception, moral character, learning, memory, sensorimotor coordination, etc., etc. These are all as common as rainfall, and of pressing practical importance to us all. But they remain largely opaque from within folk psychology.

V

Haldane diagnoses my overall metaphysical and methodological position as resulting from a fixation on the *matter* of persons, at the expense of properly considering their *form*. The truth is that I entirely share his concern with "essential form." But I am interested in getting a deeper and more accurate account of our essential form than we currently possess, and I am prepared to examine the material and functional organization of our matter in hopes of finding such an account.

There are precedents for such a methodology. Let me recall one to the reader's attention. I begin with a relevant contrast. The medieval alchemists had a taxonomy of alchemical forms ("mercury," "sulfur," "yellow arsenic," "sal ammoniac") with which they explained and manipulated the behavior of common substances. The base matter that harbored these forms was of little practical or theoretical interest to these sages, for reasons not unlike those suggested by Haldane in the case of psychology. From their perspective, it was the forms that were important, not the underlying matter.

By contrast, theorists such as Black, Boyle, Lavoisier, and Dalton focused on the *matter* of common substances, on its physical properties, and on the profile of its combinatorial behavior. They eventually came up with a conception of common substances that swept the alchemical vision permanently aside. They sought an improved account of "essential form," and they were strikingly successful.

In trying to construct a science of the mind, I embrace the methodology of Lavoisier and Dalton. Haldane appears to favor a methodology more like that of the alchemists. But Haldane, like me, is a student of history. After savoring its provenance, I doubt he will favor that methodology for long.

3

Evaluating Our Self-Conception

Paul M. Churchland

The realization that all of human knowledge is speculative and provisional is a highly liberating insight. It is also well-founded. We have the repeated empirical lessons of our own intellectual history to press the point upon us. And at both the intentional and the neural levels we have sufficient theoretical insight into the nature of human cognition to explain why its speculative and provisional character is almost certainly inevitable. This recognition encourages a modest humility about the ultimate integrity of our current conceptions and convictions, while it fosters a modest optimism about our cognitive prospects in the centuries to come.

Such liberal cognitive sentiments are widespread in the current philosophical climate. Indeed, they are almost universal. But for some philosophers they are sorely tested when the question at issue is the possible displacement of our familiar *self*-conception—a conception that portrays each human as a self-conscious rational economy of propositional attitudes. Like the self-proclaimed liberal family confronting the unexpectedly alien dinner guest (and potential son-in-law!), the discomfort level gets elevated to unseemly heights and prior principle tends to evaporate in a flurry of contrived evasions. Such "bad faith" or "inauthenticity," I shall argue here, dominates current discussions of eliminative materialism (EM).

Not all resistance is of this inauthentic kind. Some philosophers are prepared to accept and even to insist on the theoretical character of our commonsense folk psychology (FP), while maintaining that, on the whole, the empirical evidence still indicates that FP, qua theory, is at least roughly *true*. This approach at least locates the issue where it should be located—in the empirical trenches. There is no bad faith shown here. Fodor (1991) is a clear example of this position, as is Devitt (1990), Horgan and Woodward (1985), and Clark (1989).

Nor is one bound to accept the "liberal cognitive sentiments" sketched above. It is still possible, perhaps, to argue for some kind of Kantian inevitability about the framework features of FP, or some Cartesian incorrigibility in our capacity for introspection. There need be nothing inauthentic about declining EM if one declines the epistemology that makes it possible. If one is thus, shall we say, a child of an earlier era, this may seem paleolithic and regrettable to some of us, but it is not bad faith for such a philosopher to insist on some special epistemological status for FP.

Neither of these positions is the prime target of this essay, though I am deeply interested in both. I wish rather to focus on a series of objections to EM that profess to remain *faithful* to the contemporary epistemological perspective of my first paragraph while still contriving some way for our current self-conception to *evade* the standards of epistemological evaluation that naturally go with that perspective. These, I submit, are the genuinely *in*authentic objections. They have achieved some currency and they need unmasking. Let us take them in turn.

I. The "Functional Kinds" Objection

This objection proceeds from the not implausible conjecture that the taxonomy of psychological kinds embedded in FP is most accurately construed as a taxonomy of functional kinds rather than of genuinely natural kinds. It is then pointed out, quite correctly, that the ontological integrity of functional kinds—such as *chair*, *mousetrap*, or *bungalow*—is not contingent on their finding a smooth intertheoretic reduction to some natural science of the underlying substrate (because the relevant functional properties might be realizable in a variety of substrates with a variety of dynamical resources). The conclusion is then drawn that FP has nothing to fear from any future failure to find a smooth explanatory reduction within, say, computational neuroscience. The principle, "Reduce, or be eliminated," on which EM is said to rest, is rejected as unacceptable.

One will find straightforward versions of this objection in Putnam (1988) and Searle (1992). It is a popular objection and it is sufficiently obvious that my original 1981 paper on EM addressed it at some length (pp. 78–82, showing the ease of constructing a parallel "vindication" of the dear departed alchemical kinds). I stand by that original response, but let me here try a more direct approach.

In fact, the case for EM rests on no such overblown principle as "Reduce, or be eliminated," at least if this be interpreted as a demand for a type-type reduction. Such a draconian principle would banish all functional kinds at once. But the defender of EM is neither ignorant of nor hostile to the existence of functional kinds. The worry is not that FP kinds are too much like the (legitimately functional) kinds *chair* and *bungalow*; the worry is that FP kinds are too much like the (genuinely uninstantiated) kinds *phlogiston* and *caloric fluid*.

The primary worry, in other words, is that FP is a radically *false* representation of the kinematical and dynamical reality within each of us. One relevant *symptom* of FP's radical falsity would be its inevitable failure to find even a rough or disjunctive reduction within an explanatorily superior neuroscientific successor theory. Further symptoms of possible falsity would be FP's explanatory, predictive, and manipulative failures. Taken together, such symptoms could constitute a serious empirical case against FP, as they might against any other theory. That case will have to be evaluated as a whole, with the matter of reductive relations to neuroscience (or their absence) being but one very important part of it. Focusing our attention on the ontological status of chairs and bungalows simply deflects our attention away from the need and the obligation to pursue that broad empirical evaluation of FP. And it misrepresents the rationale behind EM.

It misleads in a further respect. The physical tokens of any functional kind are typically manufactured to meet our functional specifications and typically there is no intelligible question of whether our functional concept is adequate to the behavioral reality the manufactured object displays. No one feels a need to evaluate our concept *paring knife*, for example, in order to see if it lives up to the structural and behavioral reality of real paring knives. The onus of match is entirely in the other direction. Casting FP kinds as functional kinds implicitly portrays them as having a similar "authority" and empirical "invulnerability."

But human beings and animals are not artifacts. We are natural objects. Accordingly, while our internal economy may indeed be an abstract, high-level functional economy, realizable in many other substrates, *it remains a wholly empirical question whether our current FP conception of that internal economy is an accurate representation of its real structure.* Let us agree then that FP kinds are abstractly functional. This changes the situation in no relevant way. The issue of their collective descriptive integrity must still be addressed. The objection from functional kinds, as outlined above, is just a smoke screen that obscures our continuing obligation to evaluate the empirical integrity of FP and to compare its virtues and failings with competing representations of what cognitive activity consists in. It cannot serve as a *defense* of FP against real or prospective empirical criticisms.

II.   The "Self-Defeating" Objection

I am unsure who originated this one. Rudder-Baker (1987) has certainly pressed it home at greatest length, but many others have urged it in many forms, beginning with the audience at the very first public presentation of my 1981 paper, in draft, in 1980, at the University of Ottawa. A purely a priori objection, it dismisses EM as incoherent on grounds that, in arguing, stating, or embracing its case, it must presuppose the integrity of the very conceptual framework it proposes to eliminate. Consider, for example, the evident conflict between the eliminativist's apparent *belief* that FP is false, and his concurrent claim that there *are no* beliefs.

These and many other "pragmatic paradoxes" do indeed attend the eliminativist's current position. But they signal only the depth and far-reaching character of the conceptual revolution that EM would have us contemplate, not some flaw within EM itself. Logically, the situation is entirely foursquare. Assume Q (the framework of FP assumptions); argue legitimately from Q and other empirical premises to the conclusion that not-Q; and then conclude not-Q by the principle of reductio ad absurdum. [We get (Q ⊃ not-Q) by conditional proof, which reduces to (not-Q v not-Q), which reduces to (not-Q).]

If the "self-defeating" objection were correct in this instance, it would signal a blanket refutation of all formal reductios, because they all "presuppose what they are trying to deny." Such a demonstration would be a major contribution to logic, and not just to the philosophy of mind. A more balanced opinion, I suggest, is that this venerable principle of argument is threatened neither in general, nor in the case at issue.

Let us concede then, or even insist, that current FP permits no coherent or tension-free denial of itself within its own theoretical vocabulary. As we have just seen, this buys it no proof against empirical criticism. Moreover, a *new* psychological framework—appropriately grounded in computational neuroscience, perhaps—need have no such limitation where the coherent denial of FP is concerned. We need only construct it, and move in. We can then express criticisms of FP that are entirely free of internal conflicts. This was the aim of EM in the first place. (For a particularly penetrating analysis of this objection by a noneliminativist, see Devitt 1990.)

The overdrawn character of this objection shows itself in one further respect: if it were legitimate, it could be elsewhere employed to prove far too much. To see this, suppose that humankind had used—for understanding what we now call "cognition"—a conceptual framework quite different from and much less successful than our current FP. (At some point in our distant evolutionary past, we must have done so.) It uses "gruntal attitudes," let us suppose, rather than propositional attitudes.

Suppose now that some forward-looking group sets about to develop a new and better conception, one that shapes up in content and structure rather like our current FP. Contemplating the shortcomings of their older conception, and the explanatory promise of the very different new framework, these people (let us call them "eliminative intentionalists") suggest that the older framework be dismissed entirely and the new one be adopted, even in the marketplace.

But alas! A "self-defeating" objection precisely parallel to that observed above can here be constructed that will (a) block, as strictly incoherent, any attempt to reject the older framework, and (b) demand of any new cognitive theory that it be consistent with the older theory already in place. Ironically, that relocated Rudder-Baker objection would then be blocking the adoption of our current propositional-attitude FP!

In fact, such an objection could be mounted to block the displacement of any conceptual framework for cognition whatever, since the same awkwardness—formulating a rejection of a framework within the framework itself—will arise *whatever* conception of cognition one happens to be using. The objection here at issue is an empty and essentially conservative objection, in that it can be used to protect, against radical overthrow, any framework that enjoys the irrelevant distinction of being the framework in use at that time.

III.   The "What Could Falsify It?" Objection

The more modest one's imagination, the more impressive this objection is likely to seem, which should put one on guard immediately. There is more than a whiff of an argumentum ad ignorantiam about this objection ("I cannot imagine how FP could be falsified; therefore, it isn't a falsifiable theory"). Let me try to sustain this diagnosis by meeting the objection head-on, by trying to repair the very ignorance that makes it plausible.

The objector's question is rhetorical, of course, and gets its force by placing an unreasonable demand on one's imagination. With theories of the complexity and broad scope of FP, it is *in general* difficult or impossible to cite any single experiment or observation that would refute the theory at one blow. If we have learned anything from Duhem, Quine, Lakatos, and Kuhn, it is that theories, especially theories of broad scope and complexity, tend to die of slow empirical strangulation rather than by a quick observational guillotine. This is triply true if the theory is also vague, incomplete, and festooned with *ceteris paribus* clauses, as FP most famously is.

Even so, theories can have severe empirical pressure put on them, by chronic poor performance in a proprietary domain (cf. Ptolemaic astronomy); by incompatibility with closely neighboring theories that are performing extremely well (cf. vitalism vis-à-vis metabolic chemistry and molecular biology); by poor extension to domains continuous with but outside the domain of initial performance (cf. Newtonian mechanics in strong gravitational fields or high relative velocities); and finally, by the occasional empirical result carefully contrived to discriminate in some important way between competing alternatives (cf., Eddington's eclipse expedition, or the comparative statistical trials of Freudian vs. other forms of psychotherapy). All but the last mode of pressure require significant periods of time for the empirical pressure to accumulate, and tests of the last kind are relatively rare, often hard to think of, usually difficult to set up, and regularly ambiguous in their outcomes even so.

Can we imagine pressures of these four prototypical kinds building up on FP? Not only can we, but the relevant pressures are already there. Some of us think we can hear the edifice creaking even as we discuss the matter. FP's explanatory success in predicting and explaining belief acquisition, practical deliberation, emotional reaction, and physical behavior is far from zero, to be sure, but it is even farther from the possible limit of 100 percent success in the capacity to predict and explain all such activities. "The complexity of human cognition allows no more than a rough grasp of even its major activities," it is said in exculpation. Perhaps so. But that is the same apologia deployed by astrologers. And FP's marginal performance in its proprietary domains is now at least twenty centuries in evidence. This is chronically poor performance by any measure.

FP is also under pressure from computational neuroscience, whose portrayal of the fundamental kinematics and dynamics of human and animal cognition is profoundly different from the propositional-attitude psychology of FP. The brain's computational activity is no longer the smooth-walled mystery it used to be. We are now contemplating the high-dimensional vector of neuronal activation-levels as the fundamental mode of *representation* in the brain. And we are now contemplating the vector-to-vector transformation, via vast matrices of synaptic connections, as the fundamental mode of *computation* in the brain. (More on this below.) Propositions and inferences are there in the brain only in some profoundly hidden and undiscovered form, or only in some small and uniquely human subsystem, if they are there at all.

We cannot yet insist that no accommodation will be found. Nor can we insist that computational neuroscience (CN) has things right. But CN is a robustly progressive and expansionist research program. And undeniably there is a prima facie failure-of-fit between the relevant ontologies and their correlative dynamics. Here is a second dimension of empirical pressure on FP. This, incidentally, is the substance of the worry, cited earlier, that FP will fail to find a smooth reduction within a more penetrating successor or substrate theory.

FP is subject to a third dimension of empirical pressure in its failure to extend successfully to adjacent domains. FP functions best for normal, adult, language-using humans in mundane situations. Its explanatory and predictive performance for prelinguistic children and animals is decidedly poorer. And its performance for brain-damaged, demented, drugged, depressed, manic, schizophrenic, or profoundly stressed humans is pathetic. Many attempts have been made to extend FP into these domains. Freud's attempt is perhaps the most famous. They have all been conspicuous failures.

The fourth dimension of empirical pressure is the hardest to address, for the reasons outlined earlier. I shall stick my neck out even so, if only to illustrate some relevant possibilities. One way to perform an empirical test of the hypothesis that the cognition of humans and the higher animals is an inference-rule–governed dance of propositional attitudes is to construct an artifactual system that deliberately and unquestionably *does* conduct its "cognitive" affairs in *exactly* that way. The purpose is to see if such a system can then display, in real time, all of the cognitive capacities that humans and the higher animals display.

A positive result would be highly encouraging for the hypothesis, though not decisive, because of the possibility that there is more than one way to achieve such cognitive capacities, and the possibility that the human and the artifact achieve them differently. On the other hand, a persistently *negative* result in this experiment would augur very darkly for the hypothesis under test. If the relevant cognitive capacities never emerge from such a system, no matter how we tinker with it, or if they never emerge from it in anything remotely like real time, despite a blazing computational speed advantage on the part of the machine (a factor of roughly 10^6 with electronic machines over biological brains), then we have a gathering case that such a system is not in fact a reconstruction of our own computational strategy, a gathering case that our own system, and that of animals, must be using some quite different strategy.

The reader will perceive that I cite this example not just because it is a possible empirical test of the hypothesis at issue but also because the artificial intelligence (AI) community has in effect been performing and reperforming this test for something close to a quarter century now. The results have been persistently negative in just the way feared. The results are indecisive, to be sure. But there is widespread acknowledgment of and celebrated disappointment in the decreasing cognitive returns generated in the classical fashion from machines of ever-increasing speed and power. This is empirical evidence relevant to the hypothesis cited above, and it certainly is not positive.

All told then, it is indeed possible for FP to suffer disconfirmatory empirical pressure. It does so in four different dimensions, and the pressure is the more powerful for being negative in all four. It is at least arguable that FP is approaching the brink of falsification already.

IV.   The "It Serves Quite Different Purposes" Objection

This line of argument was first pressed by Wilkes (1984), and finds further expression in Hannan (1993). Both philosophers claim that the conceptual framework of FP is used for a vast range of "nonscientific" purposes beyond the prototypically "theoretical purpose of describing the ultimate nature of human psychological organization" (Hannan 1993). The idea here is that FP is up to a different game, is deployed in pursuit of different goals, from the game or the goals of a typical scientific theory. The leading examples of FP's "nontheoretical" functions concern the many practical activities that humans engage in and the many mundane purposes they address.

These premises about the manifold practical functions of FP are all true. Yet the conclusions drawn therefrom betray a narrow and cartoonish conception of what theories are and what they do. The stereotype of an abstract propositional description invented for the purpose of deep explanation far from the concerns of practical life may be popular, but it is not remotely accurate. Theory is regularly an intimate part and constituting element of people's second-by-second practical lives. Consider the role of circuit theory in the practical day of an electronics engineer designing radios, TVs, and stereos. Consider the role of geometry in the working day of a carpenter. Musical theory in the working day of a composer or jazz musician. Chemical theory in the working day of a drug engineer. Medical theory in the day of a physician. Optics in the day of a camera lens designer. Computer science in the day of a programmer. Metallurgy, mechanics, and simple thermal physics in the day of a blacksmith.

Such cases should not be set aside as the exceptional and occasional intrusions of theory into the alien realm of practice. Our best (Kuhn 1962) and most recent (P. M. Churchland 1989a, chapter 9) accounts of what learning a theory amounts to portray the process as much less the memorizing of doctrine and much more the slow acquisition and development of a host of diverse *skills*—skills of perception, categorization, analogical extension, physical manipulation, evaluation, construction, analysis, argument, computation, anticipation, and so forth. Becoming a physical chemist, for example, is very much a matter of being socialized into a community of practice with shared goals, values, techniques, and equipment. Sustaining enhanced practice is what theories typically do, at least for those who have internalized the relevant theories.

Once they have been internalized, of course, they no longer seem like theories, in the sense of the false stereotype here at issue. Yet theories they remain, however much they have become the implicit engine of intricate mundane practice. In the case of FP, we have what is no doubt the most thoroughly internalized theory any human ever acquires. Small wonder it serves the diverse practical purposes mentioned by Wilkes and Hannan. Idle spectators excepted, that is what theories are for.

In sum, the claim that FP is an empirical theory is entirely consistent with—indeed it is explanatory of—the intricate practical life enjoyed by its adepts. It is typical of theoretical adepts that their practical activities, and their practical worlds, are transformed by the relevant acquisition of knowledge. So it is with children who master FP in the normal course of socialization.

As regards immunity to elimination, we should observe that practices can be displaced just as well as theories, and for closely related reasons. Becoming a medieval alchemist, for example, was a matter of learning an inseparable mix of theory and practice. But when modern chemistry began to flower, the medieval practice was displaced almost in its entirety. Current chemical practice would be unintelligible to an alchemist. And given the spectacular power of modern chemistry, no one defends or mourns the passing of the alchemist's comparatively impotent practice, intricate and dear to him though it was.

This intimate connection of theory with practice has another side. The objection at issue wrongly characterizes the eliminativist as willing to turn her back on the intricacies of social practice in favor of an austere concern with new and abstract theory. But nothing could be further from the truth. The positive idea behind the projected displacement of FP is the hope of a comparably superior social practice rooted in a comparably superior account of human cognition and mental activity. If better chemical theory can sustain better chemical practice, then better psychological theory can sustain better social practice. A deeper understanding of the springs of human behavior may thus permit a deeper level of cognitive interaction, moral insight, and mutual care. Accordingly, a genuinely worthy scientific replacement for FP need not be "dehumanizing," as so many fear. More likely it will be just the reverse. Perversity of practice is a chronic feature of our social history. Think of trial by ordeal, purification by fire, absolution by ritual, and rehabilitation by exorcism or, currently, by long imprisonment in the intimate company of other sociopaths. Against such dark and impotent practices, any source of light should be welcomed.

V.   The "No Existing Alternatives" Objection

Near the close of her 1993 paper, Hannan remarks,

… even if all conceptual schemes, including the conceptual scheme embodying the notion of rationality, are vulnerable to revision and overthrow, we have no possible way to reject rationality and propositional attitude concepts until replacement concepts are suggested. And at this point, no replacement concepts have been suggested. …

… in the absence of plausible replacements for these concepts, or even the hint that such replacements might be on the horizon, don't we have ample reason to bet against the eliminativist? (p. 175)

I doubt Hannan is misled on the point, but it is worth emphasizing that no one is suggesting that we move out of our current house before we have constructed a new one that invites us to move in. What EM urges is only the poverty of our current home, the pressing need to explore the construction of one or more new ones, and the probability that we will eventually move into one of them.

On two other points, however, I believe Hannan is importantly misled. The second quotation embodies an argument of the form, "If FP is currently the only boat afloat, isn't this ample reason to expect that it will continue to be the only boat afloat?" The response is straightforward. No, it is not ample reason to expect that. On the other hand, it is ample reason for immediately gathering as much driftwood as we can, and for beginning the construction of alternative boats, if only to foster illuminating comparisons with our current vehicle, which after all is leaking at every seam.

Furthermore, the first quotation embodies a still more important misconception. Here in 1993, we *do* have some very specific and highly promising "replacement" concepts under active exploration. They are now the prime focus of several new journals and they have been under vigorous exploration for over a decade at several centers of cognitive and neuroscientific research. These are the ideas mentioned briefly in section III above. I can give only the flavor of this new approach here, but that much is quickly done.

One of the basic ideas of this new approach has some instances already familiar to you. Consider the momentary picture on your TV screen. That representation of some distant scene is a *pattern* of brightness levels across a large *population* of tiny pixels—about 200,000 of them on a standard set. A coherent *sequence* of such patterns represents the behavior of that distant portion of the world over time.

A very similar case, this time in you, is the momentary pattern of activation levels across the 100 million light-sensitive cells of your retina. The temporal sequence of such patterns represents the unfolding external world. A further example is the activation pattern, and the sequences thereof, across the millions of auditory cells in the cochlea of your inner ear. Here, of course, the "semantics" of the representation is not "pictorial" as in the case of vision. The information-preserving transformation from external world to internal representation is quite different in these two cases, and different again in the other modalities.

Proprietary patterns of activation across the cellular populations of your many other sensory modalities complete the story of peripheral world-representation. Prima facie, there is nothing "propositional" about any of these representations, either in their various "syntaxes" or in their diverse "semantics."

These intricate patterns—or *activation vectors*, as they are called—are projected inward from the periphery, along crowded axonal highways, to secondary cell populations within the brain called the primary sensory cortices, one for each of the sensory modalities. Here too, representation consists in the pattern of activation levels across the cortical population of neurons, patterns provoked by the arriving sensory vectors.

But the patterns at this level are not mere repetitions of the original patterns at the sensory periphery. Those patterns have been transformed during their journey to the cortical populations. They get transformed mainly by the vast filter of synaptic connections they have to traverse in order to stimulate the cortical population. The result is typically a *new* pattern across the cortical canvas, a principled *transformation* of the original sensory pattern.

Such transformations illustrate the second major idea of the new approach. *Computation* over these vectorial representations consists in their principled transformation by the vast matrix of tiny synaptic connections that intervene between any two neuronal populations. Such a process, note well, performs a prodigious number of elementary computations all at once, since each of the (possibly 10^{12}) synaptic connections does its job at the same time as all the other connections in the same matrix. This is called "massively parallel processing" and it provides us with a robust explanation of how animals can perform their extraordinary feats of computation in real time despite having "wetware" that is millions of times slower than the electronic hardware of conventional computers.

An intuitive way to think of such transformations is as follows. Consider a pictorial image projected through a nonuniform lens, or reflected from a deformed mirror. The image that comes out is quite different from the image that went in. And by configuring the surface of the lens or mirror to suit our purposes, we can produce any general transformation in the image we desire. Here the input and output images correspond to the input and output activation patterns, and the lens or mirror corresponds to the matrix of synaptic connections. Learning, incidentally, consists in modifying the configuration of synaptic connections. Learning, in other words, modifies the way we transform patterns.

The several cortical populations project in turn to further cell populations, and those to populations further still, until eventually the receiving population consists of motor cells, cells whose patterned activity is transformed by the muscle spindles into coherent bodily movement of some kind. Thus do we complete the basics of our new conception of how the nervous system works, from perception through cognition to organized behavior. It is here a stick-figure portrait, to be sure, but you will find it richly articulated in many directions in the literature. Patricia S. Churchland and Terry Sejnowski's 1992 book provides an accessible and richly illustrated entry into the current state of research. My 1989a book attempts to draw out some of its consequences for epistemology and the philosophy of science.

What is important for the issues of this paper is that the relevant sciences have indeed articulated fertile and systematic theories concerning representation and computation in the brain. From the perspective of those theories, the most general and fundamental form of representation in the brain has nothing discernible to do with propositions, and the most general and fundamental form of computation in the brain has nothing discernible to do with inferences between propositions. The brain appears to be playing a different game from the game that FP ascribes to it.

VI. Concluding Remarks

Despite the occasional polemics, the primary lesson of this paper is not that FP is already doomed, or that our current social practices are about to be swept away. The primary lesson is that we must confront the issue of the descriptive integrity and explanatory efficacy of folk psychology for what it is: an empirical question. How computational neuroscience and connectionist AI will fare in the coming years remains to be seen. How those research programes will explain our undoubted capacity for language and logic remains to be worked out. Whether folk psychological categories will find some kinematical and dynamical role within the new framework remains a strictly open question. In all of this there is plenty of empirical evidence to mull over, and ample room for reasonable people to disagree. It is an exciting period of theoretical and empirical evaluation. It would be inauthentic not to enjoy it for what it is.

4

Activation Vectors vs. Propositional Attitudes: How the *Brain* Represents Reality

Paul M. Churchland

Hilary Putnam's newest (1988) book brings several of his recent themes into an unusually clear and collective focus. It helped me to grasp certain theses I had understood only poorly before the book appeared, and to recognize several major points of agreement through the haze of our diverse concerns. Perhaps the most unexpected was the realization that I am no longer able to distinguish clearly between Putnam's newly explained and newly named *pragmatic* realism (hitherto *internal* realism) on the one hand, and the expressly antiutopian version of scientific realism that I have been defending since 1982 on the other. That shared metaphysical/ontological position will be readdressed at the close of this essay, since it represents a direct consequence of my views on the nature of mind and knowledge, just as it does for Putnam's. This convergence of principle is intriguing since we disagree substantially, even radically, on the nature of the mind and its cognitive representations, to which matter I now turn.

The bulk of Putnam's book is a defense of the integrity of the propositional attitudes, coupled with an extended argument against the idea that functionalist or other broadly "reductive" scientific stories have any realistic hope of accounting for them. Supposing that the negative second part of his position is correct, many of us would regard such a resistance to scientific explication as a sign of the *poverty* of the propositional attitudes, and as an indication that we should seek a new kinematics and dynamics on which to found a more adequate account of cognition. This is not Putnam's purpose, however, and his chapter 4 is aimed at dissuading us from this alternative.

Putnam's critique of the eliminativist approach has two main threads. The first is not very penetrating, but the second is. Putnam begins by misrepresenting the basic argument behind eliminative materialism.

Their whole argument turns on the following inference: if the instances of X do not have something in common which is *scientifically* describable ..., then X is a "mythological" entity. (p. 59)

Such a draconian principle would render "mythological" any and all purely *functional* kinds (chairs, mousetraps, valve-lifters, etc.). But eliminativists are not ignorant of or hostile to the existence of functional kinds, nor are they so careless as to embrace a principle that would banish them all at one blow.

The real motive behind eliminative materialism is the worry that the "propositional" kinematics and "logical" dynamics of folk psychology constitute a radically *false* account of the cognitive activity of humans, and of the higher animals generally. The worry is that our folk conception of how cognitive creatures represent the world (by propositional attitudes) and perform computations over those representations (by drawing sundry forms of inference from one to another) is a thoroughgoing *mis*representation of what really takes place inside us. The worry about propositional attitudes, in short, is not that they are too much like (the legitimately functional) tables and chairs, but that they are too much like (the avowedly nonexistent) phlogiston, caloric fluid, and the four principles of medieval alchemy.

These latter categories were eliminated from our serious ontology because of the many explanatory and predictive failures of the theories that embedded them, and because those theories were superseded in the relevant domains by more successful theories whose taxonomies bore no systematic explanatory or reductive relation to the taxonomies of their more feeble predecessors. In sum, eliminative materialism is not motivated by some fastidious metaphysical principle about common natures, but by some robustly factual and entirely corrigible assumptions about the failings of current folk psychology and the expected character of future cognitive theories.

On the explanatory and predictive failings of folk psychology, enough has been said elsewhere (P. M. Churchland 1981). Let me here address very briefly the positive side of the issue: the case for a novel kinematics, dynamics, and semantics for cognitive activity. Though Putnam does not explicitly rule out this possibility, his book does not take it very seriously. At one point he describes it as "only a gleam in Churchland's eye" (p. 110).

This is a serious mistake. A new kinematics and dynamics has been under vigorous exploration for roughly seven or eight years, and in its simpler forms it has been around for over three decades. No longer just a gleam in anyone's eye, it commands all or most of the attention of several recently founded journals (*Neural Networks, Journal of Neural Network Computing, Neural Computation, Cognitive Neuroscience*, to name a few), and is the prime focus of a number of recently published and currently forthcoming books.

The basic idea is that the brain represents the world by means of very high-dimensional *activation vectors*, that is, by a pattern of activation levels across a very large population of neurons. And the brain performs computations on those representations by effecting various complex *vector-to-vector transformations* from one neural population to another. This happens when an activation vector from one neural population is projected through a large matrix of synaptic connections to produce a new activation vector across a second population of nonlinear neurons. Mathematically, the process is an instance of multiplying a vector by a matrix and pushing the result through a nonlinear filter. This process is iterable through any number of successive neural populations and, with appropriate adjustment of the myriad synaptic weights that constitute the "coefficients" of these vast matrices, such an arrangement can compute, at least approximately, any computable function whatsoever. Such neural networks have been shown to be "universal approximators" (Hornik, Stinchcombe, and White 1989).

Such networks can also *learn* to approximate any desired function, from repeated presentation of its instances, by means of various automatic learning procedures that adjust the synaptic weights in response to various pressures induced by the specific input-output examples presented to the network (Rumelhart, Hinton, and Williams 1986a, 1986b; Sejnowski, Kienker, and Hinton 1986; Hinton 1989). Trained networks are fast, functionally persistent, tolerant of input degradation, sensitive to diffuse similarities, and they display complex learned prototypes. The result of training on complex discrimination problems is often an intricate and hierarchical set of partitions across the abstract activation-vector space of the network, a set of partitions that reflects the objective hierarchy of the discriminations it has just learned to make (Rosenberg and Sejnowski 1987; P. M. Churchland 1989a).

The virtues of this new research program into both artificial and biological networks cannot be effectively summarized in so short a piece as this (for a broad exposition, see P. M. Churchland 1989a). Suffice it to say that we have here a novel paradigm of extraordinary power, fertility, and biological realism, a paradigm whose kinematics and dynamics are radically *different* from those displayed in folk psychology. Whether it will prove capable of in some way reducing the familiar taxonomy of propositional attitudes is still an open question, but I am inclined to skepticism, for many of the same sorts of reasons that move Putnam. What this means, in sum, is that the current epistemic situation of folk psychology resembles more and more closely the earlier situations of alchemical theory, phlogiston theory, and caloric theory: we have a faltering old theory under siege by a new and more promising theory with an orthogonal categorial structure. That is why some of us anticipate the eventual elimination of our folk psychological ontology.

Putnam's second line of criticism is more engaging. If the unit of representation in the new paradigm is something other than the propositional attitude, then presumably its virtue will be something other than *truth*, and its relation to the world will be something other than *reference*. This is absolutely right. I was surprised, however, to find myself gently chided by Putnam as follows:

Nowhere is this selectivity [of elimination] more apparent than in the silence of both Stich and the Churchlands with respect to notions of *extensional* semantics—the notions of reference and truth .... (p. 59) ... the innocent reader of Churchland's writings is hardly aware that he is also being asked to reject the classical notion of truth! (p. 60)

In fact I have not been silent on this matter, nor tried to finesse my readers. In the final section of a paper addressed to van Fraassen (P. M. Churchland 1982, especially pp. 233–5), I drew precisely the conclusion about truth at issue and defended it at some length. (That paper is reprinted in P. M. Churchland and Hooker 1985, and in P. M. Churchland

1989a.) And in P. M. Churchland 1985b I defended the correlative conclusion about reference (pp. 4–5).

Putnam's main point, however, is not to chide me for deception but to portray the rejection of classical truth and reference as a simple reductio of the eliminativist position. I reject the reductio, since I am entirely willing to let go those notions, and to try to replace them with more worthy and more penetrating evaluative and semantical notions. This is no longer so radical a move as one might think. We can already see how to approach this most vital issue, because we already have in hand the vectorial kinematics and the synaptic weight-space dynamics to which the new evaluative-semantic notions must somehow attach. As our understanding of neural network function increases, we will be better able to define useful notions of representational success and failure, of epistemological virtue and vice. It is not even very difficult. One can see this project already launched in a recent essay (Churchland 1989a, pp. 220–3), where several dimensions of evaluation of "explanatory understanding" (there construed as "prototype activation") are defined in neurocomputational terms.

Concluding Remarks

It is a consequence of the neurocomputational conception of human cognition that the space of distinct possible theories or conceptual frameworks is almost unimaginably vast (P. M. Churchland 1989a, pp. 249–53), and that there is no real prospect either of their being, or of our ever finding, a uniquely correct Final Theory within that space, especially since one's cognitive space can in principle always be made larger and trillions of new conceptual alternatives can always be opened simply by expanding the number of processing elements in one's neural network. This neurocomputational perspective invites an antiutopian attitude toward our long-term cognitive adventure, a humility concerning the integrity of our current conceptual framework, and an optimism concerning our prospects for dramatic conceptual progress.

This brings me back to Putnam's "pragmatic realism," which I think I can and must embrace. My main worry is that he will complain that, in the neurocomputational perspective just outlined, I have *"assume[d] from the outset that there is a single system ('the organisms and their physical environment') which contains all the objects that anyone could refer to"* (p. 120). He may object, in other words, that I have violated the "humility" requirement outlined in the preceding paragraph, that I have used our current scientific ontology as if it were the Final Canvas on which all of philosophy is to be painted.

To this I reply as follows. I agree that there is no First Philosophy. I agree, moreover, that there is no Final Science either. And yet at any stage of our cognitive adventure, it is both possible and incumbent upon us to try to give the best overall account of our cognitive resources and their relation to the world that embeds them. This is all that the neuro-computational account of cognition sketched above aspires to: to be a *good theory*, better than any of its predecessors. Putnam closes his book with an arresting evocation of how the world can be endlessly recarved into new and different objects and classes as our knowledge and conceptual sophistication increases. I close this brief essay by reminding him that what is true of the "world" is also true of the "mind," and by suggesting that the occasion for a new *cognitive* taxonomy is already upon us.

II

Meaning, Qualia, and Emotion: The Several Dimensions of Consciousness

5

Could a Machine Think?

Paul M. Churchland and Patricia S. Churchland

Artificial intelligence (AI) research is undergoing a revolution. To explain how and why, and to put John Searle's argument in perspective, we first need a flashback.

By the early '50s, the old and vague question "Could a machine think?" had been replaced by the more approachable question "Could a machine *that manipulated physical symbols according to structure-sensitive rules* think?" This question was an improvement because formal logic and computational theory had seen major developments in the preceding half century. Theorists had come to appreciate the enormous power of abstract systems of symbols that undergo rule-governed transformations. If those systems could just be automated in a machine, then their abstract computational power, it seemed, would be displayed in a real physical system. This insight spawned a well-defined research program with deep theoretical underpinnings.

Could a machine think? There were many reasons for saying yes. One of the earliest and deepest reasons lay in two important results in computational theory. The first was Church's Thesis, which states that every effectively computable function is recursively computable. "Effectively computable" means that there is a "rote" procedure for determining, in finite time, the output of the function for a given input. "Recursively computable" means more specifically that there is a finite set of operations that can be applied to a given input, and applied again and again to the successive results of such applications, to yield the function's output in finite time. Since the notion of a rote procedure is nonformal and intuitive, Church's Thesis does not admit of a formal proof. But it does go to the very heart of what it is to compute, and many lines of evidence converge in supporting it.

The second important result was Alan Turing's demonstration that any recursively computable function can be computed in finite time by a maximally simple sort of symbol-manipulating machine that has come to be called a "universal Turing machine" (Turing 1950). This machine is guided by a set of recursively applicable rules that are sensitive to the identity, order, and arrangement of the elementary symbols it encounters as input.

These two results entail something remarkable, namely, that a standard digital computer, given only the right program, a large enough memory, and sufficient time, can compute any rule-governed input-output function whatever. That is, it can display any *systematic pattern of responses to the environment* whatever.

More specifically, it implies that a suitably programmed symbol-manipulating machine (hereinafter SM machine) should be able to pass the *Turing Test* for conscious intelligence. The Turing Test is a purely *behavioral* test for conscious intelligence, but it is a very demanding test even so. (Whether it is a fair test will be addressed below, where we shall also encounter a second and quite different "test" for conscious intelligence.) In the original version of the Turing Test, the inputs to the SM machine are conversational questions and remarks typed into a console by you or me, and the outputs are typewritten responses from the SM machine. The machine passes this back-and-forth test for conscious intelligence if its responses cannot be discriminated from the typewritten responses of a real, intelligent person. Of course, at present no one *knows* the function that would produce the output behavior of a conscious person. But the Church and Turing results assure us that, whatever that (presumably effective) function might be, a suitable SM machine could compute it.

This is a significant conclusion, especially since Turing's portrayal of a purely *teletyped* interaction is an unnecessary restriction. The same conclusion follows even if the SM machine interacts with the world in more complex ways: by direct vision, real speech, and so forth. After all, a more complex recursive function is still Turing-computable. The only remaining problem then is to *identify* the undoubtedly complex function that governs the human pattern of response to the environment, and then write the program (the set of recursively applicable rules) with which the SM machine will compute it. These latter goals form the fundamental research program of classical AI.

Initial results were positive. SM machines with clever programs performed a variety of ostensibly cognitive activities. They responded to complex instructions, solved complex arithmetical, algebraic, and tactical problems, played checkers and chess, proved theorems, and engaged in simple dialogue.

Performance continued to improve with the appearance of larger memories and faster machines, and with the use of longer and more cunning programs. Classical or "program-writing" AI was a vigorous and successful research program from almost every perspective. The occasional denial that an SM machine might eventually think appeared ill-motivated and uninformed. The case for a positive answer to our title question was overwhelming.

There were a few puzzles, of course. For one thing, SM machines were admittedly not very brainlike. But even here the classical approach had a convincing answer. First, the physical material of any SM machine has nothing essential to do with what function it computes. That is fixed by its program. Second, the engineering details of any machine's functional architecture are also strictly irrelevant, since different architectures running quite different programs can still be computing the very same input-output function.

Accordingly, AI sought to find the input-output *function* characteristic of intelligence, and the most efficient of the many possible programs for computing it. The idiosyncratic way in which the brain computes it just doesn't matter, it was said. This completes the rationale for classical AI, and for a positive answer to our title question.

Could a machine think? There were also some arguments for saying no. Through the '60s, interesting negative arguments were relatively rare. It was occasionally objected that thinking was a nonphysical process in an immaterial soul. But such dualistic resistance was neither evolutionarily nor explanatorily plausible. It had negligible impact on AI research.

A quite different line of objection was more successful in gaining the AI community's attention. In 1972, Hubert Dreyfus published a book that was highly critical of the parade-case simulations of cognitive activity. He argued for their inadequacy as simulations of genuine cognition, and he pointed to a *pattern* of failure in these attempts. What they were missing, he suggested, was the vast store of inarticulate background knowledge each of us possesses, and the commonsense capacity for drawing on relevant aspects of that knowledge as changing circumstance demands. Dreyfus did not deny the possibility that an artificial physical system of *some* kind might think. But he was highly critical of the idea that this could be achieved solely by symbol manipulation at the hands of recursively applicable rules.

Dreyfus's complaints were broadly perceived within the AI community, and within philosophy also, as short-sighted and unsympathetic, as harping on the inevitable simplifications of a research program still in its youth. These deficits might be real, but surely they were temporary. Bigger machines and better programs should repair them in due course. Time, it was felt, was on AI's side. Here again, the impact on research was negligible.

But time was on Dreyfus's side as well. For the rate of cognitive return on increasing speed and memory began to slacken in the late '70s and early '80s. The simulation of object recognition in the visual system, for example, proved computationally intensive to an unexpected degree. Realistic results required longer and longer periods of computer time, periods far in excess of what a real visual system requires. This relative slowness of the simulations over the real thing was darkly curious; signal propagation in a computer is roughly a million times faster than in the brain, and the clock frequency of a computer's central processor is greater than any frequency found in the brain by a similarly dramatic margin. And yet, on realistic problems, the tortoise easily outran the hare.

Furthermore, realistic performance required that the computer program have access to an extremely large knowledge base. Constructing the relevant knowledge base was problem enough, and it was compounded by the problem of how to access just the contextually *relevant* parts of that knowledge base in real time. As the knowledge base got bigger and better, the access problem got worse. Exhaustive search took too much time, and heuristics for relevance did poorly. Worries of the sort raised by Dreyfus finally began to take hold here and there among AI researchers themselves.

At about this time (1980), John Searle authored a new and quite different criticism aimed at the most basic assumption of the classical research program: the idea that the appropriate manipulation of structured symbols by the recursive application of structure-sensitive rules could constitute conscious intelligence (Searle, 1980a, 1980b).

Searle's argument rests on a thought-experiment that displays two crucial features. First, he describes a SM machine that realizes, we are to suppose, an input-output function adequate to sustain a successful Turing Test conversation conducted entirely in Chinese. Second, the internal structure of the machine is such that, however it *behaves*, we remain certain that neither the machine nor any part of it truly understands Chinese. For all it contains is a monolingual English speaker following a written set of instructions for manipulating the Chinese symbols that arrive and leave through a mail slot. In short, the system's behavior is supposed to pass the Turing Test, while the system itself lacks any genuine understanding of Chinese or real Chinese semantic content.

The general lesson drawn is that any system that merely manipulates physical symbols in accordance with structure-sensitive rules will be at best a hollow mock-up of real conscious intelligence, because you can never generate "real semantics" merely by cranking away on "empty syntax." Here, we should notice, Searle is imposing a *non*behavioral test for consciousness: the elements of conscious intelligence must possess real *semantic content.*

One is tempted to complain that Searle's thought-experiment is unfair, since his Rube Goldberg system will compute with absurd slowness. But Searle insists that speed is strictly irrelevant here. A slow thinker should still be a real thinker. Everything essential to the duplication of thought, as per classical AI, is said to be present in the Chinese Room.

Searle's paper provoked a lively reaction from AI researchers, psychologists, and philosophers alike. On the whole, however, he met an even more hostile reception than Dreyfus had experienced. Searle (1990) forthrightly lists a number of these critical responses. We think many of them are reasonable responses, especially those that bite the bullet by insisting that, although the system described is appallingly slow, the overall system of the room-plus-contents *does* understand Chinese.

We think those are good responses not because we think that the room understands Chinese. We agree with Searle that it does not. Rather, they are good responses because they reflect a refusal to accept the crucial third premise of Searle's argument: "*Syntax (in the sense of formal symbols) by itself is neither constitutive of nor sufficient for semantics*" (Searle 1990, p. 27). Perhaps this premise is true, but Searle cannot rightly pretend to know that it is true. Moreover, to assume its truth is tantamount to begging the question against the research program of classical AI, for that program is predicated on the very interesting assumption that, if we can just set in motion an appropriately structured internal dance of syntactic elements, appropriately connected to inputs and outputs, we *can* produce the same cognitive states and achievements found in humans.

The question-begging character of Searle's premise 3 becomes evident when it is compared directly with his conclusion 1: "*Programs are neither constitutive of, nor sufficient for, minds.*" (p. 27) Plainly, his third premise is already carrying ninety percent of the weight of this almost identical conclusion. That is why Searle's thought-experiment is devoted to shoring up premise 3 specifically. That is the point of the Chinese Room.

Though the story of the Chinese Room makes premise 3 tempting to the unwary, we do not think it succeeds in establishing premise 3, and we offer a parallel argument below in illustration of its failure. A single transparently fallacious instance of a disputed argument form often provides far more insight than does a book full of logic chopping.

Searle's style of skepticism has ample precedent in the history of science. The eighteenth-century bishop-philosopher George Berkeley found it unintelligible that compression waves in the air, by themselves, could constitute or be sufficient for objective *sound*. The English poet-artist William Blake and the German poet-naturalist Johann Wolfgang von Goethe found it inconceivable that, by themselves, small particles could constitute or be sufficient for the objective phenomenon of *light*. Even in this century, there were people who found it beyond imagining that inanimate matter, by itself, and however organized, could ever constitute or be sufficient for *life*. Plainly, what people can or cannot imagine often has nothing to do with what is or is not the case, even where the people involved are highly intelligent.

To see how this lesson applies to Searle's case, consider a deliberately manufactured parallel to his argument, and its supporting thought-experiment.

Premise 1. Electricity and magnetism are forces.

Premise 2. The essential property of light is luminance.

Premise 3. Forces, by themselves, are neither constitutive of, nor sufficient for, luminance.

Conclusion. Electricity and magnetism are neither constitutive of, nor sufficient for, light.

Imagine this argument raised shortly after James Clerk Maxwell's 1864 suggestion that light and electromagnetic waves are identical, but *before* the world's full appreciation of the systematic parallels between the properties of light and the properties of electromagnetic waves. This argument could have served as a compelling objection to Maxwell's imaginative hypothesis, especially if it were accompanied by the following commentary in support of premise 3.

Consider a dark room, containing a man holding a bar magnet or charged object (figure 5.1). If the man moves the magnet vigorously up and down, then, according to Maxwell's program of AL (artificial luminance), it will initiate a spreading circle of electromagnetic waves, and will thus be luminous. But as all of us who have toyed with magnets or charged pith balls well know, their forces (or any other forces for that matter), even when set in motion, produce no luminance at all. It is inconceivable that you might constitute real luminance just by moving forces around!

How should Maxwell respond to this challenge? He might begin by insisting that the Luminous Room experiment is a most misleading display of the phenomenon of luminance, because the frequency of oscillation of the magnet is absurdly low, too low by a factor of 10^{15}. This might well elicit the impatient response that frequency has nothing essential to do with it, that the room with the bobbing magnet already contains everything essential to light, according to Maxwell's own theory.

In response, Maxwell might bite the bullet and claim, quite correctly, that the room really is bathed in luminance, though of a grade or quality

THE CHINESE ROOM

Axiom 1. Computer programs are formal (syntactic).

Axiom 2. Human minds have mental contents (semantics).

Axiom 3. Syntax by itself is neither constitutive of nor sufficient for semantics.

Conclusion 1. Programs are neither constitutive of nor sufficient for minds.

THE LUMINOUS ROOM

Axiom 1. Electricity and magnetism are forces.

Axiom 2. The essential property of light is luminance.

Axiom 3. Forces by themselves are neither constitutive of nor sufficient for luminance.

Conclusion 1. Electricity and magnetism are neither constitutive of nor sufficient for light.

Figure 5.1
Oscillating electromagnetic forces constitute light even though a magnet pumped by a person appears to produce no light whatsoever. Similarly, rule-based symbol manipulation might constitute intelligence even though the rule-based system inside John Searle's Chinese Room appears to lack real understanding.

too feeble for us to appreciate. (Given the low frequency with which the man can oscillate the magnet, the wavelength of the electromagnetic waves produced is far too long and their energy is much too weak for our retinas to respond to them.) But in the climate of understanding here contemplated—the 1860s—this tactic is likely to elicit laughter and hoots of derision. "Luminous room, my foot, Mr. Maxwell. It's pitch-black in there!"

Alas, poor Maxwell has no easy route out of this predicament. All he can do is insist on the following three points. First, premise 3 of the argument above is false. Indeed, it is question-begging, despite its intuitive plausibility. Second, the Luminous Room experiment demonstrates nothing of interest one way or the other about the nature of light. And third, what *is* needed to settle the problem of light and the possibility of Artificial Luminance is an ongoing research program: to determine whether under the appropriate conditions the behavior of electromagnetic waves does indeed mirror perfectly the behavior of light.

This is also the response that classical AI should give to Searle's argument. Even though Searle's Chinese Room may appear to be "semantically dark," he is in no position to insist, on the strength of this appearance, that rule-governed symbol manipulation can never constitute semantic phenomena, especially when we have only an uninformed commonsense understanding of the semantic and cognitive phenomena that need to be explained. Rather than exploit our understanding of these things, Searle's argument freely exploits our ignorance of them.

With these criticisms of Searle's argument in place, we return to the question of whether the research program of classical AI has a realistic chance of solving the problem of conscious intelligence, and of producing a machine that thinks. We believe that the prospects are poor, but we rest this opinion on reasons very different from Searle's. Our reasons derive from the specific performance failures of the classical research program in AI, and from a variety of lessons learned from the biological brain and from a new class of computational models inspired by its structure. We indicated above some of the failures of classical AI on tasks that the brain performs swiftly and efficiently. The emerging consensus on these failures is that the functional architecture of classical SM machines is simply the wrong architecture for the very demanding jobs required.

What we need to know is this: How does the *brain* achieve cognition? Reverse engineering is a common practice in industry. When a new piece of technology comes on the market, competitors find out how it works by taking it apart and divining its structural rationale. In the case of the brain, this strategy presents an unusually stiff challenge, for the brain is the most complicated and sophisticated thing on the planet. Even so, the neurosciences have revealed much about the brain at a wide variety of structural levels (figure 5.2). Three anatomical points provide a basic contrast with the architecture of conventional electronic computers.

First, nervous systems are *parallel machines*, in the sense that signals are processed in millions of different pathways simultaneously. The retina, for example, presents its complex input to the rest of the brain not in eight-, sixteen-, or thirty-two-element chunks, as in a desktop computer, but rather in the form of almost a million distinct signal elements arriving simultaneously at the target of the optic nerve (the lateral geniculate nucleus), there to be processed collectively, simultaneously, and in one fell swoop.

Second, the brain's basic processing unit, the neuron, is comparatively simple. And its response to incoming signals is analog, not digital, inasmuch as its output spiking frequency varies continuously with its input signals.

Third, in the brain, the axons projecting from one neuronal population to a second are often matched by axons returning from their target population. These descending or *recurrent* projections allow the brain to modulate the character of its sensory processing. More important still, their existence makes the brain a genuine *dynamical system* whose continuing behavior is both highly complex and to some degree independent of its peripheral stimuli.

Highly simplified model networks have been useful in suggesting how real neural networks might work, and in revealing the computational properties of parallel architectures. For example, consider a three-layer model consisting of neuron-like units fully connected by axon-like connections to the units at the next layer (figure 5.3). An input stimulus produces some activation level in a given input unit, which conveys a signal of proportional strength along its "axon" to its many "synaptic" connections onto the several hidden units. The global effect is that a

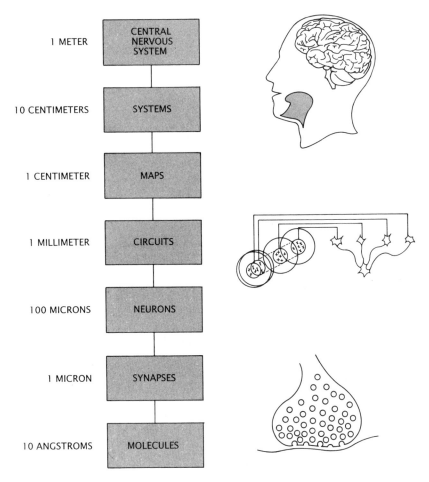

Figure 5.2
Nervous systems span many scales of organization, from neurotransmitter molecules (*bottom*) to the entire brain and spinal cord. Intermediate levels include single neurons and circuits made up of a few neurons, such as those that produce orientation selectivity to a visual stimulus (*middle*), and systems made up of such circuits such as those that subserve language (*top right*). Only research can decide how closely an artificial system must mimic the biological one to be capable of intelligence.

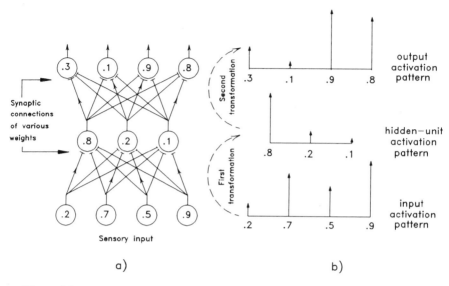

Figure 5.3
Neural networks model a central feature of the brain's microstructure. In this three-layer net, input neurons (*left*) receive a pattern of activations (*right*) and pass it along weighted connections to a "hidden" layer. Neurons in the hidden layer sum their many inputs to produce a new pattern of activations. This new pattern is passed to the output layer, where it undergoes a further transformation. Overall, the network transforms any input pattern into a uniquely corresponding output pattern, as dictated by the arrangement and strength of the many connections between neurons.

pattern of activations across the set of input units produces a distinct *pattern* of activations across the set of hidden units. Exactly what pattern is produced, for a given input, is determined by the configuration of synaptic weights meeting the hidden units.

The same story applies to the output units. As before, the global effect is that an activation pattern across the hidden units produces a distinct activation pattern across the output units. All told, this network is a device for transforming any one of a great many possible input vectors (i.e., activation patterns) into a uniquely corresponding output vector. It is a device for computing a specific function. Exactly which function it computes is fixed by the global configuration of its synaptic weights.

There are various procedures for adjusting the weights so as to yield a network that computes almost any function—that is, any vector-to-vector transformation—that one might desire. In fact, one can even impose on it a function one is unable to specify, so long as one can supply a modestly large set of examples of the desired input-output pairs. This process is called "training up the network" and it proceeds by successive adjustment of the network's weights until it performs the input-output transformations desired.

Although this model network vastly oversimplifies the structure of the brain, it does illustrate several important ideas. First, a parallel architecture provides a dramatic speed advantage over a conventional computer, for the many synapses at each level perform many small computations *simultaneously* instead of in laborious sequence. This advantage gets larger with the number of neurons at each layer. Strikingly, the speed of processing is entirely independent of both the number of units involved in each layer and the complexity of the function they are computing. Each layer could have four units (as in figure 5.3), or a hundred million (as in the brain); and its configuration of synaptic weights could be computing simple one-digit sums, or second-order differential equations. It would make no difference. The computation time would be exactly the same.

Second, massive parallelism means that the system is fault tolerant and functionally persistent, since the loss of a few connections, even quite a few, has a negligible effect on the character of the overall transformation effected by the surviving network.

Third, a parallel system stores large amounts of information in a distributed fashion, any part of which can be accessed in milliseconds. That information is stored in the specific configuration of synaptic connection strengths, as shaped by past learning. Relevant information is "released" as the input vector passes through, and is transformed by, that configuration of connections.

Parallel processing is not ideal for all types of computation. On tasks that require only a small input vector, but many millions of swiftly iterated recursive computations, the brain performs very badly where classical SM machines excel. This class of computations is very large and important, so classical machines will always be useful, indeed vital. But there is an equally large class of computations for which the brain's architecture is the superior technology. And these are the computations that typically confront living creatures: *recognizing* a predator's outline in a noisy environment; *recalling* instantly how to avoid its gaze, flee its approach, or fend off its attack; *discriminating* food from nonfood, and mates from nonmates; *navigating* through a complex and ever-changing physical and social environment; and so on.

Finally, it is important to note that the parallel system described is not manipulating symbols according to structure-sensitive recursive rules. Rather, symbol manipulation appears to be just one of many cognitive skills that a network may or may not learn to display. Rule-governed symbol manipulation is not its *basic* mode of operation. But Searle's argument is directed explicitly against rule-governed SM machines. Vector transformers of the kind described are therefore not threatened by his Chinese Room argument even if it were sound, which we have found independent reason to doubt.

Searle is aware of parallel processors, but thinks they too will be devoid of real semantic content. To illustrate their inevitable failure, he outlines a second thought-experiment, the Chinese Gym, which has a gymnasium full of people organized into a parallel network (Searle 1990, p. 28). From there his argument proceeds as in the Chinese Room experiment.

We find this second story far less responsive or compelling than his first. For one thing, it is irrelevant that no unit in his system understands Chinese, since the same is true of nervous systems: no neuron in my brain understands English, though my whole brain does. And for another, Searle neglects to mention that his simulation (using one person per neuron, plus a fleet-footed child for each synaptic connection) will require at least 10^{14} humans, since the human brain has 10^{11} neurons, each of which averages over 10^3 connections. His system will require the entire human populations of over ten thousand Earths. A single gymnasium will not begin to hold a fair simulation.

On the other hand, if such a system were to be assembled on a suitably cosmic scale, with all its pathways faithfully modeled on the human case, we might then have a large, slow, oddly made, but still functional *brain* on our hands. In that case, the default assumption is surely that, given proper inputs, it *would* think, not that it couldn't. There is no guarantee that its activity would constitute real thought, since we have no guarantee that the vector-processing theory sketched above is the *correct* theory of how brains work. But neither is there any a priori guarantee that it could *not* be thinking. Searle is once more mistaking the limits on his (or our) current imagination for the limits on objective reality.

The brain is a kind of computer, though most of its properties remain to be discovered. Characterizing the brain as a kind of computer is neither trivial nor frivolous. The brain does compute functions, functions of great complexity, but not in the classical fashion. When brains are said to be computers, it should not be implied that they are serial, digital computers, that they are programmed, that they exhibit the distinction between hardware and software, or that they must be symbol manipulators or rule followers. Brains are computers in a radically different style.

How the brain manages meaning is still unknown, but it is clear that the problem reaches beyond language use and beyond humans. A small mound of fresh dirt signifies to us, and also to coyotes, that a gopher is around; an echo with a certain spectral character signifies to a bat the presence of a moth. To develop a theory of meaning, more must be known about how sensory signals are coded and transformed by neurons, about the neural basis of memory, learning, and emotion, and about the interaction of these capacities and the motor system. A neurally grounded theory of meaning may require revision of the very intuitions that now seem so secure, and are so freely exploited in Searle's arguments. But such revisions are commonplace in the history of science.

Could science construct an artificial intelligence by exploiting what is known about the nervous system? We see no principled reason why not. Searle appears to agree, though he qualifies his claim by saying that "Any other system capable of causing minds would have to have causal powers (at least) equivalent to brains." We close by addressing this claim.

We presume that Searle is not claiming that a successful artificial mind must have *all* the causal powers of the brain, such as the power to smell bad when rotting, to harbor slow viruses such as kuru, to stain yellow with horseradish peroxidase, and so forth. Requiring perfect parity would be like requiring that an artificial flying device lay eggs.

Presumably he means only to require all of the causal powers *relevant*, as he says, to conscious intelligence. But which exactly are they? We are back to quarreling about what is and is not relevant. This is an entirely reasonable place for a disagreement, but it is an empirical matter, to be tried and tested. Since so little is known about what goes into the process of cognition and semantics, it is premature to be very confident about what features are essential.

Searle hints at various points that *every* level, including the biochemical (see figure 5.2) must be represented in any machine that is a candidate for artificial intelligence. This claim is almost surely too strong. An artificial brain might use something other than biochemicals to achieve the same ends.

This possibility is illustrated by Carver Mead's research at Cal Tech. Mead and his colleagues have used analog very-large-scale integration (VLSI) techniques to build an artificial retina and an artificial cochlea. (In real creatures, the retina and cochlea are not mere transducers: both systems embody a complex processing network at the site.) These are not mere simulations-in-a-Vax of the kind that Searle derides; they are themselves real information-processing units responding in real time to real light in the case of the artificial retina, and to real sound, in the case of the artificial cochlea. The circuitry is based on the known anatomy and physiology of the cat retina and the barn owl cochlea. And their output is dramatically similar to the known output of the organs at issue (see Mead and Mahowald 1991).

These chips do not use any neurochemicals, so they are clearly not necessary to achieve the evident results. Of course, the artificial retina cannot be said to *see* anything, because its output does not have an artificial thalamus or cortex to go to. Whether Mead's program could be sustained to build an entire artificial brain remains to be seen, but there is no evidence at this point that the absence of biochemicals renders it quixotic.

We, and Searle, reject the Turing Test as a sufficient condition for conscious intelligence. At one level, our reasons for doing so are similar: we agree that it is also very important *how* the input-output function is achieved; it is important that the right sorts of things be going on *inside* the artificial machine. At another level, our reasons are quite different. Searle bases his position on commonsense intuitions about the presence or absence of semantic content. We base ours on the specific behavioral failures of the classical SM machines, and on the specific virtues of machines with a more brainlike architecture. These contrasts show that certain computational strategies have vast and decisive advantages over others where typical *cognitive* tasks are concerned, advantages that are empirically inescapable. Clearly the brain is making systematic use of these computational advantages. But it need not be the only physical system capable of doing so. Artificial intelligence, in a nonbiological but massively parallel machine, remains a compelling and discernible prospect.

6

Intertheoretic Reduction: A Neuroscientist's Field Guide

Paul M. Churchland and Patricia S. Churchland

Might psychology someday be reduced to (= exhaustively explained by) computational neurobiology? Many still say no. We approach this question through a brief survey of some prominent intertheoretic reductions drawn from our scientific history. A general characterization of reduction is constructed from these, and some important philosophical and methodological lessons are drawn. The five most popular objections to the possibility of a neurobiological reduction of psychology are then addressed and defeated.

"Reductionism" is a term of contention in academic circles. For some, it connotes a right-headed approach to any genuinely scientific field, an approach that seeks intertheoretic unity and real systematicity in the phenomena. It is an approach to be vigorously pursued and defended.

For others, it connotes a wrong-headed approach that is narrow-minded and blind to the richness of the phenomena. It is a bullish instance of "nothing-butery," insensitive to emergent complexity and higher-level organization. It is an approach to be resisted.

One finds this latter reaction most often within the various social sciences, such as anthropology, sociology, and psychology. One finds the former attitude most often within the physical sciences, such as physics, chemistry, and molecular biology. Predictably then, the issue of reductionism is especially turbulent at the point where these two intellectual rivers meet: in the discipline of modern neuroscience.

The question at issue is whether it is reasonable to expect, and to work toward, a reduction of all psychological phenomena to neurobiological and neurocomputational phenomena. A large and still respectable contingent within the academic community remains inclined to say no. Their resistance is principled. Some point to the existence of what philosophers call *qualia*—the various subjective qualitative characters displayed in our sensations: think of pain, the smell of a rose, the sensation of redness, and so forth. These qualia, it is held, are beyond the possibility of any materialist explanation or reduction (Jackson 1982; Nagel 1974). Others point to the semantic content or *intentionality* of our thoughts, and make a similar claim about its irreducibility (Popper and Eccles 1978; Searle 1980a, 1990). Others claim that the most important aspects of human behavior are explicable only in terms of high-level *emergent properties* and their correlative regularities, properties that irreducibly encompass the social level, properties such as loyalty to a moral ideal, perception of a political fact, or the recognition of a personal betrayal (Taylor 1970, 1987). Yet others see a conflict with the important and deeply entrenched idea of *human freedom* (Popper and Eccles 1978). Finally, some materialists raise what is called the problem of *multiple instantiation*. They point to the presumed fact that conscious intelligence could be sustained by physical systems other than the biochemistry peculiar to humans—by a system of transistors, for example—just as a nation's financial economy can be sustained by tokens other than silver coins and paper bills. But no one thinks that macroeconomics can be reduced to the chemistry of metals and paper. So why think that psychology should be reducible to the neurobiology of terrestrial humans? (Fodor 1975).

Our aim in this paper is threefold. First, we try to provide a useful overview of the general nature of intertheoretic reduction, as it appears in the many examples to be found in the history of science. Expanding our horizons here is important, since little is to be learned from simply staring long and hard at the problematic case at issue, namely, the potential reduction of psychological phenomena to neural phenomena. Instead, we need to look at cases where the dust has already settled and where the issues are already clear. Second, we identify the very real virtues that such cases display, and the correlative vices to be avoided. And finally, we attempt to apply these historical lessons to the case here at issue—cognitive neuroscience—and we try to meet the salient objections listed above.

Intertheoretic Reduction: Some Prototypical Cases

A general definition would not be particularly useful at this stage. Since nothing instructs like examples, let us briefly examine some. One of the

---

Kepler's three planetary laws are:

1. All planets move on ellipses with the sun at one focus.
2. A given planet always sweeps out equal areas in equal times.
3. The square of a planet's period is proportional to the cube of its mean orbital radius.

Newton's three laws of motion are:

1. Inertial motion is constant and rectilinear.
2. Acceleration = force/mass.
3. For any change in momentum, something suffers an equal and opposite change in momentum.

To these laws we must add his gravitation law:

4. $F = Gm_1m_2/R^2$

---

earliest cases of intertheoretic reduction on a grand scale was the reduction of Kepler's three laws of astronomical motion by the newly minted mechanics of Isaac Newton. Kepler's theory was specific to the motions of the solar planets, but Newton's theory at least purported to be the correct account of bodily motions in general. It was therefore a great triumph when Newton showed that one could deduce all three of Kepler's laws from his own theory, given only the background assumption that the mass of any planet is tiny compared to the great mass of the sun.

Kepler's account thus turned out to be just a special case or a special application of Newton's more encompassing account. And astronomical motions turned out to be just a special instance of the inertial and force-governed motions of massive bodies in general. The divine or supernatural character of the heavens was thereby lost forever. The sublunary and the superlunary realms were thereby united as a single domain in which the same kinds of objects were governed by one and the same set of laws.

Newton's mechanics also provides a second great example of intertheoretic reduction, one that did not emerge until the nineteenth century. If his mechanics successfully comprehends motion at both the astronomical and the human-sized scales, then what, it was asked, about motions at the *microscopic* scale? Might these be accounted for in the same way?

The attempts to construct such an account produced another unification, one with an unexpected bonus concerning the theory of heat. If we assume that any confined body of gas consists of a swarm of submicroscopic corpuscles bouncing around inside the container according to Newton's three laws, then we can deduce a law describing the pressure they will collectively exert on the container's walls by repeatedly bouncing off them. This "kinetic" law has the form

$$PV = 2n/3 \times mv^2/2.$$

This law had the same form as the then already familiar "ideal gas law,"

$$PV = \mu R \times T.$$

Here P is pressure and V is volume. Although they are notationally different, the expressions $2n/3$ and μR both denote the *amount* of gas present in the container (n denotes the number of molecules in the container; μ denotes the fraction of a mole). The only remaining difference, then, is that the former law has an expression for the *kinetic energy of an average corpuscle* ($mv^2/2$) in the place where the latter has an expression for *temperature* (T). Might the phenomenon we call "temperature" thus *be* mean kinetic energy (KE) at the molecular level? This striking convergence of principle, and many others like it, invited Bernoulli, Joule, Kelvin, and Boltzmann to say yes. Mean molecular kinetic energy turned out to have *all* the causal properties that the classical theory had been ascribing to temperature. In short, temperature turned out to *be* mean molecular KE. Newtonian mechanics had another reductive triumph in hand. Motion at all three scales was subsumed under the same theory, and a familiar phenomenal property, *temperature*, was reconceived in a new and unexpected way.

It is worth emphasizing that this reduction involved identifying a familiar *phenomenal* property of common objects with a highly unfamiliar microphysical property. (By "phenomenal," we mean a property that is reliably discriminated in experience, but where one is unable to articulate, by reference to yet simpler discriminable elements, how one discriminates that property.) Evidently, reduction is not limited to conceptual frameworks hidden away in the theoretical stratosphere. Sometimes the conceptual framework that gets subsumed by a deeper vision turns out to be a familiar piece of our commonsense framework, a piece whose concepts are regularly applied in casual observation on the basis of our native sensory systems. Other examples are close at hand: before

Newton, *sound* had already been identified with compression waves in the atmosphere, and *pitch* with wavelength, as part of the larger reduction of commonsense sound and musical theory to mechanical acoustics. A century and a half after Newton, *light* and its various *colors* were identified with electromagnetic waves and their various wavelengths, within the larger reduction of geometrical optics by electromagnetic theory, as outlined by Maxwell in 1864. *Radiant heat*, another commonsense observable, was similarly reconceived as long-wavelength electromagnetic waves in a later articulation of the same theory. Evidently, the fact that a property or state is at the prime focus of one of our native discriminatory faculties does not mean that it is exempt from possible reconception within the conceptual framework of some deeper explanatory theory (see below).

This fact will loom larger later in the paper. For now, let us explore some further examples of intertheoretic reduction. The twentieth-century reduction of classical (valence) chemistry by atomic and subatomic (quantum) physics is another impressive case of conceptual unification. Here the structure of an atom's successive electron shells, and the character of stable regimes of electron-sharing between atoms, allowed us to reconstruct, in a systematic and thus illuminating way, the electronic structure of the many atomic elements, the classical laws of valence bonding, and the gross structure of the periodic table. As often happens in intertheoretic reductions, the newer theory also allowed us to explain much that the old theory had been unable to explain, such as the specific heat capacities of various substances and the interactions of chemical compounds with light.

This reduction of chemistry to physics is notable for the further reason that it is not yet complete, and probably never will be. For one thing, given the combinatorial possibilities here, the variety of chemical compounds is effectively endless, as are their idiosyncratic chemical, mechanical, optical, and thermal properties. And for another, the calculation of these diverse properties from basic quantum principles is computationally daunting, even when we restrict ourselves to merely approximate results, which for sheerly mathematical reasons we generally must. Accordingly, it is not true that all "chemical" knowledge has been successfully reconstructed in quantum-mechanical terms. Only the basics have, and then only in approximation. But our experience here bids us believe that quantum physics has indeed managed to grasp the underlying elements of chemical reality. We thus expect that any particular *part* of chemistry can be approximately reconstructed in quantum-mechanical terms, when and if the specific need arises. As often it does.

The preceding examples make it evident that intertheoretic reduction is at bottom a relation between two distinct *conceptual frameworks* for describing the phenomena, rather than a relation between two distinct domains of phenomena. The whole point of a reduction, after all, is to show that what we thought to be two domains is actually one domain, though it may have been described in two (or more) different vocabularies.

Perhaps the most famous reduction of all is Einstein's twentieth-century reduction of Newton's three laws of motion by the quite different mechanics of the special theory of relativity (STR). STR subsumed Newton's laws in the following sense. If we make the (false) assumption that all bodies move with velocities much less than the velocity of light, then STR entails a set of laws for the motion of such bodies, a set that is experimentally indistinguishable from Newton's old set. It is thus no mystery that those old Newtonian laws seemed to be true, given the relatively parochial human experience they were asked to account for.

But while those special-case STR laws may be experimentally indistinguishable from Newton's laws, they are logically and semantically quite different from Newton's laws: they ascribe an importantly different family of features to the world. Specifically, in every situation where Newton ascribed an intrinsic property to a body (e.g., mass, or length, or momentum, and so forth), STR ascribes a *relation*, a *two*-place property (e.g., x has a mass-relative-to-an-inertial-frame-F, and so on), because its portrait of the universe and what it contains (a unitary four-dimensional spacetime continuum with 4-D world-lines) is profoundly different from Newton's.

Here we have an example where the special-case resources and deductive consequences of the new and more general theory are not identical, but merely *similar*, to the old and more narrow theory it purports to reduce. That is to say, the special-case reconstruction achieved within the new theory parallels the old theory with sufficient systematicity to explain the old theory's apparent truth, and to demonstrate that the old theory could be displaced by the new without predictive or explanatory loss within the old theory's domain; and yet the new reconstruction is not perfectly isomorphic with the old theory. The old theory turns out not just to be narrow, but to be false in certain important respects. Space and time are not distinct, as Newton assumed, and there simply are no intrinsic properties such as mass and length that are invariant over all inertial frames.

The trend of this example leads us toward cases where the new and more general theory does not sustain the portrait of reality painted by the old theory at all, even as a limiting special case or even in its roughest outlines. An example would be the outright displacement, without reduction, of the old phlogiston theory of combustion by Lavoisier's oxygen theory of combustion. The older theory held that the combustion of any body involved the *loss* of a spirit-like substance, phlogiston, whose pre-combustion function it was to provide a noble wood-like or metal-like character to the baser ash or calx that is left behind after the process of combustion is complete. It was the "ghost" that gave metal its form. With the acceptance of Lavoisier's contrary claim that a sheerly material substance, oxygen, was being somehow *absorbed* during combustion, phlogiston was simply eliminated from our overall account of the world.

Other examples of theoretical entities that have been eliminated from serious science include caloric fluid, the rotating crystal spheres of Ptolemaic astronomy, the four humors of medieval medicine, the vital spirit of premodern biology, and the luminiferous aether of pre-Einsteinian mechanics. In all of these cases, the newer theory did not have the resources adequate to reconstruct the furniture of the older theory or the laws that supposedly governed its behavior; but the newer theory was so clearly superior to the old as to displace it regardless.

At one end of the spectrum then, we have pairs of theories where the old is smoothly reduced by the new, and the ontology of the old theory (that is, the set of things and properties that it postulates) survives, although redescribed, perhaps, in a new and more penetrating vocabulary. Here we typically find claims of cross-theoretic identity, such as "Heat is identical with mean molecular kinetic energy" and "Light is identical with electromagnetic waves." In the middle of the spectrum, we find pairs of theories where the old ontology is only poorly mirrored within the vision of the new, and it "survives" only in a significantly modified form. Finally, at the other end of the spectrum we find pairs where the older theory, and its old ontology with it, is eliminated entirely in favor of the more useful ontology and the more successful laws of the new.

Before closing this quick survey, it is instructive to note some cases where the older theory is neither subsumed under nor eliminated by the aspirant and allegedly more general theory. Rather, it successfully resists the takeover attempt, and proves not to be just a special case of the general theory at issue. A clear example is Maxwell's electromagnetic (hereinafter EM) theory. From 1864 to 1905, it was widely expected that EM theory would surely find a definitive reduction in terms of the mechanical properties of an all-pervading aether, the elastic medium in which EM waves were supposedly propagated. Though never satisfactorily completed, some significant attempts at reconstructing EM phenomena in mechanical terms had already been launched. Unexpectedly, the existence of such an absolute medium of luminous propagation turned out to be flatly inconsistent with the character of space and time as described in Einstein's 1905 special theory of relativity. EM theory thus emerged as a fundamental theory in its own right, and not just as a special case of mechanics. The attempt at subsumption was a failure.

A second example concerns the theory of stellar behavior accumulated by classical astronomy in the late nineteenth century. It was widely believed that the pattern of radiative behavior displayed by a star would be adequately explained in mechanical or chemical terms. It became increasingly plain, however, that the possible sources of chemical and mechanical energy available to any star would sustain their enormous outpourings of thermal and luminous energy for no more than a few tens of millions of years. This limited time scale was at odds with the emerging geological evidence of a history numbered in the *billions* of years. Geology notwithstanding, Lord Kelvin himself was prepared to bite the bullet and declare the stars to be no more than a few tens of millions of years old. The conflict was finally resolved when the enormous energies in the atomic nucleus were discovered. Stellar astronomy was eventually reduced all right, and very beautifully, but by quantum physics rather than by mere chemistry or mechanics. Another reductive attempt had failed, though it was followed by one that succeeded.

The Lessons for Neuroscience

Having seen these examples and the spectrum of cases they define, what lessons should a neuroscientist draw? One lesson is that intertheoretic reduction is a normal and fairly commonplace event in the history of science. Another lesson is that genuine reduction, when you can get it, is clearly a *good* thing. It is a good thing for many reasons, reasons made more powerful by their conjunction. First, by being displayed as a special case of the (presumably true) new theory, the old theory is thereby *vindicated*, at least in its general outlines, or at least in some suitably restricted domain. Second, the old theory is typically *corrected* in some of its important details, since the reconstructed image is seldom a perfect mirror image of the old theory, and the differences reflect improvements in our knowledge. Third, the reduction provides us with a much *deeper insight* into, and thus a *more effective control* over, the phenomena within the old theory's domain. Fourth, the reduction provides us with a *simpler* overall account of nature, since apparently diverse phenomena are brought under a single explanatory umbrella. And fifth, the new and more general theory immediately *inherits all the evidence* that had accumulated in favor of the older theory it reduces, because it explains all of the same data.

It is of course a bad thing to try to force a well-functioning old theory into a Procrustean bed, to try to effect a reduction where the aspirant reducing theory lacks the resources to do reconstructive justice to the target old theory. But whether or not the resources are adequate is seldom clear beforehand, despite people's intuitive convictions. And even if a reduction is impossible, this may reflect the old theory's radical falsity instead of its fundamental accuracy. The new theory may simply eliminate the old, rather than smoothly reduce it. Perhaps folk notions such as "beliefs" and the "will," for example, will be eliminated in favor of some quite different story of information storage and behavior initiation.

The fact is, in the neuroscience-psychology case there are conflicting indications. On the one side, we should note that the presumption in favor of an eventual reduction (or elimination) is far stronger than it was in the historical cases just examined. For unlike the earlier cases of light, or heat, or heavenly motions, in general terms we already know how psychological phenomena arise: they arise from the evolutionary and ontogenetic articulation of matter, more specifically, from the articulation of biological organization. We therefore *expect* to understand the former in terms of the latter. The former is produced by the relevant articulation of the latter.

But there are counterindications as well, and this returns us at last to the five objections with which we opened this paper. From the historical perspective outlined above, can we say anything useful about those objections to reduction? Let us take them in sequence.

The first concerns the possibility of explaining the character of our subjective sensory qualia. The negative arguments here all exploit the very same theme, viz., our inability to imagine how any possible story about the objective nuts and bolts of neurons could ever explain the inarticulable subjective phenomena at issue. Plainly this objection places a great deal of weight on what we can and cannot imagine, as a measure of what is and is not possible. It places more, clearly, than the test should bear. For who would have imagined, before James Clerk Maxwell, that the theory of charged pith balls and wobbling compass needles could prove adequate to explain all the phenomena of light? Who would have thought, before Descartes, Bernoulli, and Joule, that the mechanics of billiard balls would prove adequate to explain the prima facie very different phenomenon of heat? Who would have found it remotely plausible that the pitch of a sound is a frequency, in advance of a general appreciation that sound itself consists in a train of compression waves in the atmosphere?

We must remember that a successful intertheoretic reduction is typically a complex affair, as it involves the systematic reconstruction of all or most of the old conception within the resources of the new conception. And not only is it complex, often the reconstruction is highly surprising. It is not something that we can reasonably expect anyone's imagination to think up or comprehend on rhetorical demand, as in the question, How could A's *possibly* be nothing but B's?

Besides, an imagination informed by recent theories of sensory coding need not be so stumped as the rhetorical question expects. The idea that taste sensations are coded as a four-dimensional vector of spiking frequencies (corresponding to the four types of receptor on the tongue) yields a representation of the space of humanly possible tastes which unites the familiar tastes according to their various similarities, differences, and other relations such as betweenness (Bartoshuk 1978). Land's retinex theory of color vision (Land 1977) suggests a similar arrangement for our color sensations, with similar virtues. Such a theory also predicts the principal forms of color blindness, as when one's three-dimensional color space is reduced to two dimensions by the loss of one of its normal dimensions of representation.

Here we are already reconstructing some of the features of the target phenomena in terms of the new theory. We need only to carry such a reconstruction through, as in the historical precedents of the objective phenomenal properties noted earlier (heat, light, pitch). Some things may indeed be inarticulably phenomenal in character, because they are the target of one of our basic discriminatory modalities. But that in no way makes them immune to an illuminating intertheoretic reduction. History already teaches us the contrary.

The second objection concerned the meaning, or semantic content, or intentionality of our thoughts and other mental states. The antireductionist arguments in this area are very similar to those found in the case of qualia. They appeal to our inability to imagine how meaning could be just a matter of how signals interact or how inert symbols are processed. (Searle 1980a, 1990; for a rebuttal, see P. M. Churchland and P. S. Churchland 1990b. Searle, strictly speaking, objects only to a purely computational reduction, but that is an important option for neuroscience so we shall include him with the other antireductionists.) Such appeals, as before, are really arguments from ignorance. They have the form, I can't *imagine* how a neurocomputational account of meaningful representations could possibly work; therefore, it can't possibly work. To counter such appeals in the short term, we need only point this failing out.

To counter them in the long term requires more. It requires that we actually produce an account of how the brain represents the external world and the regularities it displays. But that is precisely what current theories of neural network function address. Real-time information about the world is coded in high-dimensional activation vectors, and general information about the world is coded in the background configuration of the network's synaptic weights. Activation vectors are processed by the weight configurations through which they pass, and learning consists in the adjustment of one's global weight configuration. These accounts already provide the resources to explain a variety of things, such as the recognition of complex objects despite partial or degraded sensory inputs, the swift retrieval of relevant information from a vast content-addressable memory, the appreciation of diffuse and inarticulable similarities, and the administration of complex sensorimotor coordination (P. M. Churchland 1989a). We are still too ignorant to insist that hypotheses of this sort will prove adequate to explain all of the representational capacities of mind. But neither can we insist that they are doomed to prove inadequate. It is an empirical question, and the jury is still out.

The third objection complains that what constitutes a human consciousness is not just the intrinsic character of the creature itself, but also the rich matrix of relations it bears to the other humans, practices, and institutions of its embedding culture. A reductionistic account of human consciousness and behavior, insofar as it is limited to the microscopic activities in an individual's brain, cannot hope to capture more than a small part of what is explanatorily important.

The proper response to this objection is to embrace it. Human behavior is indeed a function of the factors cited. And the character of any individual human consciousness will be profoundly shaped by the culture in which it develops. What this means is that any adequate neurocomputational account of human consciousness must take into account the manner in which a brain comes to represent not just the gross features of the physical world but also the character of the other cognitive creatures with which it interacts, and the details of the social, moral, and political world in which they all live. The brains of social animals, after all, learn to be interactive elements in a community of brains, much to their cognitive advantage. We need to know how they do it.

This is a major challenge, one that neuroscientists have not yet addressed with any seriousness, nor even much acknowledged. This is not surprising. Accounting for a creature's knowledge of the spatial location of a fly is difficult enough. Accounting for its knowledge of a loved one's embarrassment, a politician's character, or a bargaining opponent's hidden agenda, represents a much higher level of difficulty. And yet we already know that artificial neural networks, trained by examples, can come to recognize and respond to the most astonishingly subtle patterns and similarities in nature. If physical patterns, why not social patterns? We confront no problem in principle here. Only a major challenge.

It may indeed be unrealistic to expect an exhaustive global account of the neural and behavioral trajectory of a specific person over any period of time. The complexity of the neural systems we are dealing with may forever preclude anything more than useful approximations to the desired ideal account. The case of chemistry and its relation to quantum-physics comes to mind. There also, the mathematics of complex dynamical systems imposes limits on how easily and accurately we can reconstruct the chemical facts from the physical principles. This means that our reduction will never be truly complete, but we rightly remain confident that chemical phenomena are nothing but the macrolevel reflection of the underlying quantum-physical phenomena even so. As with chemical phenomena, so with psychological phenomena.

This brings us to the fourth objection, concerning the threat that a reduction would pose to human freedom. Here we shall be brief. Whether and in what sense there is any human freedom, beyond the relative autonomy that attaches to any complex dynamical system that is partially isolated from the world, is an entirely empirical question. Accordingly, rather than struggle to show that a completed neuroscience will be consistent with this, that, or the other preconceived notion of human freedom, we recommend that we let scientific investigation *teach us* in what ways and to what degrees human creatures are "free." No doubt this will entail modifications for some people's current conceptions of human freedom, and the complete elimination of some others. But that is preferable to making our current confusions into a standard that future theories must struggle to be consistent with.

The fifth and final objection claims an irreducibly abstract status for psychology, on grounds that a variety of quite different physical systems could realize equally well the abstract organization that constitutes a cognitive economy. How can we reduce psychological phenomena to neurobiology, if other physical substrates might serve just as well?

The premise of this objection will likely be conceded by all of us. But the conclusion against reduction does not follow. We can see this clearly by examining a case from our own scientific history. Temperature, we claimed earlier, is identical with mean molecular kinetic energy. But strictly speaking, this is true only for a gas, where the molecules are free to move in a ballistic fashion. In a solid, where the particles oscillate back and forth, their energy is constantly switching between a kinetic and a potential mode. In a high-temperature plasma, there are no molecules at all to consider, since everything has been ripped into subatomic parts. Here temperature is a complex mix of various energies. And in a vacuum, where there is no mass at all, temperature consists in the wavelength distribution—the "black-body curve"—of the EM waves passing through it.

What these examples show us is that reductions can be "domain specific": in a gas, temperature is one thing; in a solid, temperature is another thing; in a plasma, it is a third; in a vacuum, a fourth; and so on. (They all count as temperatures, since they interact, and they all obey the same laws of equilibrium and disequilibrium.) None of this moves us to say that classical thermodynamics is an autonomous, irreducible science, forever safe from the ambitions of the underlying microphysical story. On the contrary, it just teaches us that there is more than one way in which energy can be manifested at the microphysical level.

Similarly, visual experience may be one thing in a mammal, and a slightly different thing in an octopus, and a substantially different thing in some possible metal-and-semiconductor android. But they will all count as visual experiences because they share some set of abstract features at a higher level of description. That neurobiology should prove capable of explaining all psychological phenomena in humans is not threatened by the possibility that some *other* theory, say semiconductor electronics, should serve to explain psychological phenomena in *robots*. The two reductions would not conflict. They would complement each other.

We have elsewhere provided more comprehensive accounts of how recent work in neuroscience illuminates issues in psychology and cognitive theory (P. S. Churchland 1986; P. M. Churchland 1989a). Let us conclude this paper with two cautionary remarks. First, while we have here been very upbeat about the possibility of reducing psychology to neuroscience, producing such a reduction will surely be a long and difficult business. We have here been concerned only to rebut the counsel of impossibility, and to locate the reductive aspirations of neuroscience in a proper historical context.

Second, it should not be assumed that the science of psychology will somehow disappear in the process, nor that its role will be limited to that of a passive target of neural explanation. On the contrary, chemistry has not disappeared despite the quantum-mechanical explication of its basics; nor has the science of biology disappeared, despite the chemical explication of its basics. And each of these higher-level sciences has helped to shape profoundly the development and articulation of its underlying science. It will surely be the same with psychology and neuroscience. At this level of complexity, intertheoretic reduction does not appear as the sudden takeover of one discipline by another; it more closely resembles a long and slowly maturing marriage.

7

Conceptual Similarity across Sensory and Neural Diversity: The Fodor–Lepore Challenge Answered

Paul M. Churchland

In chapter 6 of *Holism*, Fodor and Lepore (1992) present a critical challenge to "state-space semantics," as pursued by neural network modelers. Their challenge expresses the doubt that such an approach could ever make useful sense of the notions of conceptual identity, or even conceptual similarity, in the face of the enormous functional and structural diversity across the individual networks that constitute human brains.

The present essay is the latest in a series of exchanges on this matter.[1] I stand by those earlier responses, but some new developments motivate a more ambitious and less defensive essay. Some recent theoretical insights and neuromodeling results from Laakso and Cottrell (1998) constitute a decisive answer to Fodor and Lepore's challenge, and point to new areas of semantic research. Laakso and Cottrell (hereafter: L&C) successfully deploy one member of a large family of mathematical measures of conceptual similarity, measures that see past differences—even extensive differences—in the connectivity, the sensory inputs, and the neural dimensionality of the networks being compared. The present essay explores the rationale behind these measures. L&C's application of one such measure across a diversity of real networks is sketched, and the generalization of such measures to many-layered networks and to time-series (recurrent) networks is discussed.

I. The Problem

On neural-network models of cognition, the primary unit of representation, and the primary *vehicle* of semantic content, is the overall pattern of simultaneous activation levels across the assembled neurons of a given

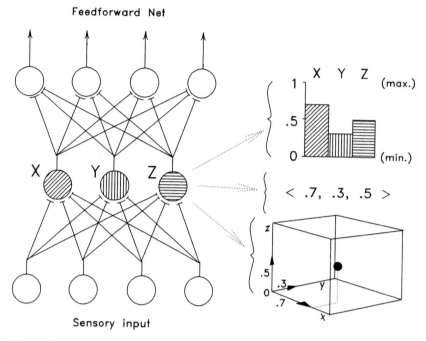

Figure 7.1
Three ways of conceiving of the current activity of a specific neuronal population: as a pattern or histogram of activation levels, as an activation vector, and as a point in an activation space.

population, such as the cells in layer 4 of the primary visual cortex, or the output cells of the motor cortex, or the "cells" in a given layer of some artificial network model (figure 7.1). Such patterns are often referred to as "activation vectors" because they can be usefully and uniquely characterized by a sequence or n-tuple of numbers, where $n = $ the number of neurons in the representing population.

To those more geometrically inclined, a specific activation pattern can also be simply and usefully characterized as a specific point in a proprietary space, an n-dimensional space with a proprietary axis for the variable activation level of each of the n neurons in the representing population. Any single point in that space will represent, by way of its unique set of n coordinate values, the simultaneous activation levels of each of the cells in the corresponding neural population.

At this level of reckoning, a specific activation *pattern* = a specific activation *vector* = a specific *point* in activation space. These are just variant ways of talking about the same thing: the unit of representation, as physically rather than semantically described.

If we are to assign specific semantical or representational *contents* to collective units of this kind, a natural first assumption is that any unit must in some way inherit its overall content from the individual and more basic representational significance of each of its many constituting elements, namely, the activation level of each of its many neurons. After all, it is these individual neurons that are the recipients of information from the environment: either directly, through their interaction with ambient light, heat, and various mechanical and chemical impingements; or indirectly, through their many synaptic connections with neurons earlier in the processing hierachy.

However, as Fodor and Lepore (hereinafter F&L) have earlier urged on me, this assumption leads quickly to a number of difficulties. In the first place, the approach to content here emerging would seem to be just another version of a Humean concept empiricism, with the "simple" concepts corresponding to whatever content or significance is assigned to the individual axes of the global activation space, that is, to whatever content or significance is assigned to the activation levels of each individual neuron in the relevant population. A "complex" concept will then be just an appropriate conjunction or configuration of the simples, a unique configuration represented by a unique point or position within the global activation space.

What was presented as new and interesting is therefore something quite old and boring, runs the objection. Worse, the emerging account leaves unaddressed the question of how each *axis* of the activation space, or each neuron of the representing population, gets *its* semantic or representational content. Presumably such "microcontent" must derive from the peculiar causal connections that a given neuron enjoys to microfeatures of the sensory environment, or, if the neuron in question is not itself a sensory neuron, then to some microfeatures of the content embodied in the activity of neurons earlier in the processing hierarchy, neurons that project axons to the specific neuron in question.

This obvious proposal, however, leads in this case to disaster. The problem is that no two people will have exactly the same set of causal dependencies across their sensory neurons, nor, a fortiori, across their subsequent neuronal layers as we climb their respective information-processing hierarchies. Even at the initial or sensory layer, there will be considerable idiosyncrasy, and that diversity will explode exponentially as the already idiosyncratic sets of microcontents get successively transformed by the profoundly idiosyncratic matrices of synaptic junctions that successively connect each layer in the neuronal hierarchy to the next layer. There is no hope, for example, of finding a mapping between the 10^{10} cells in my primary visual cortex and the 10^{10} cells in yours, such that for *every* mapped pair, your cell and mine have the *same* microcontent. The diversity in the scattered strengths or weights of our 10^{13} synaptic connections effectively precludes it. Probably we do not share a single such pair between us.

Worse still, we are all idiosyncratic in the sheer *number* of cells we have in any given neuronal population. Our respective activation spaces, therefore, do not even have the same *dimensionality*, let alone the same set of axial microcontents. Accordingly, if we cannot make sense of the notion of "same activation space" across distinct individuals, it is plain that we can make no sense of the notion of "same position in such a space" across two individuals, or even of "proximate positions." We therefore have no hope of explicating the notion of "same meaning" or "similar meaning" across distinct individuals. On such an ill-behaved neural basis, to conclude, we have no hope of constructing a workable theory of meaning.

II.   Painting a Different Picture

The short answer to this critique is that content is not in general assigned in the manner described. A point in activation space acquires a specific semantic content not as a function of its position relative to the constituting *axes* of that space, but rather as a function of

1. Its spatial position relative to all of the *other contentful points* within that space, and

2. Its causal relations to stable and objective *macrofeatures of the external environment.*

As we shall see, this very different focus takes our neural and synaptic diversity out of the semantic picture almost entirely. That undoubted diversity is without semantic significance. Two people can share a common hierarchy of partitions across their respective activation spaces, and, for each partition within that hierarchy, they can share a common causal relation to some objective environmental feature, despite the fact that those partitions and those causal relations are differently implemented across structurally idiosyncratic brains. Starting with a deliberately simple example, let me illustrate how this can happen.

Let us imagine that two identical feedforward networks, 1 and 2, are trained on the same corpus of 100 photos of each of 100 members of four extended and multigenerational hillbilly families: 25 Hatfields, 25 McCoys, 25 Wilsons, and 25 Andersons (figure 7.2). The two networks are trained—by progressive nudgings of their respective synaptic weights at the hands of the familiar backpropagation algorithm—to distinguish any input photo as a member of one of the four families. (The input layer of each network is here graphically portrayed as a line of twelve cells, but of course it would have to be a two-dimensional (2-D) grid of at least sixty-by-sixty cells to accommodate a realistic picture of each face. As well, there are far too many interlayer connections to portray all of them. Forgive the graphic license here taken.) The trained network's identification of any given face is defined as the highest of the four activation levels at the four labeled output cells. The two networks, let us suppose, are eventually trained to 100 percent accuracy on the training set of photos, and they generalize successfully to any new examples of these four extended families with greater than 90 percent accuracy.

How do they manage to perform at this high level? In real networks, the usual answer to this sort of question appeals to the coding strategy evolved, during learning, at the middle or "hidden" layer of neurons in the network involved. The idea is to look at the unique hidden-layer activation-space positions, severally displayed by the trained network, for grouping and separating the four families portrayed in the input photos. If the training was successful, the activation-space points for each of the twenty-five Hatfield faces will tend to be clustered together in a

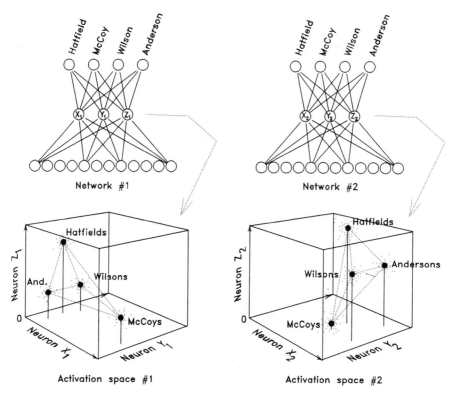

Figure 7.2
The locations of four prototype points within the hidden-layer activation spaces of two (imaginary) neural networks for recognizing the faces of four different extended families. The four points represent a prototypical Hatfield face, a prototypical McCoy face, a prototypical Wilson face, and a prototypical Anderson face.

proprietary subvolume or partition within the overall space. The face-points for other families will be similar clustered together in distinct familial clouds, as illustrated in figure 7.2.

To simplify things, let us focus our attention on the mean, average, or center-of-gravity position for all of the Hatfield face-points. This will be the *prototypical* Hatfield point, and it will represent the prototype of a Hatfield face—a face, perhaps, that no actual Hatfield actually possesses, but that every Hatfield resembles more or less closely. Let us plot this special point with a small boldface sphere in the relevant space for each network, as in figure 7.2. Do the same for the average or prototypical face of each of the other three families. The result for network 1 is the four points illustrated to the left, and the result for network 2 is the four points illustrated on the right.

As reckoned against the axes of their respective embedding spaces, each foursome is a distinct group of points. In one obvious sense, the two networks have settled on *different* coding strategies in solution to their common discriminatory problem. But a closer look reveals a residual and robust similarity in their respective coding strategies: the *relative* positions of each familial point, as reckoned against the other three familial points in each space, are obviously very similar. Indeed, they are identical across the two networks. More generally, the linear dimensions and the vertex angles of the 3-D "solids" defined by those four prototypical familial points are identical in the hidden-layer activation spaces of both networks. The solid shape at issue—an irregular tetrahedron—is both rotated and translated in space 2, relative to space 1, but it is the *same* solid shape in both spaces.

What is the significance of this isomorphic configuration of points? It means that both networks have reached a common reckoning of the *relative similarities and differences* that unite and divide the 100 faces in the training set, a common reckoning of the classes (and, as we shall see, the subclasses) into which that population divides, and a common reckoning of the numerical degree of similarity that relates any two face-points within the same activation space.

In the end it is to these common groupings, and to this common framework of similarity relations across the two hidden-layer spaces, that the final or output layer of neurons in each network gradually becomes "tuned" during training. (That is why the two networks have identical, or near identical, overall performance profiles.) The bottom half of each network manages to convert the great mass of pictorial information at the input layer into the (much lower-dimensional) form of information embodied in the two hidden-layer spaces portrayed in figure 7.2. And the top half of the network manages to convert that intermediate form of information into the labeled pigeonholes at the output layer.

Quite obviously, the intricate matrix of synaptic connections meeting both the hidden-layer neurons and the output-layer neurons will *have* to be very different across the two networks. (If they were identical, then the hidden-layer locations and orientations of the two tetrahedrons would be the same as well, and they are not.) Equally clear, the microcontents of the three axes x_1, y_1, z_1 of network 1 must be different from the microcontents of the three axes x_2, y_2, z_2 of network 2. Those two hidden layers may each be representing the same aspects of similarity and difference across the face population at issue, but clearly they are distributing the "representational load" differently across the basic axes of their representational spaces. (As causally reckoned, the respective microcontents of neurons x_1 and x_2, for example, *cannot* be the same: they are connected by a *different* family of synaptic weights to identical input layers.)

What we have, then, is a pair of networks with highly idiosyncratic synaptic connections: a pair of networks with hidden-layer neurons of quite different microcontents; a pair of networks whose input-output behaviors are nevertheless identical because they are rooted in *a common conceptual framework* embodied in the activation spaces of their respective hidden layers.

In what sense is it "the same?" In this sense: the several activation-space *distances* between the corresponding prototype positions are one and all identical, and the prototype positions identified as "corresponding" are so identified (despite their different locations in the two spaces) because each constitutes the standard causal response, at its network's hidden layer, to a typical Hatfield face (or McCoy face, and so on) presented as input to the sensory layer.

It is easy to extend this identity criterion to encompass a numerical criterion of *similarity* across such categorial frameworks. Our two tetrahedrons have six corresponding straight edges joining each of the four corresponding prototypical points. Let us ask, for each such pair of lines, AB and A'B', what is the absolute value of the difference between their lengths, and then divide it by the sum of those two lengths. This will always give us a fraction between 0 and 1, where the fraction approaches 0 as the the two lengths approach identity. Let us then take the average of all six of those fractions, as computed for each of the six pairs, and subtract it from 1. As expected, this measure will give us a similarity rating of 1 for the two identical tetrahedrons of figure 7.2. Progressively divergent shapes will get progressively lower ratings. In summary,

$$\text{Similarity} = 1 - \text{avg.}\frac{|AB - A'B'|}{(AB + A'B')}$$

Most important, this simple similarity measure will be indifferent to any translations, rotations, or mirror inversions of the solid shape in question, as that shape may find itself differently located within the diverse activation spaces of diverse neural networks. What matters is not its accidental location or orientation within any given space; what matters is its internal geometry, and the causal connections of its various vertices to objective features of the sensory environment.

Still, what of the problem of comparing such categorial frameworks across activation spaces with different *dimensionalities*? Suppose, for example, that our network 2 had four hidden-layer neurons instead of only three? That very real possibility would pose no problem at all. First, a 4-D space can obviously *contain* a 3-D tetrahedral solid. Second, nothing whatever prevents its several "prototype" vertices from being causally connected to the *same* environmental features as its 3-D cousin. Finally, and despite expectations, the similarity measure just described can be invoked, without modification, to evaluate even these dimensionally diverse cases. Let me explain.

The important point to remember is that the basic component of this similarity measure—*distance*—has the same units of measurement whatever the dimensionality of the space in which that distance happens to be reckoned. It matters not whether the spaces involved have different dimensions. Distances within them can always be directly compared across distinct spaces. For example, the line *AB* in figure 7.3a has the same length as line *A'B'* in figure 7.3b, despite their being embedded in a 2-D space and a 3-D space respectively. And the triangle *ABC* in figure 7.3c is metrically identical to the triangle *A'B'C'* in figure 7.3d, despite the different dimensionality of the two spaces that contain them.

So long as we can measure common distances across diverse spaces, we can always specify any point configuration or hyperconfiguration whatever, since the family of distances between its several vertices fixes that configuration uniquely (or rather, uniquely up to its mirror image). Dimensional differences, it emerges, matter not at all.

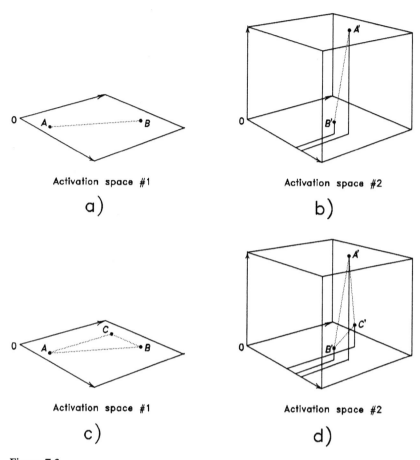

Activation space #1

a)

Activation space #2

b)

Activation space #1

c)

Activation space #2

d)

Figure 7.3
(a) A ten-inch line within a two-dimensional plane. (b) A ten-inch line within a three-dimensional volume. (c) A right-angle triangle in a 2-D plane. (d) The same right-angle triangle in a 3-D volume.

One can see this same point in another way. If a pair of dimensionally diverse spaces both contain, in some orientation or other, a same-shape n-dimensional hypersolid ("same shape" as reckoned above), then both spaces must each either constitute or contain an n-D subspace, an n-D hyperplane of some orientation or other, that confines each hypersolid at issue. Since those respective hyperplanes, at any rate, have the same dimensionality, there will be no problem in comparing the two solids. Simply superimpose the two (sub)spaces, as one might lift the plane of figure 7.3c into the space of figure 7.3d so as to coincide with the plane defined by its embedded triangle A'B'C'. If the contained shapes are indeed identical, then some relative rotation and/or translation of those two spaces will make every edge and every vertex of the two solids coincide perfectly. (Thanks to my student, Evan Tiffany, for pointing this out to me.) Once again, dimensional differences simply do not matter. They seemed to, at the outset, only against the false assumptions, concerning how conceptual similarity must be reckoned, embraced by F&L.

III. Some Precursors of These Ideas

L&C were not the first to assemble systematic distance measures to explicate important elements of conceptual structure. Sejnowski and Rosenberg confronted a scatter of seventy-nine prototypical points in the activation space of NETtalk's hidden layer, and they decided to ask how those assembled points paired off when each was coupled to its closest neighbor (Rosenberg and Sejnowski 1987). They then asked how the resulting population of pairs clustered together when closest pairs were subsequently coupled into foursomes. Repeating this process to completion resulted in a treelike structure whose trunk divides into two main branches (the grapheme-to-vowel transforms below, and the grapheme-to-consonant transforms above), and then into a series of further divisions and subdivisions, all of which grouped appropriately similar elements together while keeping dissimilar elements apart (figure 7.4).

Such *dendograms*, as they are called, are highly useful representations of the sorts of hierarchically structured sets of categories that so often emerge in the course of network training. And they express moderately well the sorts of distance relations (between prototype points) that we

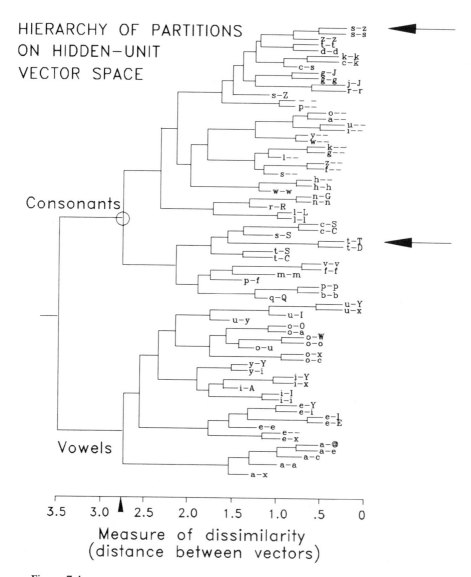

Figure 7.4
A dendogram representing the "closest-similarity" structure of the seventy-nine prototypical categories that emerged, during training, in the hidden-layer activation space of Sejnowski and Rosenberg's NETtalk, an artificial neural network that reads printed English text aloud.

have found to be so important. Locate any two disparate points at the rightmost tips of the branching tree (e.g., the two grapheme-to-phoneme transforms, s → z and t → T); trace their respective branches leftward until they meet (here marked with a circle); look at the corresponding value on the horizontal coordinate axis directly below that branch junction (here, $x = 2.75$); this will be (very roughly) the activation-space distance between the two points at issue. (Strictly speaking, this gives the distance between the *average* positions of all of the points in the two branch structures that meet at that junction. Fine-grained distance information concerning arbitrary point-pairs is thus progressively lost as one moves leftward across the diagram.)

It is worth noting that the dendogram of figure 7.4 retains no information concerning the *dimensionality* of NETtalk's activation space, the original space whose organization it so usefully represents. That space could have had two dimensions, or two million (in fact, it had twenty-four hidden-layer neurons). The dendogram doesn't care. It cares only about distances within the relevant space.

This means that dendograms are a useful device for representing both the ordinal and the metrical aspects of conceptual organization, no matter how large the representing population of neurons might be. Not so for literal spatial diagrams. Given the limits on our human imaginations, and on the graphic potential of a 2-D sheet of paper, spatial diagrams of the sort shown in figures 7.1, 7.2, and 7.3 cease to be useful when the dimensionality of the space exceeds three. It is hard to draw an effective 4-D or 5-D figure on a 2-D surface. This is a grievous limitation, since many networks will have thousands or even millions of neurons at any given layer.

Nevertheless, the 3-D spatial diagrams are a useful metaphor for what, generally speaking, is going on in the higher-D cases. Specifically, there really is an abstract space and it really does come to contain prototypical points, similarity gradients, category boundaries or partitions, and a well-defined geometrical configuration that embraces all of them. The grand picture aside, however, when we wish to specify, graphically, the actual cognitive configuration of a specific network, it is to the dendogram that we must turn.

It follows from all of this that the conceptual organizations of two distinct networks, with activation spaces of quite different dimensionalities, could be correctly represented by the very same dendogram, because the relevant family of distance relations happens to be the same for both networks. This is another instance of our earlier point that there is no problem at all in specifying conceptual identity across dimensionally diverse networks.

Strict conceptual identity, however, is not what distinct empirical networks generally give us, even if they happen to be dimensionally identical, and even if they share the same set of training examples. To illustrate, let us return to the two (imaginary) face spaces of figure 7.2. We spoke earlier of them having a "common" reckoning of the categories involved, but a fine-grained analysis would likely show some small differences. The respective dendograms for those spaces might well look as follows (figure 7.5). Note that their most basic clusterings are identical, with the Wilsons and the Andersons represented as most closely similar, with both of these families represented as slightly closer to the Hatfields than to the McCoys, and with these latter two families represented as the least similar of all.

Note, however, that some of their *peripheral* pairings for most-similar faces diverge: Jed gets paired with Bubba in net 1, but he gets paired with Festus in net 2. Such residual differences in the similarity spaces of the two trained networks are typical. They reflect small differences in the initial or naive configurations of their synaptic weights, and differences in the (random) order in which they originally encountered the faces in the training set. (In human networks, they would also reflect differences in the global corpus of faces on which they were trained.) During the learning phase, the networks end up following distinct paths through the (structural!) space of possible weight configurations, and typically they arrive at quite distinct final states. Those distinct physical states may be, and presumably will be, closely similar in their functional profiles, and relevantly similar in the conceptual organizations to which they give rise, but they need not be strictly identical in either respect.

Such idiosyncrasies should not be seen as a defect of our artificial models. People, too, display peripheral divergences in how they judge close similarities. What we have here is an explanatory account of how and why they might do so.

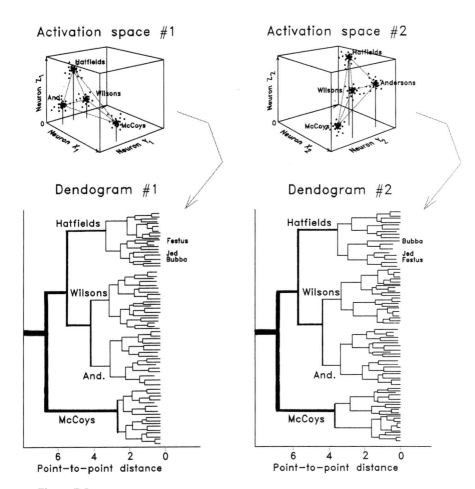

Figure 7.5
The respective dendograms for the two activation spaces of figure 7.2. Note the close similarity of their respective large-scale groupings of the 100 individual faces involved, both in who gets grouped with whom and in the relative distances that separate distinct groups. Note also the occasional small divergences in how each network pairs up "most similar" individuals at the tips of the tree's branches.

Their virtues acknowledged, dendograms have two major short-comings. As noted earlier, they positively hide information about the exact distance between any two arbitrarily chosen prototype points (because they are progressively concerned with average positions, and with averages of averages, and so on). Across distinct networks, therefore, subtly different similarity structures can be hidden behind identical dendograms.

Second, judging the global similarity of two or more conceptual organizations may be easy for the near-identical cases, but it swiftly becomes subjective and uncertain when the internal organizations of these treelike structures start to diverge, as often they do. As Cottrell remarked at the original presentation of the L&C results, "When I eyeball the dendograms for two distinct networks, I may say, 'yes, they're fairly close,' but that's just my reaction. We need an objective measure of such things."

That problem returns us to the sort of numerical similarity-measure stated in the preceding section (recall figure 7.2), where we look at the differences between the corresponding distances that spatially configure the special family of points to be compared. That simple measure provides a similarity criterion of the objective kind required: it returns a number between 0 and 1, with 1 as a perfect score. And as we saw, it is indifferent to any dimensional differences between the activation spaces being compared. But it is not the only such measure, nor perhaps the best. I have leaned on it to this point only for reasons of simplicity in exposition. Let us now look at a different but related measure, and at its application to an extended family of real empirical networks.

IV.   The Laakso-Cottrell Experiments

L&C deploy a similarity measure, apparently well-known among statisticians, called the Gutman point alienation (GPA) measure. It is applied, as in the preceding examples, to a pair of equinumerous point-families, and it, too, measures the similarity in the respective internal spatial organizations of those families. The GPA measure, however, returns a 1 for a perfect correlation between the two point-families, a 0 for a random correlation, and a −1 for a perfect anticorrelation. (See the appendix for the detailed substance of the measure.) Furthermore, unlike my fanciful

Hatfield-McCoy illustration, L&C appeal to no initial clusterings around preaveraged prototype points. They mean to apply the GPA to *all* of the actual points or activation vectors that appear in the "awake, behaving network," not just to the "prototype" points around which they may happen to cluster. This broader focus yields a much finer-grained analysis of the structure of the various similarity gradients that characterize the two spaces being compared.

Withal, deploying this measure is perhaps the least of L&C's achievements. What stands out is the series of training experiments, and the resulting family of over two dozen perceptually skilled artificial neural networks to which the GPA was subsequently applied. It is one thing to argue, as section II argues above, that there can be perfectly sensible measures of the kind denied by F&L. It is quite another to test such a measure against a large and revealing family of empirical examples. That is what L&C have done.

The target problem addressed by L&C was not facial recognition, but color recognition. They began with a data base for 627 distinct colors, a data base that provided a unique twelve-element spectral-reflectance vector for each one of those 627 colors. Those reflectance vectors were suitable for entry, as activation patterns, across the "sensory" neurons of the model network in figure 7.6. It has twelve input units, three hidden units, and five output units, whose function is to code for each of the five broad color *categories*—red, yellow, green, blue, and purple—to which the network was slowly trained. It learned to group correctly, into the categories imposed, the many elements in the test population of 627 examples.

In fact, L&C successfully trained *five* individual networks, of this same configuration, to a criterion level of competence on the color-recognition task. Each network differed only in the initial random setting of its synaptic weights, and in the random order in which the training examples were presented to it. (As usual, this yields a distinct learning excursion, in structural space, for each network.) After competence had been reached, no two networks shared the same final configuration of synaptic weights, despite the identity of their acquired discriminatory competence. The question then was, what had happened to the internal organization of the hidden-layer activation space in each network? In particular, had those activation spaces settled on the *same* organization, in the "family-of-corresponding-distances" sense that is by now becoming familiar?

The GPA was set to work comparing the geometrical similarity of the relevant point-families (families with 627 members each, instead of just 4, as in the Hatfield-McCoy example), and its answers were strongly positive. Across this set of five structurally similar networks, the lowest similarity rating returned for an activation-space pair was .93. The average pairwise similarity across this group was .97.

(A qualification needs to be made here. Computing the pairwise distances for every point-pair in a set of 627 points is computationally demanding: there are $(627 \times 266)/2$, or 196,251 such distances. For a single pair of networks you have to do it twice—once for each activation space—and then you have to compare all of the results. As well, it may be overkill, since the GPA measure is ultimately interested only in the rank ordering of the relevant distances. Choosing discretion over valor, and finesse over brute force, L&C settled for a partial computation of the all-up GPA. The point-to-point distances actually computed and compared for rank ordering were a subset of the total: those lines that shared a common vertex. This partial-GPA measure is thus less thorough than its parent, but it is still a very stern measure. L&C employed it for every example in what follows, so convey the qualification forward.)

The emergence of such close similarities is intriguing. But L&C went several steps further. In addition to the familiar twelve-element decimal fraction coding vectors described earlier, they concocted a second, a third, and a fourth scheme for encoding the same information contained in the original 627 reflectance vectors. The second coding scheme used a binary rather than a decimal code, and it yielded input vectors with *ninety-six* elements. The third coding scheme used five gaussian filters (rather like the human retinal system, but with five "cones" instead of three) and it yielded input vectors with five elements. The fourth used a simple sequential encoding from 001 to 627, and it yielded input vectors with *three* elements each.

Each sensory coding scheme, of course, required a structurally distinct network with a numerically distinct input layer to accomodate the four different forms in which the color information was coded. As they had done for the twelve-element case, L&C constructed a family of five identical networks with a ninety-six-unit input layer, five further networks with a five-unit input layer, and five more with a three-unit input layer (figure 7.6). These further networks correspond to creatures with importantly *different sense organs* for apprehending and coding color information. They give us a total of twenty networks in all.

The various networks in these further families were subjected to the same training regime as the five networks already discussed. These new networks also reached high levels of performance (although the nets using the crude three-element scheme were somewhat weaker than the others). As well, they each settled into an idiosyncratic configuration of synaptic weights. Once again, the question was, what of the internal organizations of their hidden-layer activation spaces?

Once again, the GPA returned high values in measure of their mutual similarity. Within networks using the ninety-six-element scheme, the lowest similarity rating was .89 and the average similarity was .95. For the five-element networks, the values were: lowest, .94, and average, .98. For the three-element networks, the values were: lowest, .99, and average, .99. These results parallel the outcome of the first experiment. They show, once again, that similar nets facing similar problems have a robust tendency to settle into the same abstract solution in how they structure the partitions or prototype families within their hidden-layer activation spaces.

Digging deeper, however, L&C discovered something even more interesting. They set the GPA to measuring the mutual similarity of the internal organizations of the hidden-layer activation spaces, not within, but now *across* these four (structurally diverse) families of networks. Of the ten pairwise comparisons between the ninety-six-element and the twelve-element networks, the average similarity was .95. This is the same high level of similarity that they found *within* each family of networks. The substantial structural diversity across these two families, and the diverse character of their respective sensory inputs, apparently made no difference to the activation-space solution into which they severally settled.

Other pairings across the other network families yielded comparably high measures of mutual similarity. Only when the "deliberately marginal" three-element scheme was made party to the comparisons did the

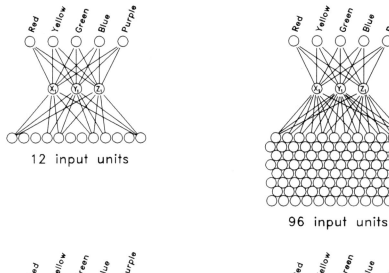

Figure 7.6
The architectures of the four main network types trained to color-recognition competence by Laakso and Cottrell. Note the differences in their respective sensory or input layers, and the corresponding differences in the number of synaptic connections that meet their respective hidden layers.

measure occasionally fall as low as .72, and even here it averaged about .8. These particular results are striking because they show that close conceptual similarity—as we are here measuring it—can and does emerge from networks with a different structural organization, and even from networks with distinct *sense organs*. (This last result is especially welcome to some of us. Readers of my 1979 book *Scientific Realism and the Plasticity of Mind* will recall that the possibility of driving the very same conceptual framework with radically different sense organs was one of the major themes of its second chapter.)

In summary, so long as the relevant information is somehow implicit in whatever sensory-input schemes happen to be employed, and so long as the training procedures impose the same requirements on recognitional performance, then diverse networks can and often will settle into almost identical abstract organizations of the similarity gradients across their hidden-layer activation spaces. During learning, that is, the networks of the four different types come to "see past" the structural idiosyncrasies of their diverse sensory manifolds, so as to achieve a common grasp of the objective features of the world that drive their several but similar behaviors. Once again,[2] and give or take a bit, this is not hello Hume; it is hello Plato.

In a final series of networks, L&C explored the consequences of expanding, beyond three, the *number* of hidden-layer neurons in such networks. The point here was to address F&L's final worry about networks whose hidden layers define spaces of different dimensionalities. Accordingly, a final family of networks, with variously expanded hidden layers, were trained to competence on the same discrimination task posed to the earlier networks, and the GPA was used to measure the similarity in the conceptual organizations that emerged during training in their several activation spaces (figure 7.7). Once more the GPA returned numbers in the range of .9 and higher, the dimensional diversity notwithstanding. The networks all had different synaptic configurations—meaning that the relevant point-families must, at the least, have different orientations in the several spaces at issue—but once more the networks were found to have settled on the same conceptual organization in response to their common discriminatory problem.

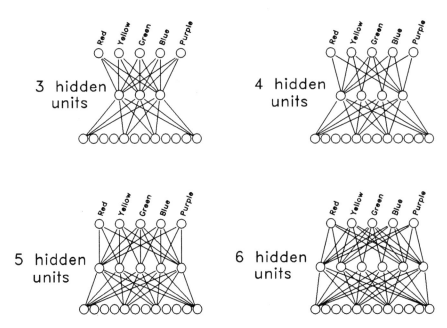

Figure 7.7
The architectures of four further color-recognition networks which have progressively larger numbers of hidden units. Despite the dimensional diversity of these four distinct representational spaces, the GPA discovered, after the networks were trained, nearly identical conceptual organizations within each.

The take-home point of the preceding pages is not that the various networks always settled on the *same* cognitive configuration in response to their shared problem. These networks did, and that fact is interesting. But networks need not and do not always show such uniformity in the "conceptual" solutions they find to common learning problems. The truly important point is that we can *tell* whether or not they did. We can say *what* their internal cognitive similarity consists in, and we can give an objective numerical *measure* of that similarity. Thanks to L&C, these are no longer purely a priori points. We now have over two dozen trained networks of whom to ask such questions, and, taking these examples pairwise, we have at least $(24 \times 23)/2 = 276$ distinct empirical applications of the similarity measure at issue. The results overturn F&L's claim that a useful measure of this kind is impossible.

V. Future Directions

These developments are encouraging, but we should remember that this is still an early skirmish in what will surely be a long campaign. The full range of semantic phenomena includes far more than the hierarchy of partitions we have discovered within the hidden-layer activation spaces of three-layer, feedforward, classifier networks. Our discussion, so far, stops there. Though I can do little more than scout the territory, I shall close this essay by looking ahead to what remains to be done.

Multilayer feedforward networks demand attention first. Few creatures have but a single neuronal layer between their sensory and their motor neurons. How, then, should we reckon conceptual similarity across networks whose input and output layers are separated not by one hidden layer, but by many? Here, I think, it is relatively easy to generalize the story of the preceding sections.

Let us assume, as before, that we are comparing two classifier networks whose learned input-output functions are close to being identical. Their gross discriminative behaviors, that is, are the same. In that case, the most obvious place to look for a pair of similarly partitioned activation spaces is at the penultimate layer of each network, since the output layer of each must base its discriminative verdicts on exactly the information that appears in the immediately preceding layer. If we want to know "where it all comes together," therefore, the *last* of the networks' hidden layers is the presumptive place to look for each network's acquired conception of how the objective world is structured.

This presumption is encouraged by the lesson of the four different network architectures trained to the same competence by L&C. The diversity across those networks lay in their earliest layers, a diversity that had disappeared by the time we reach their last (and only) hidden layers. The point is generalizable. Two networks can have many layers of hidden units preceding their penultimate layers, and yet come to exactly the same cognitive configurations within their penultimate activation spaces. Those earlier layers can be as idiosyncratic as you please, and the number of such layers may well differ from one network to another. But this need not impede the relevant application of the GPA or other similarity measure to the learned point-families within each of the two penultimate spaces. And the results of such reckoning will have the same significance they had in the original three-layer cases.

We can, of course, apply the GPA so as to compare the internal structures, across the two networks, of *any* of their corresponding layers. Simply generate a corresponding family of points in each, by presenting the "same input" to each network (as we saw, it may be differently coded), and turn the GPA loose. It may discover a series of close similarities up and down the two hierarchies in question, or it may not. (L&C actually did this for the respective input layers of their four distinct networks: the similarities here were dramatically lower.) What to make of the results of such comparisons will presumably vary from case to case, but we can be assured that we can always address such questions and hope to get a determinate answer. Multilayer networks, to conclude, seem not to present any insuperable problems, either in conceiving of similarity or in measuring it.

Recurrent networks, by contrast, launch us into a new universe of subtleties. The first major difference is structural: recurrent networks are characterized by the existence of at least some axonal projections that reach back from their originating neuronal population to make synaptic connections with some hidden layer that is earlier or below it in the processing hierarchy (figure 7.8). The result is a hidden layer whose activity is driven partly by the upward flow of sensory information, and partly by the downward flow of some already-processed information, information that is a digest of some of the network's immediately preceding activity.

Functionally, this arrangement allows for an ongoing modulation of the network's cognitive response to any sensory input, a modulation driven by a form of short-term memory of the network's proximate cognitive past. Such modulation can continue to drive the network even if its sensory layer should happen to fall silent, for the recurrent information can be quite sufficient to keep the ball rolling, once it is started.

I have elsewhere discussed at length the cognitive properties of recurrent networks,[3] and will not attempt to retell those stories here. What is important for present purposes is that a recurrent network's primary unit of representation is not the *point* in activation space, but rather the *trajectory* in activation space. It is a temporally extended *sequence* of the

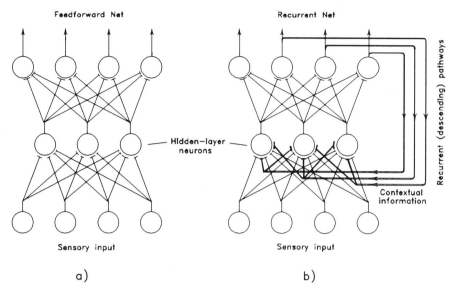

Figure 7.8
(a) A purely feedforward network. (b) A recurrent network. Note the flow of information from layer 3 back to the neurons in layer 2. This allows the network to modulate its own responses to sensory inputs, and to profit from its own immediate history.

now-familiar activation patterns across the hidden layer. The virtue of such trajectories is that they can represent objective phenomena with a *temporal* profile, such as a running animal's gait, a bouncing ball's path, or an unfolding sentence's grammatical structure. Feedforward networks represent the world as an unrelated sequence of timeless snapshots or frozen spatial structures. But recurrent networks represent the world as unfolding in time, as something that contains prototypical processes, structured sequences, and standard causal pathways.

Let us first address the similarity of such representations as it is reckoned *within* a given network's hidden-layer activation space. As expected, and as figure 7.9a illustrates, similarity consists in the spatial proximity of the trajectories being compared. The two possible trajectories there pictured represent two possible sentences that differ only in the number of their subject and in their final verb: "Boys, who boys chase, chase boy," and "Boy, who boys chase, chases boy." Elman's well-known grammar network (Elman 1992) yielded identical trajectories in its

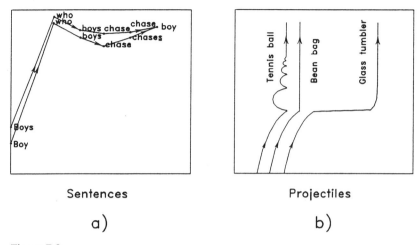

Figure 7.9
(a) The activation-space trajectories of two grammatically similar sentences in Elman's recurrent "grammar" network (after Elman 1992). (b) A family of activation-space trajectories that are similar until a critical time, at which point they diverge sharply.

representation of grammatically identical sentences entered as input. It yielded proximate trajectories in its representation of grammatically similar sentences, and it yielded distant trajectories when representing grammatically diverse sentences.

Note that similarity can be restricted to temporal segments of the compared trajectories. Figure 7.9b illustrates three trajectories that represent, respectively, a falling tennis ball that bounces several times, a falling beanbag that flattens on first impact, and a falling glass that shatters on impact. Each of the three objects is represented by a spatially distinct activation-space trajectory because the three objects are quite rightly comprehended as objects with distinct causal properties. Despite the proximity of their initial (falling) phases, therefore, they have divergent postimpact paths. Another example of this sort of restricted similarity would be the two trajectories for two sentences whose first six words were identical, but whose grammatical form diverged from the seventh word on.

We are here beginning to refine our similarity judgments to address *partial* similarities, or similarity in certain specifiable aspects. This bids me point out a second and broader way in which this can be done. Since specific hyperplanes (within the same overall activation space) regularly code for specific aspects of the global phenomenon being represented, we can make principled judgments of partial similarities between two trajectories by looking at their partial images within a specific subspace. Two trajectories may be closely proximate in one subspace, and yet be quite distant when reckoned in another. (A rough analogy here is comparing the various partial derivatives of a pair of high-dimensional functions: their slopes may be identical in one plane, but different in another.)

Elman's grammar network once more provides an illustration of this point. Similarity and difference of relative-clause structures were most saliently represented in one tilted hyperplane, and similarity and difference in noun and corresponding verb number (singular or plural) were represented in another. All of this allows us to say that two trajectories can be quite sensibly compared and contrasted in a number of distinct dimensions.

But what of the primary problem here? What of comparing trajectories across distinct networks? Here, as with the purely feedforward case, we must be mindful of the enormous neuronal and synaptic diversity in the ways in which the "same" conceptual framework can be implemented in two distinct individuals. And here, as there, what determines the semantic content or representational significance of a given trajectory will be the set of activation-space relations it bears to all of the other contentful trajectories within its home space, and the causal relations it bears to objective processes in its external environment.

The most obvious criterion of cross-person conceptual similarity for recurrent networks, accordingly, is a direct temporal generalization of the criterion we used in the feedforward case. Two networks have the same conceptual organization if and only if there is some rotation, translation, and/or mirror inversion of the prototype-trajectory family of the first network such that, when the space (or relevant subspace) of the first network is projected onto the space (or relevant subspace) of the second, all of the corresponding trajectories (as identified by what sensory inputs activate them) coincide perfectly.

I am moderately confident that this is a sufficient condition for conceptual identity, but I have a small reservation concerning its credentials as a necessary condition. The main worry is one I have discussed before, though in a different context.[4] Evidently it is possible for two people (for the sake of illustration, suppose they are Newton and Huygens) to have identical conceptions of ballistic-particle phenomena, and identical conceptions of traveling-wave phenomena, and yet differ substantially in the sensory phenomena that serve spontaneously to activate those conceptions in each of them. When Newton turns his attention to the phenomenon of light, it is his ballistic particle prototype-trajectories that standardly get activated in his brain. But when Huygens turns his attention to the same range of phenomena, it is his traveling-wave prototype trajectories that standardly get activated. Plainly said, Newton is convinced that light is a stream of particles and Huygens is convinced that light is a wave train.

This case poses a problem for the criterion just outlined because the presumed identity of conceptual machinery across these two individuals fails the requirement that identical concepts must have the same causal connections to the sensory environment. Here, they do not. The sets of connections overlap, to be sure—Newton and Huygens agree on billiard balls, comets, water waves, and sound—but they also show resolute divergences when our two heroes confront light.

The lesson of this example, and we can contrive many more, is that we should weaken the requirement that demands sameness of sensory causal connections. At the very least, we should demand such sameness across individuals only for the majority of environmental domains, and allow diverse responses within others.

For these sorts of reasons, I have always been moved to play down the semantic importance of concept-to-world connections, and moved to play up the semantic importance of the set of all concept-to-concept connections.[5] It is the sameness in the latter, across two individuals, that most decisively marks them as having the same conception of the world in which they live. This impulse toward a "purely-internal conceptual-role" theory of meaning was present in my 1979, and it moves me still, despite the substantial reconception of the basic kinematics of cognitive activity that connectionist models have introduced. I must own, however, that the considerations that motivate this tilt—namely, the desire to account for misconceptions of the phenomena, broad theoretical disagreements, and systematically false perceptual judgments—come prominently into play only when we are considering the cognitive activity of highly sophisticated intellectual creatures. For simpler creatures, it may be mostly idle to worry that the two constituting threads of semantic identity—concept-to-concept relations, and concept-to-world relations—will ever pull in opposing directions. Let me put this worry aside, then, at least for the time being, and return to a "two-aspect" approach to semantic identity, at least as a first approximation to the truth.

I make this conciliatory move for a further reason. A neglected element in the reckoning of semantic content is the set of causal connections that join cognitive states to *motor behavior*. If we have motivation for a two-aspect semantic theory, we have equal motivation for a *three*-aspect theory. It shows up even within folk-psychological reckonings of content, for, errors aside, we judge the content of an executed "intention" by the motor behavior it causes. This third aspect is highly salient from our new activation-space perspective, since in real creatures, perhaps the primary *function* of activational trajectories is to generate a corresponding sequence of motor behaviors. The administration of motor behavior is almost certainly the original function of activational trajectories, evolutionarily speaking. Neural ganglia that direct feeding behaviors, excretory behaviors, heartbeats, and basic locomotion probably antedate perceptual ganglia that track environmental events. They are in any case of equal importance to the life of any individual. We do not usually think of our internal cognitive activities as representing complex bodily behaviors—it is the perceptual end of the system that tends to dominate our philosophical attention—but most assuredly they do represent such things, and any proper account of cognitive representation in general must include the motor end of the system as well.

I close by addressing a skeptical worry from the preconnectionist semantic tradition. Specifically, what makes the preceding story of activation patterns, structured spaces, and coincident trajectories a *semantic* theory? Why isn't it just a new and unorthodox account of our underlying "syntactic" activities?

The answer, insofar as I can give one, goes something like this. The account we are currently piecing together is indeed a "syntactic" account, but it is not "just" a syntactic account. For it promises to do what we have always expected a semantic theory to do. Specifically, it gives us an account of how distinct representational contents are systematically embodied in distinct cognitive vehicles. It gives us a detailed account of how those contents are causally related to proprietary aspects of the external world, both in perception and in action. It shows us how certain aspects of the world's structure are mirrored in the relational structure of our assembled representations; that is to say, it gives us some idea of how our background conceptual framework and specific activations within it *picture* both the global structure of the world and specific things and events within it. Further, the theory gives us a detailed account of how those representations participate in a principled internal cognitive economy. And it provides a criterion for assigning the *same* contents to the representational vehicles of distinct individuals. It gives us, that is, a criterion for accurate translation across the representational/cognitive systems of distinct individuals. It may well be false, but it looks like a semantic theory to me.

It also looks like something else: it looks like a theory of perceptual *qualia* as well. In fact, and as their title and their classification task suggest, L&C first launched their investigation out of a concern for qualia, not out of a concern for concepts or universals. As well, I have long been puzzled, and a little troubled, that connectionist models fail to mark any obvious difference-of-kind between qualia and concepts. Some time ago, it occurred to me that perhaps the models were trying to tell us something: that there *is no* sharp or principled distinction between them. What we are pleased to call a perceptual quale is simply the activation of a conceptual category embodied in a hidden layer that is maximally close to the sensory transducer end of the processing hierarchy. And what we are usually pleased to call our abstract concepts (including our concepts *of* such qualia, should we happen to have developed any) are just categories embodied in some hidden layer rather higher up in the same hierarchy. If so, the connectionist approach can lay claim to an unexpected unification in our understanding of cognitive phenomena.

Appendix: The Gutman Point-Alienation Measure

As applied to a pair of networks, X and Y, the GPA takes the following form. (Save for some trivial simplifications, the following is drawn from

Laakso and Cottrell.) For network X, there will be a matrix X whose columns represent specific input stimuli and whose rows represent the hidden-layer activation pattern produced thereby. There will be a related matrix Y for network Y. We can compute the similarity or correlation $\mu_{X,Y}$ between their respective modes of hidden-layer representation as follows:

$$\mu_{X,Y} = \frac{\sum\limits_{r=1}^{m} \sum\limits_{p=1}^{m} \sum\limits_{q=1}^{m} (d_{X_r X_p} - d_{X_r X_q})(d_{Y_r Y_p} - d_{Y_r Y_q})}{\sum\limits_{r=1}^{m} \sum\limits_{p=1}^{m} \sum\limits_{q=1}^{m} |d_{X_r X_p} - d_{X_r X_q}| \, |d_{Y_r Y_p} - d_{Y_r Y_q}|}$$

where

X, Y are the two matrices,
m is the number of rows in the two matrices,
X_r is the rth row of matrix X, and
$d_{X_r X_p}$ is the distance between the rth row and the pth row of matrix X.

The Euclidean distance $d_{X_p X_q}$ between two vectors of n elements is defined as the square root of the sum, over all n elements, of the squares of the differences of the elements of each vector, as follows:

$$d_{X_p X_q} = \left[\sum_{i=1}^{n} (X_{pi} - X_{qi})^2 \right]^{1/2}$$

where

X is an m by n matrix,
$d_{X_p X_q}$ is the Euclidean distance between rows p and q of matrix X,
p, q are indices for the rows of matrix X,
i is an index for the columns of matrix X,
n is the number of columns in matrix X, and
X_{pi} is the ith element of row p of matrix X.

The two matrices, X and Y, are determined empirically, by presenting a common range of inputs to each network and determining the hidden-layer activation-space point that results, for each input, in each network. The global correlation between those two point-families can then be calculated as indicated.

The GPA has the disadvantage of deliberately losing metrical information because it eventually turns its attention to comparing only the *rank* orderings of the respective activation-space distance-families across the two networks. For this reason, I am inclined to think that a similarity measure of the sort suggested in section II will provide a more penetrating measure of conceptual similarity. Unlike the GPA, that measure does not lose metrical information in computing its assessment. However, this virtue comes with what may be a residual vice: as it stands, the metrical measure (unlike the GPA) is *not* blind to differences in *scale*. Two hypersolids, shape-identical but different in absolute size, will receive a low similarity rating. If we wish, this sensitivity to global scale is easily repaired. Simply sum all the lengths of the first hypersolid, and divide it by the sum of all of the lengths of the second hypersolid, to obtain a "correction factor," *c*, thus:

$$c = \Sigma(\text{AB})/\Sigma(\text{A}'\text{B}')$$

Then insert that correction factor into the original metrical measure, as follows:

$$\text{Similarity} = 1 - \text{avg.} \; \frac{|\text{AB} - c(\text{A}'\text{B}')|}{(\text{AB} + c(\text{A}'\text{B}'))}.$$

This measure will give a similarity rating of 1 for two hypersolids whose *relative* internal distances are all identical, but which differ globally in absolute scale.

8

Betty Crocker's Theory of Consciousness

Paul M. Churchland

John Searle is known primarily for his extensive corpus in the philosophy of language, but in recent years he has penned some celebrated if iconoclastic essays in the philosophy of mind. For example, his provocative "Minds, Brains, and Programs" (Searle 1980a) challenged the fundamental assumption of the classical research program in artificial intelligence, viz., that cognition can be recreated by the manipulation of physical symbols according to a formal program. This essay of Searle's provoked a broad range of refutory responses from champions of all forms of artificial intelligence (AI), responses notable mostly for their unexpected and embarrassing lack of unanimity concerning just where and how his critique was mistaken.

Searle's new book provides a much broader canvas, as it contains the first book-length exposition of his own positive account of the mind and its place in nature, and it contains systematic criticisms not just of classical AI but of all existing forms of philosophical materialism, and of several research programs in linguistics and psychology as well.

Inevitably, the book will set many people's teeth on edge. Its content aside, Searle's text is abrasive, peremptory, and occasionally unfair. Withal, the book remains worth reading, for it is lucidly written, passionately inspired, and it constitutes an unusual position piece that is sure to provoke controversy. It pulls together Searle's earlier work in the philosophy of language and integrates it with his matured position in the philosophy of mind. Unexpectedly, that position recalls to me the earlier position of René Descartes.

Like Descartes, John Searle is an eloquent and evidently sincere spokesman for what was then loosely called "the mechanical philosophy" and is now loosely called "materialism." Yet Searle, like Descartes, balks "at the very door of the mind" and declares conscious, intentional phenomena to be wholly real, yet distinct from and irreducible to the non-mental physicalistic features of the brain. Like Descartes, Searle has here a profound tension on his hands, and he never entirely succeeds in resolving it.

To be sure, Searle's rejection of all forms of reductive materialism concerning the mind is much more circumspect than was Descartes'. Searle wants no part of any dualism of substances. Rather, Searle makes the bold assertion that mental phenomena are entirely natural phenomena *caused by* the neurophysiological activities of the physical brain. He calls this position "biological naturalism": mental states are natural states of biological organisms.

What distinguishes Searle from other contemporary materialists (identity theorists, functionalists, and eliminative materialists), and what unites him with Descartes, is his firm insistence that mental phenomena form an *ontologically distinct class of natural phenomena*, phenomena that causally arise from and interact with, but cannot be reduced to, any of the familiar classes of physical phenomena—dynamical, electrical, chemical, biological, etc. Here again we may feel the tension that goes unfelt by Searle: how can mental phenomena *fail* to be reducible to physical phenomena within the brain if, as Searle himself asserts, mental phenomena ultimately arise, evolutionarily and ontogenetically, from nothing other than the complex interaction of those physical phenomena with one another and with the environment?

Searle's position, however, is no oversight. The supposed ontological gulf fixed between mental phenomena and physical phenomena forms the fulcrum of his book-length argument. Here arises both the motive and the systematic basis for his deepest criticisms of various recent orthodoxies in AI, cognitive psychology, semantic theory, transformational grammar, and the philosophy of mind. Searle has a comprehensive critical vision that he wishes to urge on researchers in all of these areas. Let me try to outline what his vision is.

A theme familiar from Searle's earlier writings is his position concerning what philosophers call "intentionality." This is a technical term for what you or I would call the *meaning* or *content* of a thought or sentence. Searle insists on a distinction between the genuine or "intrinsic" intentionality of real mental states, as contrasted with the merely "as if" or "derivative" intentionality of the physical states of various nonmental systems such as thermostats, heliotropic sunflowers, and classical digital computers.

In the present book, this distinction is claimed by Searle to be tightly connected with a second distinction—that between the conscious states (actual or potential) of any individual, as contrasted with the deeply or essentially *non*conscious states of that individual. Intrinsic or genuine intentionality, says Searle, is a property exclusively of states that actually *are* a part of someone's current consciousness (conscious states), and of states that *could be brought* to consciousness by memory, prompting, attention, and so forth ("shallowly unconscious" states). States that do not meet the disjunctive demands of this Connection Principle are denied anything beyond "as if" intentionality. Intrinsic meaning on the one hand, and consciousness on the other, are thus claimed to be essentially connected with one another.

Since thermostats, sunflowers, and computers have no conscious states at all, reasons Searle, their internal states must lack intrinsic intentionality. Accordingly, no form of explanation that presupposes intrinsic intentionality can ever provide more than a metaphorical explanation of their behavior. Literal explanations of their behavior must always be drawn instead from physics, biology, and the other nonmental sciences. The same lesson, urges Searle, applies to the explanation of all aspects of human cognition that fall strictly outside the domain of the actually or potentially conscious.

Searle's demand that nonconscious phenomena receive their literal explanation in appropriate nonmental terms is mirrored in the complementary demand that genuinely conscious intentional phenomena receive their literal explanation in appropriately mental terms. Just as it is wrong to try to explain the lowly sunflower's heliotropic behavior in terms of desires, perceptions, and actions, so is it wrong to try to explain a genuinely conscious creature's perceptions, deliberations, and behavior in terms appropriate solely to the nonmental physical substrate that causes such conscious activity.

This conviction forms the basis of Searle's criticism of all current forms of materialism. They have all of them, he avers, lost sight of the central importance of the phenomenon of consciousness. Or worse, they deliberately downplay its importance by refocusing our attention on the more obviously formal or structural features of cognition such as grammar, logic, problem solving, and learning. It is high time, insists Searle, that the several cognitive sciences rediscover the importance of consciousness itself, and refocus their explanatory efforts appropriately. Thus the title of his book; it is as much exhortation as description.

It is hard not to resonate with a clarion call to readdress consciousness. Indeed, why ever should we resist? We would all dearly love to understand consciousness better. And yet, Searle's readers are hereby advised to proceed with considerable caution as they follow Searle in pursuit of this worthy goal. Other major positions, materialist to the core but no less interested in consciousness, are summarily dismissed on flimsy grounds. And in the end, Searle himself fails to achieve that goal. Moreover, the interim position he takes is inadequately motivated, doctrinally unstable, and flatly contradicted by every relevant lesson of our scientific history.

Consider first its motivation. The focal issue is Searle's claim that mental phenomena are irreducible to the objective features of the physical brain. The sticking point here, according to Searle, is the *subjective* character of mental states, as opposed to the *objective* character of any and all physical states. In the face of this "rock-bottom" divergence of character on each side of the alleged equation, how could mental phenomena possibly be identical with, or somehow constituted from, sheerly physical phenomena? They are as different as chalk from cheese.

The argument, let us admit, is beguiling. That is why it is famous. Searle is not offering us a new argument, but an old one, one made famous in the modern period by Thomas Nagel and Frank Jackson.

There is also a standard and quite devastating reply to this sort of argument, a reply that has been in undergraduate textbooks for a decade. On the most obvious and reasonable interpretation, to say that John's mental states are *subjective* in character is just to say that John's mental states are *known-uniquely-to-John-by-introspection*. And to say that John's physical brain states are objective is just to deny that his physical brain states have the hyphenated property at issue. Stated carefully, the argument thus has the following form:

1. John's mental states are known-uniquely-to-John-by-introspection.
2. John's physical brain states are *not* known-uniquely-to-John-by-introspection.
Therefore, since they have divergent properties,
3. John's mental states cannot be identical with any of John's physical brain states.

Once put in this form, however, the argument is instantly recognizable to any logician as committing a familiar form of fallacy, a fallacy instanced more clearly in the following two examples.

1. Aspirin is known-to-John-as-a-pain-reliever.
2. Acetylsalicylic acid is *not* known-to-John-as-a-pain-reliever.
Therefore, since they have divergent properties,
3. Aspirin cannot be identical with acetylsalicylic acid.

Or,

1. The temperature of an object is known-to-John-by-simple-feeling.
2. The mean molecular kinetic energy of an object is *not* known-to-John-by-simple-feeling.
Therefore, since they have divergent properties,
3. Temperature cannot be identical with mean molecular kinetic energy.

Here the conclusions are known to be false in both cases, despite the presumed truth of all of the premises. The problem here is that the so-called "divergent properties" consist in nothing more than the item's being *recognized, perceived, or known*, by somebody, by a specific means and under a specific description. But no such "epistemic" property is an intrinsic feature of the item itself, one that might determine its possible identity or nonidentity with some candidate thing otherwise apprehended or otherwise described. Indeed, as the two clearly fallacious parallels illustrate, the truth of the argument's premises need reflect nothing more than John's overwhelming *ignorance* of what happens to be identical with what. And as with the parallels, so with the original. Despite its initial appeal, the argument is a non sequitur.

Though he makes no attempt to protect the reader from it, Searle's text indicates that he is aware of this familiar fallacy, for he briefly insists

(p. 117) that he does not intend an "epistemic" construal of subjectivity, which is precisely what the above reconstruction of the Subjectivity Argument involves. But beyond this most natural and familiar construal, what other construal is there?

Searle intends an ontological construal. The Subjectivity Argument, he explains, is meant to make "a point about what real features exist in the world and not, except derivatively, about how we know about those features." Fine. Now we need to know which features—beyond the illicit "epistemic features" just discussed—are supposed to discriminate mental states as being forever distinct from physical brain states. Searle answers this question as follows.

"Suppose we tried to say that pain is really 'nothing but' the patterns of neuron firings. Well, if we tried such an ontological reduction, the essential features of the pain would be left out. No description of the third-person, objective, physiological facts would convey the subjective, first-person character of the pain, simply because the first-person features are different from the third-person features." (p. 117) Of this reconstructed version of the Subjectivity Argument, Searle comments, "It is ludicrously simple and quite decisive" (p. 118).

This last remark is an apt characterization of any argument that establishes its conclusion by the simple expedient of assuming as its premise (viz., "the first-person features are different from the third-person features") a thinly disguised restatement of the very conclusion it aims to establish (viz., "a pain and its subjective features are not identical with a brain state and its objective features"). Searle's brief preamble about what certain descriptions can or cannot "convey" is just more "epistemic" smoke screen creeping illegitimately back into the picture. What remains beyond that is a stark example of begging the question. Whether or not the subjective mental features one discriminates in introspection are identical with some objective features of one's brain that might eventually be discriminated in some objective fashion is exactly what is at issue.

What will determine the answer to this question is not whether our subjective properties intuitively *seem* to be different from neural properties, but whether cognitive neuroscience eventually succeeds in discovering suitably systematic neural analoges for all of the intrinsic and causal properties of mental states.

Remember the case of light, to choose one of many historical examples. From the standpoint of uninformed common sense, light and its manifold properties certainly *seem* to be utterly different from anything so esoteric and alien as orthogonal electric and magnetic fields oscillating at a million billion cycles per second. And yet, our strong intuitions of ontological differences notwithstanding, that is exactly what light turns out to be. Who will be so bold as to insist, just as the neuroscientific evidence is starting to pour in, that mental states cannot find a similar fate?

John Searle, apparently. And he cites one final consideration in support of this antireductionist position. Borrowing once again from an earlier argument of Tom Nagel's, Searle points out, as a presumptive final symptom of the alleged ontological distinction enjoyed by mental phenomena, that in historical cases of the scientific reduction of some objective physical property (such as temperature, sound, color, etc.), the reduction always "leaves aside," as something so far unexplained and unreduced, the subjective effects of that objective physical property on the conscious experience of humans.

In fact, this is not entirely true, but it is close enough to the truth to merit being dealt with on that assumption. What Searle sees as a symptom of ontological distinction is a reflection of something much simpler: once again, Our Ignorance. Why is it that statistical mechanics (the nineteenth-century theory that successfully reduced heat and temperature) does not also account for the subjective effects of temperature on human consciousness? Plainly, because such an account would require, in *addition* to Statistical Mechanics, an adequate theory of the human brain and its cognitive activities, something we have only recently begun to construct. Similarly, why is it that wave mechanics (the eighteenth-century theory that successfully reduced acoustic phenomena) does not also account for the subjective effects of sound on human consciousness? Plainly, because such an account would require, in *addition* to wave mechanics, an adequate theory of the human brain and its cognitive activities, something we have only recently begun to construct. And so on.

Note well that all of these theories "leave aside," as unexplained and unreduced, a vast variety of other esoteric properties beyond those found in human consciousness. Statistical Mechanics (SM), for example, also leaves aside the effects of heat and temperature on the GNP of Peru, on bluebirdegg cholesterol levels, on pneumonic infections in infants, on Antarctic anchovy production, on the rotting of forest-floor vegetable matter, and so forth. Each of these phenomena requires some additional theory beyond SM if it is to be successfully addressed. So it is no surprise that each is "left aside" by SM itself. And no one is tempted to insist, on these grounds, that such phenomena must be counted as ontologically distinct, irreducible, nonphysical features of reality. The effects of heat and temperature on human conscious perception are in exactly the same position. Only a man who had *prejudged* the ontological issue would make the mistake of seeing any ontological significance in the historical pattern at issue.

To summarize the motivation behind Searle's antireductionism, it has come apart in our hands. The Subjectivity Argument exploits a familiar fallacy or it falls back on a simple begging of the question. And the "leaves aside" argument is a faulty induction from a misapprehended historical pattern. So far as positive motivation is concerned, I am unable to find further considerations of any significance in Searle's book. My judgment, then, is that his positive position is badly undermotivated.

But the situation is darker than this. For there are independent negative considerations facing a position like Searle's. I mentioned earlier that it is an unstable position. By this I mean the following.

Searle is attempting to embrace both the biologically natural character of mental states, and their physical irreducibility. But one or other of these has to go. As Searle fits these strange bedfellows together, the relation between the neural and mental is said to be causal. Neural phenomena do not *constitute* mental phenomena, according to Searle, but they do *cause* them (p. 125).

The difficulty for Searle is that every last one of the many available real scientific examples of what he calls "micro-to-macro forms of causation" are also cases where the macroproperty at issue is *constituted* by some feature of the underlying microreality. For example, the swift compression of the molecules of a gas into a smaller volume will indeed *cause* the temperature of the gas to increase, but temperature is *constituted* by the mean kinetic energy of those molecules. The subtraction of kinetic energy from the molecules of a tray of water will indeed *cause* the water to become solid (to form ice), but the solidity of the ice is *constituted* by the matrix of positionally stable bonds into which the now more quiescent molecules settle. Raising the hydrogen-ion concentration of one's stomach acids will indeed *cause* one's digestion to accelerate, but digestion is *constituted* by the complex chemical decomposition of one's food.

Similarly, while a retinal activation pattern will indeed *cause* a conscious visual image to occur—in the primary visual cortex, perhaps—it will be because the conscious visual image is *constituted* by something like an activation pattern across the cortical neurons, and because the retina is causally connected to those cortical neurons via the optic nerve.

Searle's robust persistence in thinking of mental states as ontologically distinct from, yet causally produced by, physical brain states reminds me of a comparable persistence of thought in a comparable domain. It appears in the introduction to *Betty Crocker's Microwave Cooking* (New York: Golden Press, 1977), a book published soon after microwave ovens began to appear in every American kitchen. ("Betty Crocker" is a major American brand name for sundry baking products.) Before turning to the endless recipes, the authors attempt a brief explanation of how such newfangled devices manage to produce heat in the foodstuffs we put inside them. I quote.

The magnetron tube converts regular electricity into microwaves.... When [the microwaves] encounter any matter containing moisture—specifically food—they are absorbed into it.... The microwaves agitate and vibrate the moisture molecules at such a great rate that friction is created; the friction, in turn, creates heat and the heat causes the food to cook. (p. 4)

The decisive failure of comprehension begins to appear halfway through the last sentence. Instead of asserting that the induced motion of the moisture molecules already *constitutes* heat, and gracefully ending their explanation there, the authors benightedly continue to discuss heat as if it were an ontologically distinct property. They then fall back on their folk understanding of one of the many things that can *cause* heat: friction. The result is massively misleading to the innocent reader, who is left with the impression that rubbing two molecules together causes heat in the same way that rubbing your two hands together causes heat. In this confusion, the real nature of heat—the motion of the molecules themselves—is left entirely out of the account.

I have always treasured this example, since it illustrates the way in which our folk conceptions can blithely persist, even in the face of clean and established scientific reductions. How much firmer their grip, then, when the relevant reduction is still no more than in prospect? What Searle has written, I suggest, is something not too far from *Betty Crocker's Philosophy of Mind*. As a recipe for addressing the true nature of conscious phenomena, it is a bust. What Searle's book resolutely rediscovers is not the mind, but our commonsense, prescientific, folk-psychological conception of the mind. The aim of science, by contrast, is to discover a new and better conception. In this endeavor, Searle's book is not likely to help.

9

The Rediscovery of Light

Paul M. Churchland

There is a family of seven arguments advanced by John Searle urging the ontologically distinct and physically irreducible nature of conscious phenomena. These are joined by three arguments from Frank Jackson and David Chalmers which tend to the same conclusion. My aim in what follows is to construct systematic and unitary analogs of all ten of these arguments, analogs that support a parallel family of antireductive conclusions about the nature of light. Since those analogous conclusions are already known to be false in the case of light (its physicalist reduction is one of the many triumphs of electromagnetic [EM] theory), it becomes problematic whether the integrity of the original family of antireductionist arguments is any greater than the purely specious integrity of their deliberately constructed analogs.

I. A Searle-like Family of Arguments Concerning the Nature of Light

A. A fundamental distinction:

original (intrinsic) visibility vs. *derivative* (secondary) visibility.

Only light itself has original visibility. For light alone is visible, when directed into the eyes, without the causal intervention of any mediating agent. By contrast, any physical object, physical configuration, or physical event is visible only when and only because light is somehow reflected from or emitted by that object, configuration, or event. Such physical items have at most *derivative* visibility, because they are utterly and forever *in*visible, save as they interact appropriately with the one thing that has *original* visibility, namely, light itself.

These conclusions reflect the obvious fact that, if the universe contained no light at all, then absolutely nothing would be visible, neither intrinsically nor derivatively.[1]

B. The original visibility of light marks it off as belonging to a *unique ontological category*, distinct in its essential nature from the essential nature of any physical phenomenon, which must always *lack* original visibility. In other words, for any physical object, configuration, or event, it is always a contingent matter whether or not it happens to be visible on this occasion (it is a matter of whether or not it happens somehow to be illuminated). By contrast, light itself is always and essentially visible. The ontology of light is an ontology of things and features that are uniquely accessible from the visual point of view.

This means that the phenomenon of light must be *irreducible* to any complex of purely physical or not-essentially-visible phenomena. You simply cannot get *original* visibility from things that have, at most, derivative visibility.[2]

C. The consequence just reached is denied by a celebrated research program called "Strong EM." This program claims not only that light can be "instructively simulated" by the behavior of interacting electric and magnetic fields (to which all may agree); it makes the stronger claim that light is actually *identical with* EM waves. The folly of Strong EM can be seen in the following obviously sound argument.

1. Electricity and magnetism are physical forces.
2. The essential nature of light is original visibility.
3. Physical forces, no matter how they are deployed, are neither identical with, nor sufficient for, original visibility.
Therefore,
4. Electricity and magnetism are neither identical with, nor sufficient for, light.

Premises (1) and (2) are obvious. That premise (3) is obvious can be seen by the following thought-experiment. According to EM theory, an oscillating magnet or charged particle will generate an expanding sphere of oscillating EM fields: an EM wave front. And by the same theory, this is strictly sufficient for the existence of light. But imagine a man in a pitch-black room who begins to pump a bar magnet back and forth (see figure 5.1, p. 54). Clearly it will do nothing to illuminate the room. The room will remain wholly devoid of light.[3]

D. The ontologically distinct nature of light is further reflected in the fact that the distinction between (visual) appearance and reality, which holds for any broadly physical phenomenon, cannot be drawn in the case of light itself. It there disappears. For while light is an agent that typically *represents* the physical objects, configurations, or events from which it has been differentially reflected or emitted, light does not represent *itself.* It is neither reflected nor emitted from itself. It thus cannot possibly *mis*-represent itself, as it may occasionally misrepresent things other than it-self from which it has been reflected or emitted. Accordingly, where the reality at issue is light itself (as opposed to any and all physical phe-nomena), the appearance just *is* the reality.[4]

E. The irreducibility here claimed can be further seen as follows. Sup-pose we tried to say that the redness or blueness of light was *nothing but* a specific wavelength of EM waves. Well, if we tried such an ontological reduction, the essential features of the light would be left out. No de-scription of the extrinsic wavelengths of EM waves could possibly convey the intrinsic character of (objective) visible redness and visible blueness, for the simple reason that the *visible* properties of light are distinct from the *physical* properties of EM waves. This argument is ludicrously simple and quite decisive.[5]

F. Light is always and necessarily visible: there can be no such thing as *invisible* light. Granted, not all light is visible at any given time or place: light can be "shallowly" invisible to me simply because its path does not lead into my eyes. But if light exists at all, then there is some perspective from which it will be directly visible. Let us call this "The Connection Principle," since it unites (i) being light and (ii) being accessible-from-the-visual-point-of-view.[6]

G. Considerations (A) through (F) indicate that light is a phenomenon that is ontologically distinct from and irreducible to any purely physical phenomena. And yet, while nonphysical in itself, light is plainly *caused* by certain special physical phenomena, such as very high temperatures or the electrical stimulation of gases. Let us call our position here "non-reductive physical naturalism": it holds that light is a natural (but irre-ducible) phenomenon caused to occur within certain special kinds of physical systems—specifically, within *self-luminous* objects such as the sun, fires, and incandescent filaments. The aim of a scientific account of light should be to explain how such a nonphysical phenomenon is *caused* to occur within such highly special physical systems as stars and light bulbs.[7]

II.   Three Jackson-Chalmers–like Arguments Concerning the Nature of Light

H. In the study of the nature of light, there is a distinction to be drawn between the "easy" problems and "The Hard Problem." The first class concerns such problems as the emission, propagation, and absorption of light, its reflection and refraction, its velocity, its carrying energy, its self-interference, and so forth. These are all causal, relational, functional, and in general *extrinsic* features of light, features variously accessible by a wide variety of physical instruments and techniques, and it may well be that someday they will all be satisfactorily explained in terms of, for example, the propagation and interactions of EM fields.

But there remains a highly special *intrinsic* feature of light whose explanation must be found along some other path. This intrinsic feature is *luminance*, and it is what is responsible for the "original visibility" that is unique to light. Unlike all of the extrinsic (i.e., physical) features of light listed above, luminance is unique in being epistemically accessible only from "the visual point of view."[8]

I. We can illustrate and reinforce the contrast just drawn with a thought-experiment about a physicist named Mary who is completely blind, but comes to know everything physical there is to know about EM waves, about their internal structure and their causal behavior. And yet, because she is blind and thus has no access at all to "the visual point of view," she cannot know about, she must remain ignorant of, the special intrinsic feature of light—luminance—which is accessible from that point of view alone. Evidently, even complete knowledge of the physical facts must still leave her ignorant of the nature of luminance. Luminance must therefore be, in some way, *non*physical.[9]

J. As just illustrated, any possible physicalist story about the structure and causal functions of EM waves must still leave open an "explanatory gap" between the physical processes and luminance. In particular, it leaves unanswered the following question: Why should mutually inducing electric and magnetic fields (for example) oscillating at a million billion hertz and propagating at 300,000 kilometers per second ever give rise to the intrinsic feature of *luminance*? After all, we can easily imagine a universe which is filled with oscillating EM fields propagating back and forth all over the place, a universe which is nonetheless utterly *dark*, because it is devoid of the additional feature of luminance. We need to know how, when, and why oscillating EM fields *cause* the ontologically distinct feature of intrinsic luminance. Until we understand *that* mysterious causal relation, we shall never understand the ground and real nature of light.[10]

III. Critical Commentary

Concerning (A)

As an exercise in term introduction ("original" visibility, etc.), this is strictly harmless, perhaps. But it falsely elevates an extremely peripheral feature of light—namely, its capacity to stimulate the idiosyncratic rods and cones of terrestrial animals—into a deep and presumptively defining feature of light. This is thrice problematic. First, it is arbitrarily selective. Second, it is strictly false that *only* light will stimulate rods and cones (charged particles of suitable energy will also do so, though at some cost to the retina). And third, infrared and ultraviolet light are quite *in*visible to terrestrial eyes. Our eyes evolved to exploit a narrow window of EM transparency in the Earth's idiosyncratic atmosphere and oceans. Nothing of ontological importance need correspond to what makes our rods and cones sing.

Concerning (B)

The dubious distinction legislated in (A) is here deployed to consign all physical phenomena to a class (things with merely derivative visibility) that *excludes* the phenomenon of light. This division certainly appeals to our default stereotype of a physical object (a tree, or a stone, has merely derivative visibility), but it begs the question against the research program of physicalism, because some unfamiliar physical things may indeed have original visibility, our commonsense expectations notwith-standing. As it turns out, EM waves with a wavelength between 0.4 and 0.7 μm are capable of stimulating the retina all by themselves, and thus have original visibility as defined in (**A**). The argument of (**B**) is thus a question-begging exploitation of superficial stereotypes and electro-magnetic ignorance.

Concerning (C)

The crucial premise of this argument (premise 3) may seem highly plau-sible to those who have a commonsense prototype of forces and who are ignorant of the details of EM theory, but it plainly begs the central question against physicalism. (Premise 3 is the direct denial of the basic physicalist claim.) Moreover, it is false. As mentioned in the preceding paragraph, EM waves of suitable wavelength *are* sufficient for original visibility. The Luminous Room thought-experiment, concerning the oscillating bar magnet in the pitch-black parlor, is designed specifically to make premise 3 plausible, but that prejudicial story illegitimately exploits the fact that some forms of EM radiation have wavelengths that are simply too long to *interact* effectively with the rods and cones of terres-trial retinas (figure 9.1). The darkened parlor may *look* to be devoid of

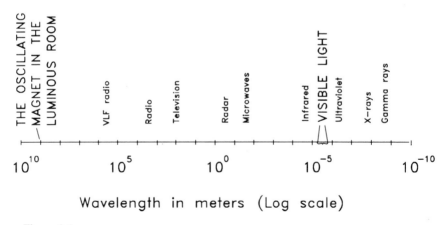

Figure 9.1
The place of visible light in the extended electromagnetic spectrum, and, at an energy level fourteen orders of magnitude lower, the place of the oscillating magnet's almost undetectable output.

light, but, thanks to the oscillating magnet, a very weak form of light is there regardless.

Concerning (D)

While superficially plausible, perhaps, this argument refuses to take into account the many ways in which we can be mistaken or misled about the character of the light entering our eyes (e.g., the light from a cinema screen appears continuous, but is really discontinuous at 36 frames per second; the light of an incandescent automobile headlight, while really yellowish, looks white at night; and so forth). Its brief plausibility is a reflection of nothing more than our unfamiliarity with how light is perceptually apprehended and with how that intricate process can occasionally produce false perceptual beliefs. It is a reflection of our own ignorance, rather than of any unique ontological status had by light.

Concerning (E)

This argument is sheer question-begging assertion rather than instructive argument. Whether objective properties of light such as spectral redness or spectral blueness are identical with, or distinct from, specific wavelengths of EM radiation is precisely what is at issue. And in this case, it has been plain for a century that these properties are identical. It is also plain that spectral redness, spectral blueness, and their various causal properties—their refractive and absorptive behavior, their velocity and interference effects—are positively *explained* by, rather than impotently "left out" by, their smooth reduction to electromagnetic features.

The point about what an electromagnetic vocabulary can or cannot "convey" about certain perceptual properties is a distinct point (and a red herring) to be dealt with below in (I).

Concerning (F)

This argument also would be found plausible by someone still imprisoned by prescientific prototypes of light. *Invisible light* may well be a conceptual impossibility against the assumptions of the story just told, but we now know better. Indeed, we have learned that *most* light is invisible—and not just "shallowly" invisible, but permanently beyond

human visual apprehension (see figure 9.1). Once again, we find ignorance being paraded as positive knowledge.

Concerning (G)

This summary attempts to find a proper place in nature for the phenomenon touted as ontologically distinct and physically irreducible in arguments (A) through (F). The place suggested is that of a nonphysical *causal*
consequence of certain special but purely physical events.

Such a move threatens to violate well-established laws concerning the
conservation of both energy and momentum, at least if light is presumed
to have any causal powers of its own. But we need not enter into these
matters here, for as the critical commentary to this point shows, there is
no significant motivation for any such antireductionist research program
in the first place. And in the second place, the proper place in nature of
light has already been made clear: it has been smoothly and systematically reduced to EM waves.

Concerning (H)

Light is here conceded to have a wide variety of physical features—its so-
called "extrinsic" or "structural/functional" features—to which some
sort of physical explanation is deemed appropriate. But light is also assigned an allegedly special or "intrinsic" feature, a feature that is epistemically accessible through vision, but not through the "structural/
functional" stories to which current physical science (alas) is limited.

Once again, our prescientific noninferential epistemic access (namely,
vision) to certain entirely physical properties is portrayed as a unique
window onto an ontologically special domain. And to further compound
the felony, the potential reach of physical explanation is restricted, by
arbitrary fiat at the outset (rather than by any empirical failures revealed
during the course of ongoing research), so as inevitably to fall short of
the so-called "intrinsic" features within the "special" domain at issue.

The "Hard Problem" is thus *made* transcendently hard at the outset by
presumptive and question-begging fiat, rather than by any substantive
considerations. As EM theory has taught us, *there is no* "Hard Problem"
here at all, and no defensible ontological distinction between intrinsic
and extrinsic features. "Luminance"—if we concede the integrity of this

notion at all—is just the normal and entirely physical capacity of EM waves to excite our own rods and cones (and to induce chemical changes in photographic film, to free electrons in a TV camera, and so forth).

Concerning (I)

This "knowledge" argument equivocates on "knows about." It elevates two distinct modes of epistemic access to light into a false dichotomy of distinct phenomena thereby accessed—physical features by scientific description, and a special range of nonphysical features by normal human vision. But for light, at least, we know perfectly well that there is only one thing here rather than two, only one class of objective features rather than two.

What Blind Mary is missing is one common *form* of knowledge about light: she lacks perceptual/discriminative knowledge of light. And yet, people who have such knowledge are accessing the very same features of reality that she is obliged to access in other ways. The difference lies in the manner of the knowing, not in the nature of the thing(s) known. It is true that no amount of propositional knowledge of light will ever *constitute* the visual apprehension of light, but that is entirely to be expected. They are different forms of knowledge; they operate with different representational "palettes" inside Mary's brain. But they both represent, each in its own distinct way, one and the same entirely physical thing: light.

Our contemporary scientific knowledge about light aside, one can see immediately that the crucial divergence here is merely epistemic rather than ontological (as the argument pretends). For while it is indeed true that Blind Mary does not know what it is like to *see* spectral-red light, it is equally true, and for exactly the same reasons, that she does not know what it is like to *see* EM waves at 0.65 μm. The deficit here evidently lies with Mary and her epistemic failings, not with EM waves and their ontological shortcomings vis-à-vis light. For Mary would continue to have her deficit even if light *were* (as it is) identical with EM waves. Her deficit, therefore, can hardly weigh against that identity.

Concerning (J)

This "open question" argument begs the question in favor of the ontological distinctness of "luminance," and then insists on our providing a *causal* account of how EM waves might produce it. This gets everything backward. We no longer have need for an account of how EM waves might "cause" the various phenomena associated with light, because the systematic reconstruction of optical phenomena within EM theory leads us to believe that light is simply identical with EM waves, and that the assembled properties of light are identical with, rather than caused by, the corresponding properties of EM waves.

The conceivability of a dark universe filled with EM waves shows only that the various cross-theoretic identities motivated by the electromagnetic reduction are, as they should be, contingent rather than necessary identities. It should also be pointed out that such an "open question" argument will be maximally appealing to one who is minimally instructed in EM theory. This is because the more one learns about EM waves, about their effects on matter in general and on our eyes in particular, the *harder* it becomes to imagine a consistent scenario in which a universe abuzz with EM waves of all wavelengths remains dark even so. Here, as in so many of the earlier arguments, the audience's presumed ignorance is once more a lubricant that smooths the path of a worthless argument.

This concludes my attempt to construct, and to deflate, a systematic analog for the family of arguments currently so influential in the philosophy of mind. My point, of course, is that the family of arguments on which they are modeled is just as empty of real virtue.

IV.   A Final Nagel-Searle Argument for Irreducibility

A question will inevitably arise over the fairness of the global analogy deployed above. In particular, it will be complained that the global analogy is faulty in placing the *objective* properties of "original visibility" and "luminance" in the role played by the *subjective* properties of original intentionality and inner qualia in the arguments under attack.

The analogy deployed does indeed proceed in precisely this fashion, but this assimilation is the central point of the exercise. It should at least give us pause that the original family of arguments can be collectively and successfully mirrored in a ten-dimensional analogy that deliberately and self-consciously concerns "objective" features. After all, if the analog arguments are at all compelling—and to the electromagnetically uninformed, they will be—then the essential appeal of both families of arguments presumably derives from something other than the unique status of the "subjective."

Second, there is no mystery about what drives the plausibility of the analog arguments. It is the ignorance-fueled appeal of the idea that the epistemic modality of vision is or might be a unique window onto an ontologically distinct class of properties. But in the case of light it is also plain, at least in retrospect, that nothing substantive motivates that repeated insistence. We have to wonder if the same failure might be true of the original family of arguments. After all, and whatever else it might be, introspection *is* an epistemic modality, or perhaps a family of them. And while it may have its own quirks and distinguishing profile, it is entirely unclear whether it, alone among all of our epistemic modalities, constitutes a window onto a unique *ontological* domain of nonphysical properties. None of our other epistemic modalities has any such distinction: they all access some aspect or other of the purely physical world. Why should introspection be any different?

Searle has a further argument, unaddressed to this point, whose burden is to illustrate the ontological cleft he sees between the domain of "outer sense" and the domain of "inner sense," as Kant called them. Searle's argument here appeals, uncharacteristically, to the history of science. The argument originally appeared, very briefly, in Nagel (1974), but Searle has more recently developed it in detail.

Premise 1. We must draw a distinction between the real and objective properties of objects and the contingent subjective effects those properties happen to have on the conscious processes of humans. For example, objective heat (molecular kinetic energy [KE]) is one thing; the subjective feeling of warmth in humans *produced by* objective heat is quite another.

Premise 2. The scientific reduction of observable phenomena typically ignores or "carves off" their contingent subjective effects on the conscious processes of humans, and reduces only the nonsubjective aspects of the phenomena. (For example, kinetic theory successfully reduces objective heat to molecular KE, but leaves its *subjective conscious effects* on humans aside. EM theory successfully reduces objective spectral colors to different wavelengths of EM radiation, but leaves their *subjective conscious effects* on humans aside. And so forth.)

Premise 3. When we attempt to provide a physicalistic reduction of those subjective conscious effects themselves, we must realize that here we *cannot* "carve off" their subjective-effects-on-us from their objective properties, and reduce only the latter, because it is precisely those subjective-effects-on-us that we wish to understand. Here, inside the mind, there is no longer any meaningful or defensible distinction between the "objective" and the "subjective" that would allow us to repeat the pattern of reduction described above. The subjective phenomena are exclusively and *essentially* subjective. Any alleged "reduction" would simply leave out what is essential to their nature.

Therefore, mental phenomena are irreducible to physical phenomena. The proper pattern of a physicalist reduction (an "objective"-to-"objective" mapping) uniquely precludes any reduction of the subjective.[11]

What is going on here? Simply this. The Nagel-Searle argument treats a contingent, minor, and remediable feature (of a handful of historical examples of reductions) as if it were a necessary, central, and permanent feature of any possible physicalistic reduction. Specifically, the merely contingent feature that is paraded as essential is the feature: *leaves aside the-effects-on-human-consciousness* (the "C-effects," for short). The argument then points out that this "essential" feature of physicalistic reduction precludes any such reduction in the unique case of C-effects themselves, since "leaving the C-effects aside" is here not an option.

It is indeed true that historical property reductions pay little or no attention to, or provide us with little or no insight into, the C-effects of the various phenomena being reduced. Searle and Nagel seem antecedently convinced that this historical fact is the inevitable reflection of an ontological gulf already fixed between "objective" phenomena and "subjective" phenomena.

That is one (distant) possibility. But there is an obvious alternative explanation of why physicalistic reductions so regularly leave out any account of the human C-effects of the phenomena being reduced, as the historical reduction of heat to molecular energy made no attempt to account for the subjective sensation of warmth, or as the historical reduction of light to EM waves made no attempt to account for the subjective sensation of redness.

The obvious alternative explanation is that *such C-effects are the proper province of a distinct science*, a science such as cognitive neurobiology or computational neuroscience. Searle is wrongly demanding that the kinetic theory of heat do, all by itself, something that clearly requires, in addition, an adequate theory of the brain. The fact is, during the late nineteenth century, we were too ignorant about neurobiology for the kinetic theory to suggest any worthwhile hypotheses about the human C-effects of molecular energy. It is no surprise then, that physicists simply walked past that arcane problem, if it ever occurred to them to address it in the first place. The same is true for the electromagnetic theory of light and the problem of our subjective sensations of redness.

Accordingly, this incidental "leaving-aside" need have no metaphysical or ontological significance. This deflationary view is further encouraged by the fact that physicalistic reductions such as the kinetic theory also "leave aside" any explanatory account of millions of other phenomena, so there is no automatic reason to find any special significance in its ignoring of human C-effects in particular. If I may give several examples, historical reductions of heat typically leave aside any attempt to account for

- Heat's effect on Antarctic anchovy production, or for
- Heat's effect on bluebird egg cholesterol levels, or for
- Heat's effect on pneumonial infections, or for
- Heat's effect on the GNP of Peru, or for
- Heat's effect on the rotting of vegetable matter, or for
- Heat's effect on the conscious states of humans, or for
- (This list is extendible indefinitely).

The great reductions of classical and modern physics *typically* leave out any account of heat's (or light's, or sound's) effect on all of these things, and of millions more, because no reduction all by itself can presume to account for the ever-more-distant causal effects of its proprietary phenomena as they are progressively articulated into all possible causal domains. There are far too many domains, and causal understanding of the phenomena within those other domains will typically require the resources of further theories in addition to the theory that achieves the local reduction at issue.

It is in no way noteworthy or ontologically significant, then, that the kinetic theory of heat, all by itself, provides no account of any of the arcane phenomena listed above, nor of thousands of others as well. In particular, it is neither noteworthy nor ontologically significant that the kinetic theory of heat provides no account of the human conscious response to heat. This marginal and idiosyncratic phenomenon has no more ontological significance than any of the other arcane phenomena just listed. And they all require the resources of theories beyond the kinetic theory of heat to address them adequately. Specifically, heat's effect on

- Anchovy production needs *ecology*,
- Egg cholesterol levels needs *metabolic chemistry*,
- Pneumonia needs *immunology* and *bacteriology*,
- Peru's GNP needs *biology* and *economics*,
- Vegetable rotting needs *bacteriology* and *cell chemistry*, and
- Human conscious experience needs *cognitive neurobiology*.

My counterclaim, then, against Nagel and Searle, is that it is *not* an essential feature of physicalistic reductions that they always "leave aside" human C-effects, or any of the many other effects cited. It is a merely contingent and wholly explicable fact that historical reductions have so far done so. It is not an essential pattern that all physicalistic reductions are doomed-by-nature to follow, nor is it a self-imposed definitional stipulation on what counts as a reduction, as Searle at one point inexplicably suggests.[12] Once we begin to address human C-effects with some appropriately focused science—as neuronal vector-coding theories are already doing, with striking success (Clark 1993)—then that earlier "pattern" will be well and truly broken. For that pattern reflected only our own scientific ignorance, not some ontological division in nature.

In sum, human conscious experience has no quicksilver history of darting off to one side each time our reductive scientific thumb has tried to pin it down. There have *been* no significant reductive attempts at that target, not, at least, within the grand historical reductions of physics and chemistry. Instead, the phenomena of human conscious experience have quite properly been waiting, patiently and at the sidelines, for the maturation of the only theory that has any realistic hope of providing such a reductive account, namely, an adequate theory of the brain. If and when *that* approach has been fully tried, and proves a failure, *then*, perhaps, it will be time to insist on nonphysical approaches.

Both the appeal to ignorance and the question-begging nature of the Nagel-Searle argument become finally vivid if one plays at constructing a series of parallel arguments to "establish" the physicalistic irreducibility of whatever arcane, complex, and puzzling phenomenon one might choose to consider (something from the preceding list, for example). Simply note that historical reductions of various important phenomena have invariably left that particular phenomenon aside as an unaddressed mystery; pretend that this is an essential pattern, a reflection of an antecedent metaphysical division or the result of some appropriately exclusive definition of "reduction"; note that said "leave-aside" pattern (surprise!) precludes any similar reduction of *exactly* the phenomenon at issue, and you are home free. You will then have performed for us the same empty service that Nagel and Searle have performed.

V. Some Diagnostic Remarks on Qualia

There is a chronic temptation among philosophers to assign a special epistemological, semantical, or ontological status to those features or properties that form the "discriminational simples" within each of our several sensory or epistemic modalities, such as brightness and colors in the case of vision, sweetness and sourness in the case of taste, and so on. These are the features of the world where one is unable to *say* how it is that one discriminates one such feature from another; one simply can. As well, one is unable to *say* how the meaning of "red" differs from the meaning of "green"; one simply has to point to appropriate exemplars.

Such discriminational simples are typically contrasted with properties such as "being a horse," where one can usually articulate the more elemental constituting features that make up the type in question: size, shape, configuration, color, texture, and so forth, which more elemental features lead us stepwise back toward the discriminational simples.

Too much has been made of these "simples," for the existence of such discriminable but inarticulable features is entirely inevitable. Such features must exist, if only to prevent an infinite regress of features discriminated by constituting subfeatures discriminated by constituting *sub*-subfeatures and so on (see Hesse 1970). And their existence is inevitable even on wholly physicalist conceptions of cognition. It simply cannot be the case that *all* conscious feature-discriminations are made on the basis of distinct conscious (sub)feature-discriminations. Given any person at any time, there must be some set of features whose spontaneous or noninferential discrimination is currently basic for that person, a set of features whose discrimination does not depend on the conscious discrimination of any more elemental perceptual features. In short, there must be something that counts, for that person, as a set of inarticulable qualia.

Accordingly, we should not be tempted to find anything physically irreducible or ontologically special about such inarticulable features. They need reflect nothing more than the current and perhaps changeable limits of the person's capacity for epistemic and semantic articulation, the current limits, that is, of the person's *knowledge* of the world's fine structure and his own epistemic access to it. Most important, there is no reason to expect that the current limits of the typical person's knowledge must mark the boundary of a distinct ontological domain. This is just as true, note, for the epistemic modalities that underwrite (what we loosely call) "introspection" as it is for the epistemic modalities of vision, taste, and audition.

And yet, philosophers have regularly been tempted here, some beyond redemption. Bishop Berkeley rejected the identification of sound with atmospheric compression waves; Blake and Goethe rejected the identification of light with Newton's ballistic particles; and Nagel, Jackson, Searle, and Chalmers reject the proposed reduction of inner qualia to physical states of the brain.

There is an important factor here that may help to explain why such features have so frequently been held to be beyond the reach of any physicalist reduction. Specifically, any reduction succeeds by reconstructing, within the resources of the new theory, the antecedently known nature, structure, and causal properties of the target phenomena. That is what intertheoretic reduction is. But if the target phenomena—such as sensory qualia—are features whose internal structure (if any) we are currently unable to articulate, and whose causal properties (if any) are largely unknown to us, then the target phenomena will inevitably seem to offer *the minimum purchase possible* for any aspirant reducing theory. They will display no structure worth reconstructing. They will present themselves as smooth-walled mystery. They will appear to be irreducible to any "structural-functional" theory from conventional science.

But the appearance of seamless simplicity need reflect nothing more than our own ignorance, an ignorance, we should note, that already holds promise of repair. In sum, we should not be too quickly impressed by qualia, whether outer or inner. If cognitive creatures exist at all, then the existence of inarticulable qualia is inevitable, even in a purely physical universe.

If ultimately they are physical, then inner qualia ought to be epistemically accessible from more than just the first-person or "subjective" point of view; they ought to be accessible as well from one or more "objective" points of view, via some appropriate instruments that scan brain activity, for example.

Some will continue to find this implausible on its face. That is mainly because the terms "objective" and "subjective" are commonly used in mutually *exclusive* contrast. But the default implication of mutual exclusivity may well be inappropriate in precisely the case at issue. After all, we know that the two epistemic modalities of vision and touch, for example, are not mutually exclusive in the phenomena that they access— one can both see and feel the shape of an object, see and feel that the sun is out, see and feel that rain is falling, and so forth. Why should it be impossible *a priori* that the epistemic modality we call "introspection" have some similar overlap with one or more of our other epistemic modalities?

Indeed, such overlap appears actual, even by the standards of common sense. One can tell by introspection that one's own bladder is full, but an ultrasound image will tell anyone the same thing. One can tell by introspection that and where one's retinal cells are photo-fatigued (we call it an "afterimage"), but that too is accessible by nonsubjective means. One can tell by introspection that the cochlear cells of one's inner ear are firing randomly (the condition is called "tinnitus"), but others can access their behavior instrumentally. There are, of course, thousands more such examples.

It would seem, then, that the "subjective" and the "objective" are not mutually exclusive after all. In at least some cases, one and the same (physical) state can be known both subjectively *and* objectively, from both the first-person perspective *and* the third-person perspective. Further, it would seem that the extent and location of the overlap is somewhat fluid, and that it varies as a function of how much background knowledge, conceptual sophistication, and recognitional skill the person has acquired. The process is called "coming to understand explicitly what was hitherto inarticulate," and it is entirely to be encouraged. The more epistemic modalities we can bring to bear on any puzzling phenomenon, the deeper our understanding will become. To insist, in *advance* of real understanding, that a given phenomenon is locked forever within its own epistemic box serves only to block the very research that might dissolve such a prejudicial conception.

VI.   A Final Point About Light

In closing, let me return to the opening family of arguments concerning the irreducibility of light. Someone may remark that, with light, I have used an example that is antithetical to my own reductive inclinations in the philosophy of mind. For while light reduces cleanly to EM waves, light is still famous for having escaped the various *mechanical* reductions (ballistic particle theories, elastic media theories) that everyone in the nineteenth century expected. And it is still famous for having thus emerged as one incarnation of a fundamental and nonmechanical aspect of reality: electromagnetism.

This is quite true, and more than a little instructive. But in the present context it is also instructive that (1) while nonmechanical, light remains an entirely physical phenomenon, and (2) more important, the modestly special status that light eventually discovered had *absolutely nothing to do* with any of the considerations urged in the family of antireductive arguments in my opening parody. Light's nonmechanical status emerged primarily as a consequence of Special Relativity, as a consequence of the unity of spacetime and the impossibility of a universal elastic aether. It was not a consequence or reflection of any of the arguments offered above. It is ironic that, even though light did turn out, unexpectedly, to be a rather special kind of physical phenomenon, the parody arguments (A) through (J) did nothing whatever to herald it, and they are, after the fact, quite irrelevant to it.

The parallel lesson about mental states is that, even if conscious phenomena are ontologically special in some way, roughly analogous to the case of light, there is no reason to think that the arguments of Searle, Jackson, and Chalmers do anything to illustrate or establish it. Those arguments are no more instructive about the ultimate nature of mental phenomena than arguments (A) through (J) are instructive about the ultimate nature of light.

10

Knowing Qualia: A Reply to Jackson

Paul M. Churchland

In a recent paper concerning the direct introspection of brain states (1985a) I leveled three criticisms against Frank Jackson's "knowledge argument" (Jackson 1982). At stake was his bold claim that no materialist account of mind can possibly account for all mental phenomena. Jackson has replied to those criticisms in "What Mary Didn't Know" (1986). It is to those replies, and to the issues that prompted them, that the present note is directed.

Jackson concedes the criticism I leveled at my own statement of his argument—specifically, that it involves an equivocation on "knows about"—but he insists that my reconstruction does not represent the argument he wishes to defend. I accept his instruction, and turn my attention to the summary of the argument he provides at the bottom of p. 293. Mary, you will recall, has been raised in innocence of any color experience, but has an exhaustive command of neuroscience.

1. Mary (before her release) knows everything physical there is to know about other people.

2. Mary (before her release) does not know everything there is to know about other people (because she *learns* something about them on her release).

3. There are truths about other people (and herself) which escape the physicalist story.

Regimenting further, for clarity's sake, yields the following:

1. $(x)[(Hx \ \& \ Px) \supset Kmx]$
2. $(Ex)[Hx \ \& \ {\sim}Kmx]$ (namely, "what it is like to see red")
3. $(Ex)[Hx \ \& \ {\sim}Px]$

Here m = Mary; $Kyx = y$ knows about x; $Hx = x$ is about persons; $Px = x$ is about something physical in character; and x ranges over "knowables," generously construed so as not to beg any questions about whether they are propositional or otherwise in nature.

Thus expressed, the argument is formally valid: the salient move is a *modus tollens* that applies the second conjunct of premise (2), "$\sim Kmx$", to the waiting consequent of premise (1), "Kmx". The question now is whether the premises are jointly true, and whether the crucial notion "Kmx" is univocal in both of its appearances. Here I am surprised that Jackson sees any progress at all with the above formulation, since I continue to see the same equivocation found in my earlier casting of his argument.

Specifically, premise (1) is plausibly true, within Jackson's story about Mary's color-free upbringing, only on the interpretation of "knows about" that casts the object of knowledge as something propositional, as something adequately expressible in an English sentence. Mary, to put it briefly, gets 100 percent on every written and oral exam; she can pronounce on the truth of any given sentence about the physical characteristics of persons, especially the states of their brains. Her "knowledge by description" of physical facts about persons is without lacunae.

Premise (2), however, is plausibly true only on the interpretation of "knows about" that casts the object of knowledge as something nonpropositional, as something inarticulable, as something that is non-truth-valuable. What Mary is missing is some form of "knowledge by acquaintance," acquaintance with a sensory character, prototype, or universal, perhaps.

Given this prima facie difference in the sense of "knows about" or the kind of knowledge appearing in each premise, we are still looking at a prima facie case of an argument invalid by reason of equivocation on a critical term. Replace either of the "K"'s above with a distinct letter, as acknowledgment of the ambiguity demands, and the inference to (3) evaporates. The burden of articulating some specific and unitary sense of "knows about," and of arguing that both premises are true under that interpretation of the epistemic operator, is an undischarged burden that still belongs to Jackson.

It is also a *heavy* burden, since the resources of modern cognitive neurobiology already provide us with a plausible account of what the difference in the two kinds of knowledge amounts to, and of how it is possible to have the one kind without the other. Let me illustrate with a case distinct from that at issue, so as not to beg any questions.

Any competent golfer has a detailed representation—perhaps in his cerebellum, perhaps in his motor cortex—of a golf swing. It is a *motor* representation and it constitutes his "knowing how" to *execute* a proper swing. The same golfer will also have a discursive representation of a golf swing—perhaps in his language cortex, or in the neighboring temporal and parietal regions—which allows him to describe a golf swing or perhaps draw it on paper. The motor and the discursive representations are quite distinct. Localized brain trauma, or surgery, could remove either one while sparing the other. Short of that, an inarticulate golf champion might have a superb representation of the former kind, but a feeble representation of the latter kind. And a physicist or sports physiologist might have a detailed and penetrating representation of the mechanics of a good swing, and yet be unable to duff the ball more than ten feet, by reason of lacking an adequate *motor* representation, of the desired behavioral sequence, in the brain areas that control his limbs. Indeed, if our physicist is chronically disabled in his motor capacities, he may have no motor representation of a golf swing whatsoever. In one medium of representation, his representational achievements on the topic may be complete, while in another medium of representation, he has nothing.

A contrast between "knowing how" and "knowing that" is one already acknowledged in common sense, and thus it is not surprising that some of the earliest replies to Jackson's argument (Nemirow 1980; Lewis 1983) tried to portray its equivocation in these familiar terms, and tried to explicate Mary's missing knowledge solely in terms of her missing some one or more *abilities* (to recognize red, to imagine red, etc.). While the approach is well motivated, this binary distinction in types of knowledge barely begins to suggest the range and variety of different sites and types of internal representation to be found in a normal brain. There is no reason why we must be bound by the crude divisions of our prescientific idioms when we attempt to give a precise and positive explication of the equivocation displayed in Jackson's argument. And there are substantial grounds for telling a somewhat different story concerning the sort of nondiscursive knowledge at issue. Putting caution and qualification momentarily aside, let me tell such a story.

In creatures with trichromatic vision (i.e., with three types of retinal cone), color information is coded as a pattern of spiking frequencies across the axonal fibers of the parvocellular subsystem of the optic nerve. That massive cable of axons leads to a second population of cells in a central body called the lateral geniculate nucleus (LGN), whose axonal projections lead in turn to the several areas of the visual cortex at the rear of the brain's cerebral hemispheres, to V1, V2, and ultimately to V4, which area appears especially devoted to the processing and representation of color information (Zeki 1980; Van Essen and Maunsell 1983; Hubel and Livingstone 1987). Human cognition divides a smooth continuum of color inputs into a finite number of prototypical categories. The laminar structure at V4 is perhaps the earliest place in the processing hierarchy to which we might ascribe that familiar taxonomy. A creature competent to make reliable color discriminations has there developed a representation of the range of familiar colors, a representation that appears to consist in a specific configuration of weighted synaptic connections meeting the millions of neurons that make up area V4.

That configuration of synaptic weights partitions the "activation-space" of the neurons in area V4: it partitions that abstract space into a structured set of subspaces, one for each prototypical color. Inputs from the eye will each occasion a specific pattern of activity across these cortical neurons, a pattern or vector that falls within one of those subspaces. In such a pigeonholing, it now appears, does visual recognition of a color consist (see P. M. Churchland 1989a, chapters 9 and 10, for the general theory of information processing here appealed to). This recognition depends upon the creature possessing a prior representation—a learned configuration of synapses meeting the relevant population of cells—that antecedently partitions the creature's visual taxonomy so it can respond selectively and appropriately to the flux of visual stimulation arriving from the retina and LGN.

This distributed representation is not remotely propositional or discursive, but it is entirely real. All trichromatic animals have one, even those without any linguistic capacity. It apparently makes possible the many abilities we expect from color-competent creatures: discrimination, recognition, imagination, and so on. Such a representation is presumably what a person with Mary's upbringing would lack, or possess only in stunted or incomplete form. Her representational space within the relevant area of neurons would contain only the subspace for black, white, and the intervening shades of gray, for the visual examples that have shaped her synaptic configuration were limited to these. There is thus more than just a clutch of abilities missing in Mary: there is a complex representation, a processing framework that deserves to be called cognitive, which she either lacks entirely or has in severely reduced form. There is indeed something she "does not know." Jackson's premise (2), we may assume, is thus true on these wholly materialist assumptions.

These same assumptions are entirely consistent with the further assumption that elsewhere in Mary's brain—in the language areas, for example—she has stored a detailed and even exhaustive set of discursive, propositional, truth-valuable representations of what goes on in people's brains during the experience of color, a set she has brought into being by the exhaustive reading of authoritative texts in a completed cognitive neuroscience. She may even be able to explain her own representational deficit, as sketched above, in complete neurophysical detail. Jackson's premise (1), we may thus assume, is also true on these wholly materialist assumptions.

The view sketched above is a live candidate for the correct story of sensory coding and sensory recognition. But whether or not it is true, it is at least a logical possibility. Accordingly, what we have sketched here is a consistent but entirely *physical* model (i.e., a model in which Jackson's conclusion is false) in which both of Jackson's premises are true under the appropriate interpretation. They can hardly entail a conclusion, then, that is inconsistent with physicalism. Their compossibility, on purely physicalist assumptions, resides in the different character and the numerically different medium of representation at issue in each of the two premises. Jackson's argument, to refile the charge, equivocates on "knows about."

An argument form with one invalid instance can be expected to have others. This was the point of a subsidiary objection in my 1985 paper: if valid, Jackson's argument, or one formally parallel, would also serve to refute the possibility of *substance dualism*. I did not there express my point with notable clarity, however, and I accept responsibility for Jackson's quite missing my intention. Let me try again.

The basic point is that the canonical presentation of the knowledge argument, as outlined on p. 143 above, would be just as valid if the predicate term "P" were everywhere replaced by "E". And the resulting premises would be just as plausibly true if

i. "E" stood for "is about something ectoplasmic in character" (where "ectoplasm" is an arbitrary name for the dualist's nonphysical substance), and

ii. the story is altered so that Mary becomes an exhaustive expert on a completed *ectoplasmic* science of human nature.

The plausibility would be comparable, I submit, because a long discursive lecture on the objective, statable, law-governed properties of ectoplasm, whatever they might be, would be exactly as useful, or use-*less*, in helping Mary to *know-by-acquaintance* "what it is like to see red," as would a long discursive lecture on the objective, statable, law-governed properties of the physical matter of the brain. Even if substance dualism were true, therefore, and ectoplasm were its heroic principal, an exactly parallel "knowledge argument" would "show" that there are some aspects of consciousness that must forever escape the *ectoplasmic* story. Given Jackson's antiphysicalist intentions, it is at least an irony that the same form of argument should incidentally serve to blow substance dualism out of the water.

Though I am hardly a substance dualist (and neither is Jackson), I do regard substance dualism as a theoretical possibility, one that might conceivably succeed in explicating the psychological ontology of common sense in terms of the underlying properties and law-governed behavior of the nonmaterial substance it postulates. And I must protest that the parallel knowledge argument against substance dualism would be wildly unfair, for the very same reason that its analog against physicalism is unfair. It would equivocate on "knows about." It would be no more effective against dualism than it is against materialism.

The parallel under examination contains a further lesson. If it works at all, Jackson's argument works against physicalism not because of some defect that is unique to physicalism; it works because no amount of discursive knowledge, on *any* topic, will *constitute* the nondiscursive form of knowledge that Mary lacks. Jackson's argument is one instance of an indiscriminately anti*reductionist* form of argument. If it works at all, an analog will work against any proposed reductive, discursive, objective account of the nature of our subjective experience, no matter what the reducing theory might happen to be. I see this as a further symptom of the logical pathology described earlier. Since the argument "works" for reasons that have nothing essential to do with physicalism, it should "work" against the explanatory aspirations of other ontologies as well. And so it does. The price of embracing Jackson's argument is thus dramatically higher than first appears. For it makes *any* scientific account of our sensory experience entirely impossible, no matter what the ontology employed.

We can appreciate the equivocation more deeply if we explore a version of Jackson's argument that does *not* equivocate on "knows about." The equivocation can quickly be closed, if we are determined to do so, and the results are revealing. Given that the problem is a variety in the possible forms of knowing, let us simply rewrite the argument with suitable quantification over the relevant forms of knowing. The first premise must assert that, for any knowable x, and for any form f of knowledge, if x is about humans and x is physical in character, then Mary knows(f) about x. The second premise is modified in the same modest fashion, and the conclusion is identical. Canonically,

1′. $(x)(f)[(Hx \;\&\; Px) \supset K(f)mx]$
2′. $(Ex)(Ef)[Hx \;\&\; \sim K(f)mx]$
_____
3′. $(Ex)[Hx \;\&\; \sim Px]$

This argument is also formally valid, and its premises explicitly encompass whatever variety there may be in forms of knowing. What can we say about its soundness?

Assume that Mary has had the upbringing described in Jackson's story, and thus lacks any knowledge-by-acquaintance with "what it is like to see red." Premise (2′) will then be true, as and for the reasons that Jackson's story requires. What will be the truth-value of premise (1′) on these assumptions?

Premise (1′) is now a very strong claim indeed, much stronger than the old premise (1), and a materialist will be sure to insist that it is false. The reason offered will be that, because of her deprived upbringing, Mary quite clearly *lacks one form* of knowledge of a certain physical aspect of people. Specifically, she lacks a proper configuration of synaptic connections meeting the neurons in the appropriate area of her visual cortex. She thus lacks an apropriately partitioned activation vector space across those neurons, and therefore has no representation, at that site, of the full range of sensory coding vectors that might someday come from the retina and the LGN. In other words, there is something physical about persons (their color sensations = their coding vectors in their visual pathways), and there is some form of knowledge (an antecendently partitioned pre-linguistic taxonomy), such that Mary lacks that form of knowledge of that aspect of persons. Accordingly, premise (1′) is false and the conclusion (3′) is not sustained.

From a materialist's point of view, it is obvious that (1′) will be false on the assumptions of Jackson's story. For that story denies her the upbringing that normally provokes and shapes the development of the relevant representation across the appropriate population of cortical neurons. And so, of course, there is a form of knowledge, of a physical aspect of persons, that Mary does not have. As just illustrated, the materialist can even specify that form of knowledge, and its objects, in neural terms. But this means that premise (1′), as properly quantified at last, is false. Mary does *not* have knowledge of everything physical about persons, in every way that is possible for her. (That is why premise [2′] is true.)

There is of course no guarantee that the materialist's account of sensations and sensory recognition is correct (although the experimental and theoretical evidence for a view of this general kind continues to accumulate). But neither is Jackson in a position to insist that it must be mistaken. That would beg the very question at issue: whether sensory qualia form a metaphysically distinct class of phenomena beyond the scope of physical science.

To summarize. If we write a deliberately nonequivocal form of Jackson's argument, one that quantifies appropriately over all of the relevant forms of knowledge, then the first premise must almost certainly be false under the conditions of his own story. So, at any rate, is the materialist in a strong position to argue. Jackson's expressed hope for "highly plausible premises" is not realized in (1′). The original premise (1) was, of course, much more plausible. But it failed to sustain a valid argument, and it was plausible only because it failed to address all the relevant forms of knowledge.

My final objection to Jackson was aimed more at breaking the grip of the ideology behind his argument than at the argument itself. That ideology includes a domain of properties—the qualia of subjective experience—that are held to be metaphysically distinct from the objective physical properties addressed by orthodox science. It is not a surprise then, on this view, that one might know all physical facts, and yet be ignorant of some domain of these nonphysical qualia. The contrast between what is known and what is not known simply reflects an antecendent metaphysical division in the furniture of the world.

But there is another way to look at the situation, one that finds no such division. Our capacity for recognizing a range of (currently) inarticulable features in our subjective experience is easily explained on materialist principles—the relevant sketch appears earlier in this essay, and elsewhere in this volume (chapters 7 and 9). Our discursive inarticulation on those features is no surprise either, and signifies nothing about their metaphysical status. Indeed, that veil of inarticulation may itself be swept aside by suitable learning. What we are now able spontaneously to report about our internal states and cognitive activities need not define the limit on what we might be able to report, spontaneously and accurately, if we were taught a more appropriate conceptual scheme in which to express our discriminations. In closing, let me again urge on Jackson this exciting possibility.

The intricacies of brain function may be subjectively opaque to us now, but they need not remain that way forever. Neuroscience may appear to be defective in providing a purely "third-person account" of mind, but only familiarity of idiom and spontaneity of conceptual response are required to make it a "first-person account" as well. What makes an account a "first-person account" is not the *content* of that account, but the fact that one has earned to *use* it as the vehicle of spontaneous conceptualization in introspection and self-description.

We all of us, as children, learned to use the framework of current folk psychology in this role. But it is entirely possible for a person or culture to learn and use some other framework in that role—the framework of cognitive neuroscience, perhaps. Given a deep and practiced familiarity with the developing idioms of cognitive neurobiology, we might learn to discriminate by introspection the coding vectors in our internal axonal pathways, the activation patterns across salient neural populations, and myriad other things besides.

Should that ever happen, it would then be obvious, to everyone who had made the conceptual shift, that a completed cognitive neuroscience would constitute not a pinched and exclusionary picture of human consciousness, one blind to the subjective dimension of self, as Jackson's argument suggests. Rather, it would be the vehicle of a grand reconstruction and expansion of our subjective consciousness, since it would provide us with a conceptual framework which, unlike folk psychology, is at last equal to the kinematical and dynamical intricacies of the world within. (See also P. M. Churchland 1979, section. 16; 1981.)

Real precedents for such a reformation can be drawn from our own history. We did not lose contact with a metaphysically distinct dimension of reality when we finally stopped seeing an immutable, sparkle-strewn quintessential crystal sphere each time we looked to the heavens, and began to see instead an infinite space of gas and dust and giant stars structured by gravitational attractions and violent nuclear processes. On the contrary, we now see far more than we used to, even with the un-aided eye. The diverse "colors" of the stars allow us to see directly their absolute temperatures. Stellar temperature is a function of stellar mass, so we are just as reliably seeing stellar masses. The intrinsic luminosity or brightness of a star is tightly tied to these same features, and thus is also visually available, no matter how bright or faint the star may appear from Earth. Its "visual magnitude" or "apparent" brightness is visually obvious also, of course, and the contrast between the apparent and the intrinsic brightnesses gives you the star's rough distance from Earth. In this way is the character and three-dimensional distribution of complex stellar objects in a volume of interstellar space hundreds of light-years on a side made visually available to your unaided eyes from your own back yard, given only the right conceptual framework for grasping it, and observational practice in using that framework. From within the new framework, one finds a systematic significance in experiential details that hitherto went largely or entirely unnoticed (cf. Feyerabend 1963b; P. M. Churchland 1979).

The case of inner space is potentially the same. We will not lose contact with a metaphysically distinct dimension of self when we stop introspecting inarticulable qualia, and start introspecting "instead" sensory coding vectors and sundry activation patterns within the vector spaces of our accessible cortical areas. As with the revolution in astronomy, the prospect is one we should welcome as metaphysically liberating, rather than deride as metaphysically irrelevant or metaphysically impossible.

Postscript: 1997

The following remarks concern the attempt to repair or avoid the charge of equivocation by quantifying over the possible diversity in any relevant forms of knowing, as briefly discussed two sections ago. Some time after publishing the original version of this paper, I discovered there was yet more to be learned from this exercise. Let me begin by giving the proof for the original version of the multiply quantified argument. (As before, $Hx = x$ is a fact about humans; $Px = x$ is a physical fact; $K(f)mx =$ Mary knows$_f$ x.)

ATTEMPT No. 1

1. $(x)(f)[(Hx \& Px) \supset K(f)mx]$		**False !**
2. $(Ex)(Ef)[Hx \& \sim K(f)mx]$	___/	..$(Ex)[Hx \& \sim Px]$
3. $(Ef)[Hr \& \sim K(f)mr]$		2, E.I. (flag constant r)
4. $Hr \& \sim K(i)mr$		3, E.I. (flag constant i)
5. $(f)[(Hr \& Pr) \supset K(f)mr]$		1, U.I.
6. $(Hr \& Pr) \supset K(i)mr$		5, U.I.
7. $\sim K(i)mr \& Hr$		4, Comm.
8. $\sim K(i)mr$		7, Detach
9. $\sim (Hr \& Pr)$		6,8, M. Tollens
10. $\sim Hr \lor \sim Pr$		9, DeMorgan
11. Hr		4, Detach
12. $\sim \sim Hr$		11, Dbl. Neg.
13. $\sim Pr$		10, 12, Dis. Syl.
14. $Hr \& \sim Pr$		11, 13, Conj.
15. $(Ex)[Hx \& \sim Px]$		14. E.G.

As remarked in the original paper, this argument is valid, but premise (1) is clearly false. The universal quantifier, (f), claims far too much about Mary's knowledge (because there *is* a form of knowledge about red sensations that Mary most famously *lacks*: introspective knowledge or knowledge-by-acquaintance).

But there are other possibilities here. Perhaps Jackson can get by with a slightly weaker first premise. To this end, let us replace the universal quantifier, (f), with an existential quantifier, (Ef). Premise (1) is now circumspect enough to be perfectly true on the assumptions of Jackson's story; for the specific case of *propositional* knowledge, Mary knows all there is to know.

Moreover, it might seem that this (true) premise is adequate to sustain a closely parallel argument.

ATTEMPT No. 2

1. $(x)(Ef)[(Hx \ \& \ Px) \supset K(f)mx]$	
2. $(Ex)(Ef)[Hx \ \& \sim K(f)mx]$ ———/	.. $(Ex)[Hx \ \& \ \sim Px]$
3. $(Ef)[Hr \ \& \sim K(f)mr]$	2, E.I. (flag constant r)
4. $Hr \ \& \sim K(i)mr$	3, E.I. (flag constant i)
5. $(Ef)[(Hr \ \& \ Pr) \supset K(f)mr]$	1, U.I.
6. $(Hr \ \& \ Pr) \supset K(i)mr$	5, E.I. **Invalid !**
7. $\sim K(i)mr \ \& \ Hr$	4, Comm.
8. $\sim K(i)mr$	7, Detach
9. $\sim (Hr \ \& \ Pr)$	6,8, M. Tollens
10. $\sim Hr \ V \sim Pr$	9, DeMorgan
11. Hr	4, Detach
12. $\sim \sim Hr$	11, Dbl. Neg.
13. $\sim Pr$	10, 12, Dis. Syl.
14. $Hr \ \& \sim Pr$	11, 13, Conj.
15. $(Ex)[Hx \ \& \sim Px]$	14. E.G.

Unfortunately, this argument is invalid by reason of violating (in line [6]) the standard restriction on Existential Instantiation to an already instantiated individual constant: in this case, the constant i. This failure is not random. It is revealing. The inference from (5) to (6) invalidly assumes that the form of knowledge, i, of which line (6) presumes to speak, is the *same thing* as the introspective form of knowledge of which line (4) quite correctly speaks. If these are indeed the premises from which Jackson wishes to proceed, then even the blind machinery of the predicate calculus finds him guilty of the classic charge against him—the illegitimate conflation of two possibly distinct (indeed, presumptively distinct) forms of knowledge.

There remains the possibility that, while the specific deduction of attempt no. 2 is invalid, there is some other deductive route that *will* take us validly from its two premises to its conclusion. But this hope is vain also, since the two premises are formally and jointly consistent with the negation of the conclusion. As I showed above (pp. 146–7), there exists a model—indeed, a purely physical model—in which both premises are true and yet the conclusion is false.

Still, perhaps the logical gap here can be closed and the argument's validity recaptured by leaning, this time, on a stronger version not of the first, but rather of the *second* premise. Specifically, let us replace the existential quantifier, (Ef), with a universal quantifier, (f). This will yield the following argument:

ATTEMPT No. 3

1. $(x)(Ef)[(Hx \ \& \ Px) \supset K(f)mx]$		
2. $(Ex)(f)[Hx \ \& \sim [K(f)mx]$	**False, or Question-Begging**	
3. $(f)[Hr \ \& \sim K(f)mr]$	2, E.I. (flag constant r)	
4. $Hr \ \& \sim K(i)mr$	3, U.I.	
5. $(Ef)[(Hr \ \& \ Pr) \supset K(f)mr]$	1, U.I.	
6. $(Hr \ \& \ Pr) \supset K(i)mr$	5, E.I. (flag constant i)	
7. $\sim K(i)mr \ \& \ Hr$	4, Comm.	
8. $\sim K(i)mr$	7, Detach	
9. $\sim (Hr \ \& \ Pr)$	6, 8, M. Tollens	
10. $\sim Hr \ V \sim Pr$	9, DeMorgan	
11. Hr	4, Detach	
12. $\sim \sim Hr$	11, Dbl. Neg.	
13. $\sim Pr$	10, 12, Dis. Syl.	
14. $Hr \ \& \sim Pr$	11,13, Conj.	
15. $(Ex)[Hx \ \& \sim Px]$	14. E.G.	

As expected, this new argument is formally valid. The problematic restriction on instantiating to the constant i in line (6) has now disappeared, because i was never flagged in any earlier line. In this argument, its first appearance came by U. I. rather than by E. I.

Alas, premise (2) is now a very strong claim indeed, and deeply problematic as a result. The materialist can plausibly maintain that it is false, and it begs the question in any case. As stated here, it claims that there is a fact or facts about humans (e.g., the character of their red sensations) that is unknown to Mary, not just via her introspection, but via *any* form of knowledge whatsoever. The materialist, however, is bound to claim that Mary does indeed know about sensations and their qualities (the alleged lacuna) via a discursive or propositional form of knowledge, namely, her exhaustive and completed neuroscience. The materialist's position, after all, is that sensations and their qualities are (either type- or token-) *identical* with brain states and their properties, something of which it has been stipulated that Mary has extensive, indeed, exhaustive, knowledge. *If* this identity claim is correct, then knowledge of the latter is *bound to be* knowledge of the former, despite the doubly opaque epistemic context arising from two distinct *forms* of knowledge (knowledge-by-acquaintance vs. knowledge-by-description) and two distinct descriptive vocabularies: folk psychology on the one hand, and cognitive neuroscience on the other. Accordingly, premise (2) would then be false: Mary would know a great deal—indeed, *everything*—about the qualitative characters of people's sensations, but only as those characters get represented within a single (discursive) form of knowledge, and only under a set of (scientific) descriptions mostly unfamiliar to the rest of us.

Materialists have also argued that, with nothing more than extensive practice on our part, the originally "unfamiliar" neuroscientific descriptions can come to displace entirely the more primitive vocabulary of our current folk psychology, even as the conceptual vehicle for our spontaneous self-conscious introspections. In that event, the descriptive opacity here lamented would disappear entirely. (Good riddance, too, if all it represented was our own ignorance.)

To be sure, the materialist cannot simply insist that Mary's neuroscientific knowledge truly constitutes a knowledge of sensations and their qualities: that would beg the question against the property dualist. Whether such identities do or do not hold is for our unfolding science to show in the fullness of time. But equally sure, neither can Jackson simply insist that neuroscience must *fail* to encompass qualia, which is precisely what the inflated version of premise (2) is attempting to blow past us.

That would be to *assume at the outset* that materialism is false, rather than to *show* that it must be false.

We have now explored three of the four combinations possible. There are two premises in Jackson's argument, and two forms of quantification over *f* for each. The last and least of the possible combinations deploys the strong version of both premises.

ATTEMPT No. 4

1. $(x)(f)[(Hx \ \& \ Px) \supset K(f)mx]$ **False !**
2. $(Ex)(f)[Hx \ \& \sim K(f)mx]$ **False, or Question-Begging**

$\vdots$

15. $(Ex)[Hx \ \& \sim Px]$

As in attempts no. 1 and no. 3, the ensuing argument will be valid, but here the premises make up the least compelling package of all, for the reasons already discussed singly.

In summary, then, the only argument whose premises are broadly and uniformly acceptable is attempt no. 2, but that argument is formally invalid by reason of conflating possibly distinct (presumptively distinct) forms of knowledge. And the only valid argument whose premises have even an outside chance of being true is attempt no. 3, but its second premise blithely begs the very question at issue.

As I remarked earlier in a similar context, Jackson has surely profited from the ambiguities here. The difference between attempts no. 2 and no. 3 is subtle—an (Ef) vs. an (f) buried within premise (2). Further, attempt no. 2 clearly has true premises, and attempt no. 3 is clearly valid. What is important, however, is that neither attempt meets both conditions, and so nothing whatever has been accomplished.

Curiously, Jackson's "color-blind Mary" argument is still regularly cited as a decisive critique of reductive materialism (e.g., Chalmers 1996; Searle 1992). It is curious because this somewhat vague and elusive argument shows up as either invalid, unsound, or question-begging on every rigorous interpretation in the neighborhood. If Jackson has some further version of the argument he would like to propose—preferably in canonical form, for clarity's sake—we should all be eager to address it. As it stands, we seem to have exhausted the available possibilities. None of them teaches us anything about the status of materialism: only about the dangers of equivocation, conflation, and begging the question at issue.

11

Recent Work on Consciousness: Philosophical, Theoretical, and Empirical

Paul M. Churchland and Patricia S. Churchland

Broad-spectrum philosophical resistance to physicalist accounts of conscious awareness has condensed around a single and clearly identified line of argument. Philosophical analysis and criticism of that line of argument has also begun to crystallize. The nature of that criticism coheres with certain theoretical ideas from cognitive neuroscience that attempt to address both the existence and the contents of consciousness. As well, experimental evidence has recently begun to emerge that will serve both to constrain and to inspire such theorizing. The present paper attempts to summarize the situation.

The Loyal Opposition

The possibility, or impossibility, of a neurobiological account of consciousness has been a hot topic of late, in both the public and the academic presses. A variety of theoretical overtures on the positive side (Edelman 1989; Baars 1988; Llinás and Ribary 1993; Llinas etal. 1994; Dennett 1991; P. M. Churchland 1995; Crick and Koch 1990) have provoked a gathering resistance focused on a single topic, namely, the ineffable qualitative characters of one's sensations, and their accessibility to no one but oneself. To use the current code words, the core problem for all aspiring physical accounts is said to be the undeniable existence of sensory *qualia* and the fact of their unknowability by any means except the subjective, introspective, or *first-person point of view*. This is sometimes referred to as "the Hard Problem," to distinguish it from the allegedly easier problems of memory, learning, attention, and so forth.

Sensory qualia are thought by many (Nagel 1974; Jackson 1982; Searle 1992; McGinn 1982; Chalmers 1996) to pose a problem for physicalist accounts—indeed, an insuperable problem—as follows. The intrinsic qualitative character or *quale* (pronounced *kwah-lee*) of a pain is to be sharply distinguished from the many causal, functional, and relational features of a pain. Examples of the latter are familiar: pain is typically caused by bodily stress or damage; pain typically causes unhappiness and avoidance behavior; pain disappears under analgesics. These are all extrinsic features of pain, accessible to everyone. They can be revealed in public experiments, they are known to every normally socialized person, and they play a central role in our public explanations and predictions of one another's behavior. Moreover, these causal/relational features of pain form a legitimate target for the reductive/explanatory aspirations of a growing neuroscience. The only requirement is to discover whatever states of the brain display exactly the *same* causal/relational profile antecedently accepted by us as characteristic of the state of pain. This is what would constitute, here, as elsewhere in science, a *reductive explanatory account*. If the discovered parallel of profiles were suitably systematic, we could then legitimately claim to have discovered what pains really *are*: they are states of the brain, the states captured by the neurobiological theory imagined.

Or rather, we could make that claim, except for one glaring difficulty: the intrinsic quale of pains would inevitably be left out of such an account, as would each person's unique knowledge of his pain qualia. It is evident, runs the argument, that our reductive aspirations here confront a problem not encountered in any other scientific domain. Specifically, the phenomena involved in conscious awareness are not *exhausted* by the fabric of causal and other relations in which they are embedded. In all other domains, the essential nature of the phenomena are so exhausted. But in the unique case of conscious awareness, there is a family of intrinsic properties—the subjective qualia that enliven our inner lives—whose essence cannot be captured in any causal, functional, structural, or relational story.

To drive its point home, the antireductionist argument continues as follows. The sciences, or at any rate, the *physical* sciences, are limited by nature to providing stories of this latter kind, stories that reconstruct the causal/relational reality of the target phenomena. They are therefore doomed to failure in precisely the case at issue, for the subjective qualia of one's sensations are something distinct from and additional to whatever causal/relational roles those sensations might happen to play in one's overall biological and cognitive economies. Such intrinsic qualia, though easily discriminable from the first-person point of view, are structureless simples in and of themselves. Accordingly, they can offer no "reconstructive purchase" for the aspirations of any physical science. They are the wrong kind of explanatory target. They are (i) metaphysically simple and (ii) exclusively subjective, whereas any physical reconstruction of them would have to be (i) based on causal/relational structures and (ii) entirely objective.

Thus the core resistance of the loyal philosophical opposition. A survey of the literature will find a variety of "thought-experiments" whose function it is to illustrate or highlight, in some way or other, the essentially elusive nature of our subjective qualia, as they are addressed by any third-person, physicalist point of view. For example, we have Nagel's impenetrably alien bat (1974), Jackson's neurobiologically omniscient but color-blind Mary (1982), Chalmers' functionally normal but qualia-deprived zombies (1996), and everyone's puzzle about whether one's subjective color space might be inverted relative to that of one's fellows. Each such story depends, in its own way, on the set of convictions outlined in the preceding two paragraphs. In the end, it is these shared convictions that do the real antireductive work. Let us take a closer look at them.

The Loyal Opposition Disarmed

We must concede, I think, that the quale of a pain, or of the sensation of red, or of the taste of butter, certainly *seems* to be simple and without hidden structure. So far as my native introspective capacities are concerned, they reveal nothing whatever in the way of constituting elements or relational structure. I can recognize and discriminate such qualia— spontaneously, reliably, and noninferentially—but I am quite unable to say *how* or *on what basis* I am able to identify them. So far, then, they seem to be intrinsic simples. And my knowledge of them would seem to be as direct and as fundamental as it could possibly be.

But we are here in danger of being seduced by that favorite of freshman logic classes: an Argument from Ignorance. That we are *unaware* of any hidden structure in the qualia of our sensations, that we *do not know* how our conscious awareness manages to discriminate among different sensations, these admitted facts about our own *lack* of knowledge do not entail that such qualia must therefore be free of underlying structure, nor that our first-person recognition of such qualia does not depend on some mechanism keyed to the relational features of that underlying structure.

Indeed, they do not even suggest such a view, because we know by sheerly logical considerations that, for any cognitive creature capable of discriminating among aspects of its experience, there must be some relatively low level of property-discrimination that is currently "basic" for that creature, in the weak sense that he is *ignorant of and unable to articulate* the possibly quite complex underlying causal basis on which those discriminations are made. The denial of this inevitable limitation would commit us to an infinite regress of discriminative levels, for each of which levels the creature can *always* articulate an account of the yet more basic level of properties on which his discriminations within the target level of properties consciously depends. Barring such infinities, for each creature there must be some level of property discrimination where his capacity for articulation runs out.

This logical fact is reflected in many familiar limitations. For example, you can recognize your youngest child's voice. You can discriminate it instantly from hundreds of her school chums. But you cannot articulate the acoustic basis of that discrimination. You can recognize suspicion in a person's face, instantly. But you will do very poorly at articulating the complex facial profile that prompts that judgment. Such judgments plainly *have* an underlying physical basis, but our ability to make them does not require that we be consciously aware of that basis.

It is both familiar and inevitable, then, that we be ignorant, at the level of conscious awareness, of the basis or etiology of at least *some* of our property-discriminations. And those inarticulated properties may well present themselves to us as being "simple," however complex their underlying nature might be. And this is so for reasons that have nothing to do with any issues that might divide materialists from dualists. We should not be too quickly impressed, then, that our discrimination of the qualia of our sensations turns up as constituting such a currently "basic" level. The "simplicity" of our sensory qualia need reflect nothing more than our own predictable ignorance about how we manage to discriminate them.

This does not show that the antireductionists must be wrong. But it does show that one of their crucial premises—concerning the intrinsic, nonrelational, metaphysical *simplicity* of our sensory qualia—is a question-begging and unsupported assumption. Whether qualia have that character is a matter for ongoing research to discover, one way or the other, not a matter on which partisan enthusiasts can pronounce from the armchair.

There is a further reason we should resist the premise of structureless simplicity. There is a robust historical precedent for the scientific issue here at stake. It is instructive to recall it.

Consider a familiar family of qualitative features, not of our internal states, but of external physical objects. Specifically, consider the *colors* that enliven the surfaces of apples and flowers and stones. These, too, are features we can learn to discriminate—spontaneously, reliably, and noninferentially. These, too, are features that present no internal causal/relational structure to our conscious apprehension. These, too, are features that are discriminationally "basic" for us in the weak sense outlined above. These, too, have been described as something we apprehend "directly" (the position is called "direct realism," and it survived into the present century). And these, too, have been defended as physically irreducible "simples" (by thinkers such as William Blake, and Goethe, both of whom were reacting against Newton's newly published particle theory of light). Finally, these features, too, might have been plausibly claimed to be epistemically accessible from but a single epistemic standpoint, viz., the "visual point of view." (Call such epistemically isolated properties "visjective" properties.)

Despite all these antireductive presumptions, a century's scientific research has taught us that the surface colors of external objects do indeed have a rich internal causal/relational structure, a structure, moreover, that is systematically related to our native mechanisms for color discrimination. *External* color qualia, at least, are not metaphysical simples at all, despite a fairly convincing first impression. To a first approximation, an object's color is constituted by its differential capacity to absorb and reflect diverse wavelengths of incident electromagnetic radiation. Colors have been successfully reduced to, or better, re-constructed as, appropriate families of *reflectance vectors*. The "tri-chromatic" retinal cells of humans are differentially responsive to these reflectivity profiles of external objects, and that is how we discriminate objective colors.

The lessons here are obvious, but worth enunciating. While it may occasionally seem plausible to insist on a heavy-duty metaphysical dis-tinction between the "causal/relational" and the "intrinsic" features of some domain of phenomena, that distinction may well be ignorance-driven and entirely empty. And while it may seem doubly plausible to insist on some such distinction when we also possess a native epistemic access to precisely the "intrinsic" features of the relevant domain, that native access does nothing whatever to assure the problematic contrast at issue. It need mark nothing but the current limits of our discriminatory understanding.

In sum, nothing about the case of our internal sensory qualia guaran-tees their structureless simplicity, or even suggests it. In fact, such histor-ical precedents as lie at hand (see above) suggest precisely the opposite conclusion. Our subjective sensory qualia may each have a rich internal structure, and thus it remains entirely possible that a matured neuro-science will eventually discover that hidden structure and make it an in-tegrated part of the overall reconstruction of mental phenomena in neurobiological terms. On this, more below.

But what of the peculiarly *exclusive* character of one's epistemic access to sensory qualia? What of their inaccessibility to any apprehension or instrumental detection from the objective or "third-person" point of view? Does not this show, all by itself, that internal qualia must lie be-yond the reach of any physicalist reduction?

No, because this exclusivity premise is no more substantial or com-pelling than the simplicity premise we have just dismissed. To illustrate, recall once more the case of the external colors and our "exclusively" *visual* access to them. The theoretically motivated claim that external colors might also be detected by some *non*visual artificial instruments—instruments that respond to an object's electromagnetic reflectance vector—would no doubt be dismissed by Blake and Goethe as a case of confusing the essentially "*vis*jective" property of color with the wholly "nonvisual" property of electromagnetic reflectance profiles. Alternatively, our two antireductive stalwarts might simply dismiss such a claim as "changing the subject" away from the properties that really interest us (the visible colors) and toward something else (reflectivity profiles) that is only contingently related to colors, at best. Such digging in of the heels is perhaps only to be expected. So long as one is antecedently convinced that external colors are ontologically distinct and physically irreducible properties, then so long will one be inclined to dismiss any novel and unexpected epistemic access to them as being, in truth, an access to something else entirely.

But it need not be so. In the case of external colors, it is now plain that it was not so. Insofar as color exists at all, to access an object's reflectivity profile *is* to access its objective color. And in the currently spotlighted case of *internal* sensory qualia, we must be sensible that something similar may happen. When the hidden neurophysiological structure of qualia (if there is any) gets revealed by unfolding research, then we will automatically gain a new epistemic access to qualia, above and beyond each person's native and currently exclusive capacity for internal discrimination. As aspiring reductionists, we cannot insist that this will happen. That is for research to determine. But neither can the antireductionist insist that it will not. His second premise, therefore—the epistemic exclusivity premise—is as question-begging and as ignorance-driven as the first.

We conclude that no substantive considerations currently block the reductive and explanatory aspirations of the neurosciences. The celebrated arguments that attempt to do so derive their plausibility from our current ignorance, from our limited imaginations, and from a careless tendency to beg the very questions at issue. We should not be taken in by them.

A final caution. A complete knowledge of the neurophysiological basis of our conscious awareness of sensory qualia—such as might be acquired by Frank Jackson's utopian neuroscientist, Mary (1982)—would of course not *constitute* our normal native capacity for the spontaneous, noninferential discrimination and recognition of sensory qualia. Though aimed at the same epistemic target—sensory qualia—this native capacity is a *distinct* cognitive capacity. (Evolutionarily, it antedates our capacity for discursive science by hundreds of millions of years.) Mary could have the scientific story down pat, and yet, because of a congenital color-blindness perhaps, lack the native capacity entirely. This possible dissociation has often been appealed to as proving that phenomenal facts about consciousness are distinct from physical facts about the brain (see again Jackson 1982; Chalmers 1996). But it shows nothing of the sort. The dissociation described is entirely possible—indeed, it is cleanly explicable—even on a purely physical account of mental phenomena. It can hardly *entail*, therefore, the falsity of reductive materialism.

Phenomenal Qualia: Theory and Data

Defending the abstract possibility of a neurobiological reduction of mental phenomena is one thing. Actually providing such an explanatory reduction is quite another. These closing sections address work that is already underway. We shall try to sample some recent results as they bear on the antireductive worries so widespread in the literature.

We begin with what seems to us an irony: of the many problems confronting our explanatory ambitions in neuroscience, the so-called Hard Problem—the problem of subjective sensory qualia—appears to be one of the easiest and closest to a stable solution. As we see it, the much harder family of problems is the clutch that includes short-term memory, fluid and directable attention, the awake state vs. sleep, and the unity of consciousness. These come up in the next section. For now, let us examine some representative work that bears on qualia.

Neurobiology aside, psychophysics has long been in the business of exploring the structure of our perceptual "quality spaces." Without ever sinking an electrode, one can systematically explore the relative similarity relations and betweenness relations among hundreds of color samples, as they are spontaneously judged by a large sample of experimental subjects. For each subject, those judgments allow the experimenter to locate every color sample in a unique position relative to all of the others. For normal humans, the structure of that quality space is well-defined and uniform across subjects. It is roughly as portrayed in figure 11.1. (A similar story can be told for the other sensory modalities, but we here choose to mine a single example in some depth.)

Phenomenological Space

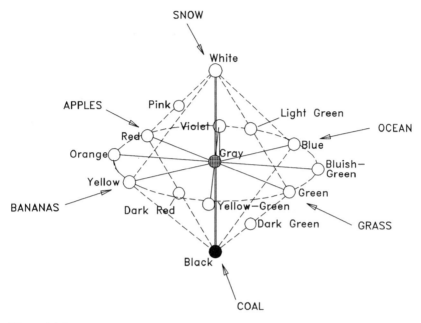

Figure 11.1
The intrinsic order of the human quality space for color. Some of the standard causal relations that connect it to the external world are indicated at its periphery. (A caution: this figure wrongly portrays our quality space as symmetric or homotopic. Importantly, it is not, and its internal asymmetries provide one way to address worries about so-called "inverted spectra." Hardin [1988] and Clark [1993] provide the best discussions on this topic. But I am here trying to pose the problem in its most difficult form, in order to outline an independent solution.)

Here we have, already, some systematic structure that unites the set of visual qualia, a structure that the neurobiology of vision can hope (and must try) to reconstruct. Incidentally, the "inverted spectrum" puzzle is here quickly characterized. Evidently, the mirror image of the double cone in figure 11.1 would capture the internal relations of that color space equally well, and one might wonder whether, and how to tell whether, one's own color space is causally attached to the external world in the same way as everyone else's. Single-axis inversions are not the only possibility here: partial rotations of the entire space, around arbitrary

axes, are quite conceivable also. One wonders how we can get an independent handle on everyone's internal color space in such a way as to
settle such questions.

One possible way is to find some determinate and accessible internal or
*intra*qualia structure that is variable across qualia, a structure that gives
rise to the same interqualia relations as are displayed in figure 11.1. This
internal structure would give us a means of identifying an individual internal quale, a means that is independent of both its relations to other
internal qualia and its problematic causal connections with external
stimuli. The existence of such an intraqualitative structure, of course, will
be rejected as impossible by the antireductionist of the preceding sections,
but we have learned not to be buffaloed by such insistence. Let us now
look at a live candidate.

Our current "best theory" for the neuroanatomy and neurophysiology
of human and primate color vision is the so-called *opponent processes*
theory. On this proposal, color is coded as a three-element vector of
activation levels within three proprietary types of cells synaptically
downstream (perhaps in the lateral geniculate nucleus, or LGN) from the
familiar three types of retinal cone cells. Those three downstream cell
types are each the locus of an excitatory vs. inhibitory tug of war (hence,
"opponent processes"), as indicated in figure 11.2. As a result of the
connections there portrayed, the leftmost cell type ends up coding the
relative dominance of yellow light over blue; the middle cell type ends up
coding the relative dominance of red light over green; and the rightmost
cell type ends up coding the relative dominance of brightness over dark-
ness roughly summed over all wavelengths.

Here we can determine, experimentally, exactly what signature activation triplet is produced across the opponent-color cells by any given
external color sample. We have, that is, an independent access to the internal structure of the creature's neurophysiological response, and we
can make determinate judgments of what external objects produce that
response. Let us now ask how those proprietary coding triplets are
globally organized, within the vector space of all possible triplets, according to their Euclidian proximity to and distance from each other.
The answer is portrayed in figure 11.3, and what is salient is that the
coding scheme at issue produces the *same* global organization of features

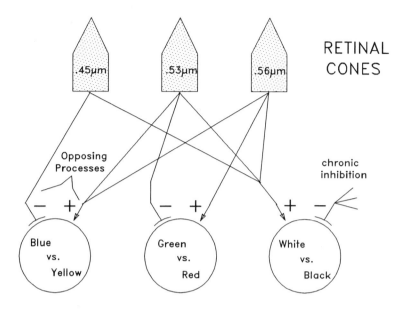

RETINAL
CONES

VISUAL OPPONENT CELLS

Figure 11.2
A schematic of the proposed visual opponent processes for coding color in
the human and primate visual systems. (After Clark 1993; Hardin 1988; and
Hurvich 1981.)

found in the psychophysically determined quality space of figure 11.1, an
organization that enjoys the *same* pattern of causal connections to the
external world.

As in the historical case of *external* color qualities, such a systematic
coincidence of causal and relational structures suggests a reductive explanation of the original quality space, and a corresponding identity
claim, viz., that one's internal or subjective color qualia *are identical with*
one's coding triplets across the three types of opponent cells. If that is
what sensory qualia really are, then we have, in the story just outlined, a
systematic explanation of the specific contents and rich internal structure
of our native quality space for color, an explanation that also accounts
(via the electromagnetic theory of light) for its specific causal connections
with the objective colors of objects in the external world.

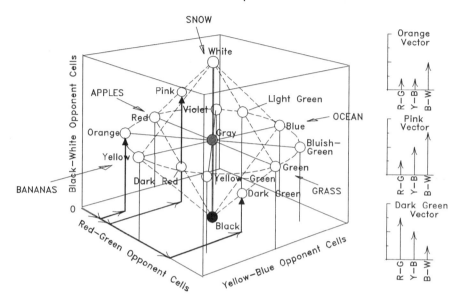

Figure 11.3
The vector space of opponent-cell coding, with some of the standard causal connections it bears to the external world. Note the isomorphism with the quality space of figure 11.1, both in its internal relations and its external connections. Sample vectors—for orange, pink, and dark green—are displayed as histograms at the side. These vectors are also traced within the color space proper.

Does this explanation allow for the possibility of "inverted spectra," as mooted in the traditional philosophical puzzle? Indeed it does, and it even entails how to produce that effect. Take a normal adult observer and, while holding all other neural connections constant, take all of the axons currently synapsing onto his blue/yellow opponent cells and exchange them with the axons currently synapsing onto his red/green opponent cells. That will do it. Upon awakening from this (highly fanciful) operation, our observer will see things quite differently, because his internal color space has been surgically remapped onto the external world. It has been "rotated" 90 degrees around the black/white axis, relative to the "external causes" in figure 11.1.

Alternatively, a mirror inversion of the original space, along one axis, could be achieved by an (even more demanding) surgery that inverted the polarity of all of the existing synapses onto exactly one of the three populations of opponent cells. *Of course* such "inverted spectra" are conceptually possible! It is even possible that we might detect them experimentally in the details of our neural wiring, or manipulate them as indicated .

Note that the present account also entails the existence of a variety of suboptimal color spaces for that small percentage of humans who are missing one or other of the normal populations of retinal cones. Their opponent cells thus end up denied important dimensions of information. If this vector-coding approach to qualia is correct, then psychophysical mapping of these nonstandard quality spaces will also have to match up with these nonstandard vector spaces at the cellular level. So far as I am aware, such experimental work on the varieties of color blindness remains to be done, at least as concerns the cellular level, but it offers a clear test of the theory.

The vector-coding approach to the inner nature of sensory qualia can be further tested as follows. As mentioned earlier in a figure legend, the normal human quality space for color is importantly asymmetric. The actual profile of that asymmetry is something that the opponent-cell theory must also aspire to explain, perhaps in terms of the nonuniform response profiles of the human opponent cells involved.

Should our growing neurophysiological reconstruction of human color space succeed in accounting even for this level of detail, then we would have a gathering case that our internal color qualia are indeed identical with coding vectors across the opponent cells in our LGN. It would not cinch the case, but we would here have the same sorts of systematic evidence that justify reductive explanatory claims elsewhere in science. And, dualist enthusiasms aside, it should be accorded the same weight that such evidence possesses elsewhere in science. No more. But no less.

Another caution is in order here. For we are not urging the *truth* of the preceding account as the refutation of the antireductionist's trenchant skepticism. Sensory qualia may yet be metaphysical simples forever inaccessible to neuroscience. But the antireductionist arguments addressed at the beginning of this paper made the very strong claim that (1) we *already* know that they are structureless simples, and that (2) no theory from the physical sciences has any hope of even *addressing* the phenomena in this area. Against this, we are claiming only that (1) we know no such thing, and (2) a perfectly respectable theory from the physical sciences already addresses the relevant phenomena, in considerable detail and with some nontrivial success.

Our caution is well advised for a further reason. While the opponent-cell story appears correct as far as it goes, it may be that we should resist identifying our conscious color quality space with the specific vector space of those relatively peripheral LGN opponent cells. They may be entirely too peripheral. A more plausible candidate vector space, for the physical embodiment of our color qualia space, might well be the activation space of some neuronal population two or three synaptic steps *downstream* from the LGN's opponent cells, a subpopulation of the primary visual cortex, for example, or perhaps the cells of area V4. Such higher-level vector spaces, boasting more highly processed information, may allow a more faithful reconstruction of the fine-grained features of our actual color qualia space, both in normals and in abnormals. And they may locate the relevant vectors in a processing arena more plausibly implicated in the phenomenon of conscious awareness. To which topic we now turn.

Consciousness and Attention: Theory and Data

Sensory qualia aside, why and how does anything *at all* ever make its way into conscious awareness? Vector coding is something that occurs at all levels of the nervous system, in thousands of distinct neuronal populations which represent an enormous range of information concerning the state of one's body and the state of the world around it, only a small percentage of which information is ever present to conscious awareness. What distinguishes this preferred class of conscious representations from the much larger class of representations that never see the light of consciousness?

This matter is no longer the smooth-walled mystery it used to be. A growing appreciation of the brain's neuronal organization, and enhanced access to brain activity in awake behaving creatures, has produced an

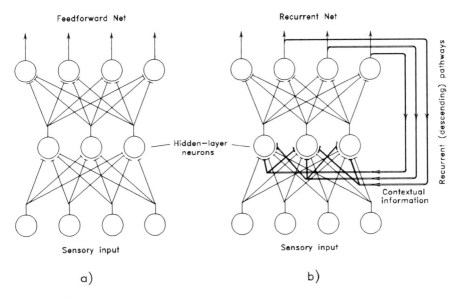

Figure 11.4
(a) The architecture of a standard feedforward network. Its response, at the middle layer, to a specific input activation vector, is some unchanging activation vector across that second population. (b) The architecture of a recurrent network. Its response, at the middle layer, can be an unfolding sequence of activation vectors, since that second population is also subject to subsequent and repeated input activity returned to it from a cell population one or more levels higher in the processing hierarchy.

environment in which responsible theoretical activity can at least get off the ground. The critical elements, it seems to us, are as follows.

Since the mid-'80s, there has been a groundswell in the construction of artificial neural networks and in the exploration of their pattern-recognizing capacities. A prototypical feedforward architecture appears in figure 11.4a. Modelers quickly learned, however, that for the great many important patterns that have a *temporal* dimension—such as typical motor sequences and typical causal processes—a purely feedforward network is representationally inadequate. One must move to networks that have descending or recurrent pathways, as in figure 11.4b, in addition to the standard ascending ones.

These additional pathways yield a network whose vectorial response, at the middle layer, to sensory-layer input, is partly a function of the concurrent activational or cognitive state of the third layer, which state is the result of still earlier inputs and earlier processing. A recurrent network's response to a given stimulus, therefore, is not fixed solely by the structural features of the network, as in a feedforward network. The response varies as a function of the prior dynamical or cognitive context in which the input stimulus happens to occur.

This middle-layer response can also unfold continuously over time, as the middle-layer cells receive an ever-changing set of modulating influences, from the downstream cognitive activity, via the recurrent pathways. For such a recurrent system, the middle-layer response is typically a *sequence* of activation vectors. That is to say, the response is a *trajectory* in activation space, rather than a point.

What is charming about such networks is that, by adjusting the weights and polarities of their synaptic connections appropriately, we can train them to respond to various input stimuli with proprietary activational trajectories. These vector sequences can represent salient causal sequences in the network's perceptual environment, sequences that the network has been trained to recognize. Alternatively, they can serve as generators for well-honed motor sequences that the network has been trained to produce. In both the perceptual and the motor domains, therefore, recurrent networks achieve a command of temporal patterns as well as spatial patterns—a command of time as well as space. More generally, they hold out a powerful set of theoretical resources with which to understand the phenomena of learning, memory, perception, and motor control.

They may also help us get an opening grip on consciousness, as follows. If a reductive explanatory account of consciousness is our aim, then here, as elsewhere in science, we must try to *reconstruct* the known features of the target phenomena using the resources of the more basic science at hand. (See P. M. Churchland and P. S. Churchland 1990 and chapter 6, this volume for an accessible account of the nature of intertheoretic reduction.) What features of consciousness stand out as salient targets for such reconstruction? While they are hardly exhaustive, the following would likely be included on anyone's list.

Consciousness involves short-term memory. Consciousness does not require concurrent sensory input. Consciousness involves directable attention. Consciousness can place different interpretations on the same sensory input. Consciousness disappears in deep sleep. Consciousness reappears, in somewhat altered form, in dreaming. Consciousness brings diverse sensory modalities together in a single, unified experience.

Recurrent networks have reconstructive resources that might eventually prove relevant to all of the elements of this list. First, any recurrent net already embodies a form of short-term memory: the information embodied in the middle-layer activation vector gets processed at the next layer and is then sent back to its origin, perhaps in modified form. That information may cycle through that recurrent loop many times while it slowly degrades. If some of it is important, the network may even be configured to retain that information, undegraded, through many cycles, until the unfolding cognitive context no longer values it. Such a system provides, automatically, a short-term, content-sensitive, variable decay-time memory.

A recurrent network can also engage in cognitive activity in the absence of current stimulation at the input layer, because activity in the recurrent pathways can be sufficient to keep the system humming away all on its own. It can also modulate, via those same pathways, the manner in which it reacts to sensory-layer stimuli, and the salience that certain aspects of that input will command. This gives us a crude analog for both the plasticity of conceptual interpretation, and the capacity for steering one's perceptual attention.

Moreover, a recurrent network can have its recurrent pathways selectively disabled for a time, and it will temporarily revert to a purely feedforward network, in which condition it will lose or suspend all four of the cognitive capacities just described. Perhaps deep sleep in humans is some peculiar instance of this highly special form of cognitive shutdown. Correlatively, it may well be that dreaming consists in the spontaneous or self-driven activity of a richly recurrent network that wanders among the learned trajectories that have come to dominate its normal waking operation, a meander that is temporarily free of the coherent guidance of sensory input from a stable external world, a meander that is also temporarily detached from the motor effectors it would normally drive.

Finally, a recurrent network can integrate information from different sensory modalities by delivering such information, directly or indirectly, back to a common cell population. The activations vectors at such a population will thus embody multimodal information. The Damasios (1994) call such brain areas "convergent zones."

Though vague, these assembled reconstructive suggestions are more than just suggestions. We know that the brain is a profoundly recurrent neuronal system, and there is experimental evidence that provides some initial support for the conjectures about the dynamical contrasts between deep sleep, dream sleep, and the awake state (Llinás and Ribary 1993; Llinás et al. 1994). Guided by neuroanatomy, we can at least see how we might sharpen the vague proposals just displayed. And guided by neurophysiology, we can at least see how progressively to test them.

A possible answer, therefore, to the question that opened this section, is as follows. A representation is an element of one's current conscious awareness just in case that activation vector occurs at the focal population of a suitably central recurrent system in the brain, a system that unites the several sensory modalities and dominates the control of motor behavior.

This may or may not be true. But it is a reductive hypothesis that explicitly addresses both of the central concerns of the antireductionist, the concerns that introduced this paper. First, we can indeed give an illuminating physical account of the "intrinsic" nature of our various sensory qualia. In short, they are activation vectors, one and all. And second, we can indeed suggest a possible account of when such vectors are a part of one's current conscious awareness. They must occur as part of the representational activity of a suitably recurrent network meeting the functional and anatomical constraints outlined above. The antireductionist's counsel of despair was never well-founded, as we saw earlier in our second section. And it came with no competing framework with which to sustain a viable tradition of research. Best we should put that counsel behind us then, and go where the recent progress pulls us.

12

Filling In: Why Dennett Is Wrong

Patricia S. Churchland and V. S. Ramachandran

It comes as a surprise to discover that the foveal area in which one has high resolution and high acuity vision is minute: it encompasses a mere 2 degrees of visual angle—roughly, the area of a thumbnail at arm's length. The introspective guess concerning acuity in depth likewise errs on the side of extravagance; the region of crisp, fused perception is, at arm's length, only a few centimeters deep; closer in, the area of fused perception is even narrower. The eyes make a small movement—a saccade— about every 200 to 300 milliseconds, sampling the scene by continually shifting the location of the fovea. Presumably, interpolation across intervals of time to yield an integrated spatiotemporal representation is a major component of what brains do. Interpolation in perception probably enables generation of an internal representation of the world that is useful in the animal's struggle for survival.

The debut demonstration of the blind spot in the visual field is comparably surprising. The standard setup requires monocular viewing of an object offset about 13 to 15 degrees from the point of fixation (figure 12.1). If the object falls in the region of the blind spot of the viewing eye, the object will not be perceived. Instead, the background color and texture will be seen as uniform across the region. This is generally characterized as "filling in" of the blind spot. The existence of the perceptual blind spot is owed to the specific architecture of the retina. As shown in figure 12.2, each retina has a region where the optic nerve leaves the retina and hence where no transducers (rods and cones) exist. This region is the blind spot. Larger than the fovea, it is about 6.0 degrees in length and about 4.5 degrees in width.

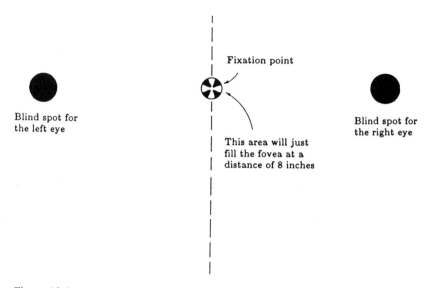

Figure 12.1

Instructions: close your right eye. Hold the page about eight inches in front of you. Hold the page very straight, without tilting or rotating it. Stare at the fixation point. Adjust the distance of the page until the black spot on the left disappears. Repeat with the left eye closed. (After Lindsay and Norman, 1972.)

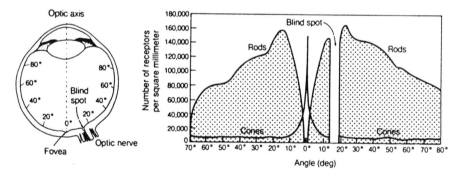

Figure 12.2

(*Left*) The human eye. The blind spot (optic disk) is that region on the retina where the ganglion cells leave the retina and project to the lateral geniculate nucleus of the thalamus. (*Right*) The packing density of light-sensitive cones is greatest at the fovea, decreasing sharply in the peripheral field. Rod density is greatest in the region that immediately surrounds the fovea, and gradually decreases in the more peripheral regions. Note that the region of the blind spot is in the peripheral field, and is larger than the foveal area.

Relying on two eyes, a perceiver—even a careful and discerning perceiver—will fail to notice the blind spot, mainly because the blind regions of the two eyes do not overlap. If light from a thimble, for example, falls in the blind spot of the left eye, it will nevertheless be detected normally by the right retina, and the viewer sees a thimble. Even in the monocular condition, however, one may fail to notice the blind spot because objects whose borders extend past the boundaries of the blind spot tend to be seen as filled in, as without gaps.

I. Dennett's Hypothesis

What is going on when one's blind spot is seen as filled in—as without gaps in the scene? Is it analogous to acquiring the nonvisual representation (belief) that Bowser, the family dog, is under the bed, on the basis of one's visual perception of his tail sticking out? Or is it more akin to regular visual perception of the whole Bowser in one's *peripheral but nonblind field*? That is, is the representation itself a visual representation, involving visual experiences? In *Consciousness Explained* (1991) Dennett favors the first hypothesis, which he sums up in his discussion of filling in: "The fundamental flaw in the idea of 'filling in' is that it suggests that the brain is providing something when in fact the brain is ignoring something" (p. 356).

We understand Dennett to mean that in the monocular condition the person may represent that there is a non-gappy object, say a vertical bar, in his visual field, but not because his brain generates a non-gappy *visual* representation of the vertical bar. In explicating his positive view on filling in, Dennett invites us to understand filling in of the blind spot by analogy to one's impression on walking into a room wallpapered with pictures of Marilyn Monroe:

Consider how the brain must deal with wallpaper, for instance... Your brain just somehow represents *that* there are hundreds of identical Marilyns, and no matter how vivid your impression is that you see all that detail, the detail is in the world, not in your head. And no figment gets used up in rendering the seeming, for the seeming isn't rendered at all, not even as a bit map. (pp. 354–5)

If, as instructed, we are to apply this to the case of filling in of the blind spot, presumably Dennett's point is that no matter how vivid one's impression that one sees a solid bar, one's brain actually just represents that there is a solid bar. Dennett's claim, as he clarifies later, is that the brain ignores the absence of data from the region of the blind spot. In what follows, we shall show that, contrary to Dennett, the data strongly imply that at least some instances of filling in do indeed involve the brain "providing" something.

One preliminary semantic point should be made to forestall needless metaphysical tut-tutting. Hereafter, in discussing whether someone's perception of an object, say an apple, is filled in, we shall, *as a convenient shorthand*, talk about whether or not "the apple is filled in." In availing ourselves of this expedient, we do *not* suppose that there might be a little (literal) apple or (literal) picture of an apple in someone's head which is the thing that is filled in. Rather, we refer merely to some property of the brain's *visual* representation such that the perceiver sees a non-gappy apple.

Very crudely speaking, current neurobiological data suggest that when one sees an apple, the brain is in some state that can be described as representing an apple. This representation probably consists of a pattern of activity across some set of neurons, particularly those in the visual cortex, that have some specific configuration of synaptic weights and a specific profile of connectivity (P. M. Churchland 1989b). Given this general characterization of a representation, the question we want to address can now be rephrased: Does filling in an apple-representation consist in the visual cortex generating a representation which more closely resembles the standard case of an apple-representation of an apple in a peripheral visual field? Or does it consist, as Dennett (1991) suggests, in a nonvisual representation rather like one's nonvisual representation of the dog under the bed?

Our approach to these questions assumes that a priori reflection will have value mainly as a spur to empirical investigation, but not as a method that can be counted upon by itself to reveal any facts. Thought-experiments are no substitute for real experiments. To understand what is going on such that the blind spot is seen as filled in (non-gappy), it will be important to know more about the psychological and neurobiological parameters. In addition to exploring filling in of the blind spot, other versions of visual filling in, such as the filling in experienced by subjects

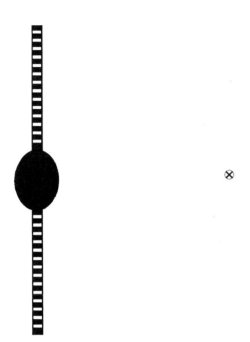

Figure 12.3
Subjects are presented with a display consisting of two vertical bar segments, separated by a gap of about 5 degrees, and this gap is positioned to coincide with the subject's blind spot. Fixation is to the right for left-eye viewing. Subjects report seeing an uninterrupted bar.

with cortical lesions, can also be studied. Although a more complete study would make an even wider sweep, embracing modalities other than vision, for reasons of space we narrow the discussion to visual filling in.

II. Psychophysical Data: The Blind Spot

To investigate the conditions of filling in, Ramachandran (1992) presented a variety of stimuli to subjects who were instructed to occlude one eye and fixate on a specified marker. Stimuli were then presented in various parts of the field in the region of the subject's blind spot. If a bar extends to the boundary on either side of the blind spot, but not across it, will the subject see it as complete or as having a gap (figure 12.3)? Subjects see it as complete. If, however, only the lower bar segment or the upper bar segment is presented alone, the subject does not see the bar

Figure 12.4
If only the upper segment of the bar is presented, subjects do not complete across
the blind spot.

as filled in across the blind spot (figure 12.4). What happens when the
upper bar and the lower bar are different colors; for example, upper, red;
lower, green? Subjects still see the bar as complete, with extensions of
both the red and green bar, but they do not see a border where the red
and green meet, and hence they cannot say just where one color begins
and the other leaves off. (For the explanation of nonperception of a border
in terms of semisegregated pathways for functionally specific tasks, see
Ramachandran 1992.)

Ramachandran also found that spokes extending to but not into the
blind-spot boundary were filled in, demonstrating that filling in can be
very complex. Suppose there is a kind of competition between completion of a black bar across the blind spot, and completion of an illusory
contour lengthwise across the blind spot. Will the illusory contour or the
real contour complete? Ramachandran discovered that in this test, the
illusory contour typically completes (figure 12.5).

Ramachandran next explored the relation between subjective completion of a figure, and that figure's role in illusory motion (figure 12.6).
The basic question is this: Does the brain treat a filled-in bar like a solid
bar or like a gappy bar? In the control case, the upper gappy bar is replaced with the lower gappy bar (delay about 100 to 200 ms). Because
the gap in the upper bar is offset with respect to the gap in the lower
bar, subjects see illusory motion in a diagonal direction from left to right.

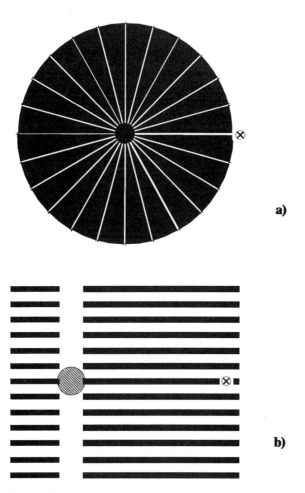

Figure 12.5
(a) Subjects reported perceptual completion of the spokes. (b) An illusory vertical strip was displayed so that a segment of the illusory contour fell on the blind spot. Subjects reported completion of the illusory strip rather than completion of the horizontal lines.

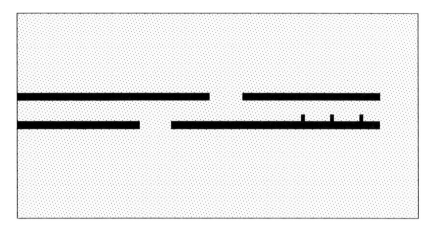

Figure 12.6
To generate illusory motion, the upper bar is replaced by the lower bar. When the gaps in both bars are located outside the blind spot, subjects see diagonal movement. When the gap in the upper bar coincides with the subject's blind spot, the movement appears to be vertical.

In the experimental (monocular) condition, the gap in the upper bar is positioned so that it falls in the subject's blind spot, and the subject sees a completed bar. Now when the upper bar is replaced by the lower bar to generate illusory motion, subjects see the bar moving vertically, *nondiagonally*, just as one does if a genuinely solid bar is replaced by the lower bar. This experiment shows that the brain treats a completed bar just at it treats a genuinely non-gappy bar in the perception of illusory motion.

According to Dennett's characterization of filling in (1991, p. 356), the brain follows the general principle that says, in effect, "just more of the same inside the blind spot as outside." Several of Ramachandran's results are relevant to this claim. If filling in is just a matter of continuing the pattern outside the blind spot, then in figure 12.7 subjects should see an uninterrupted string of red ovals, as a red oval fills the blank space where the blind spot is. In fact, however, subjects see an interrupted sequence; that is, they see two upper red ovals, two lower red ovals, and a white gap in between. In a different experiment, subjects are presented with a display of "bagels," with one bagel positioned so that its hole falls within the subject's blind spot (figure 12.8). The "more of the same" principle

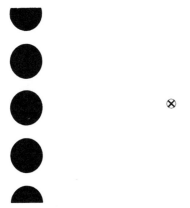

Figure 12.7
If the display is positioned so that a circle falls in the blind spot, subjects report a gap, not completion.

Figure 12.8
The display consists of yellow bagels and a fixation marker. The hole in one bagel (labeled *b*) coincides with the subject's blind spot. Subjects report seeing a yellow disk at this location, indicating that the yellow bagel is filled in.

presumably predicts that one will see only bagels in the display, as one apparently sees "more Marilyns." So the blind spot should not fill in with the color of its surrounding bagel. In fact, however, this is not what happens. Subjects see bagels everywhere, *save in the region of the blind spot*, where they see a disk, uniformly colored.

III.   Psychophysical Data: Cortical Scotomata

A lesion to early areas of visual cortex (V1, V2; i.e., areas 17, 18) typically results in a blind area in the visual field of both eyes. The standard optometric test for determining scotomata consists in a flashing point of light in various locations of the visual field. Subjects are instructed to indicate, verbally or by pressing a button, when they see a flash. Using this method, the size and location of a field defect can be determined. Ramachandran (1992, 1993) explored the spatial and temporal characteristics of filling in of the scotoma in two patients (B. M. and J. R.).

B. M. had a right occipital-pole lesion caused by a penetrating skull fracture. He had a paracentral left hemifield scotoma, 6 × 6 degrees with clear margins. J.R. had a right occipital lesion caused by hemorrhage and a left visual field scotoma 12 degrees in width and 6 degrees in height. The locations of the lesions were determined by magnetic resonance (MR) scanning. Both patients were intelligent and otherwise normal neurologically. Vision was 20/20. B. M. was tested six months and J. R. eight months after the lesion events. Neither patient experienced his scotoma as a gap or hole in his visual field, but each was aware of the field defect. For example, each noticed some instances of "false" filling in of a real gap in an object. Additionally, they noticed that small, separable components of objects were sometimes unperceived, and noticed as missing. For example, one subject mistook the women's room for the men's room because the "Wo" of "Women's" fell into the scotoma. Seeing "men's," the subject walked directly in and quickly discovered his mistake.

In brief, the major findings of Ramachandran are as follows:

1. A 3-degree gap in a vertical line is completed across the scotoma, the completion taking about 6 seconds. The duration was determined by asking the patients to press a button when the line segment was completely filled in. Even with repeated trials, the latency remained the same.

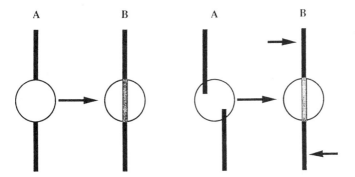

Figure 12.9
Schematic illustration of the stimuli shown to patients. The circle represents (roughly) the region of the patient's scotoma; fixation was approximately center field. (*Left*) Two bar segments were displayed on either side of the scotoma. The bar was vividly completed; the process of completion took about 6 seconds. (*Right*) The vertical bar segments were misaligned in the horizontal plane. After a few seconds of viewing, patients reported the lines moving toward each other until they became colinear. Then they gradually began to complete across the scotoma.

2. One patient (J. R.) reported that his perception of the filled-in line segment *persisted* for an average of 5.3 seconds after the upper and lower lines were turned off. The delay in completion as well as the persistence of "fill" is intriguing, and it is not seen in nontraumatic blind-spot filling-in.

3. When the top and bottom segments of the line were misaligned horizontally by 2 degrees, both patients first reported seeing two misaligned segments separated by a gap. After observing this for a few seconds, they spontaneously reported that the upper and lower line segments began to drift toward each other, moving into alignment, then slowly (over a period of about 10 seconds) the line segments filled in to form a single line spanning the scotoma (figure 12.9). The realignment and visual completion took 6.8 seconds on average.

4. When viewing dynamic two-dimensional noise (e.g., "snow" on a television screen), one patient reported that the scotoma was first filled in with static (nonflickering) noise for 7 or 8 seconds before the random spots began to move and flicker. When the noise was composed of red pixels of randomly varying luminance, J. R. reported seeing the red color bleeding into the scotoma almost immediately, followed about 5 seconds later by the appearance of the dynamic texture.

5. When a vertical column of spots (periodicity greater than 2 degrees) was used instead of a solid line, both patients clearly saw a gap. When

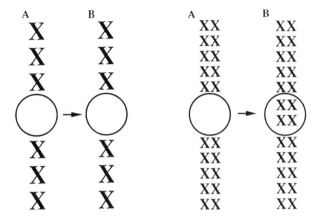

Figure 12.10
(*Left*) A column of large X's was not completed across the scotoma. (*Right*) A column of small X's did complete. If the column consisted of small horizontal line segments, the results were similar.

the spacing was reduced (periodicity less than 0.3 degree), patients reported seeing completion, across the scotoma, of a dotted line. These conditions were repeated using X's instead of spots, and the results were comparable (figure 12.10). Presented with a wavy, vertically oriented sinusoidal line (0.5 cycle per degree) with a gap matching the height of the patient's scotoma, both patients reported clearly seeing a non-gappy sinusoidally wavy line.

6. Each patient reported seeing illusory contours filled in across his scotoma. The experiment was similar to that performed with normal subjects (see again figure 12.5) save that the display was positioned so that the scotoma lined up with the gap in the stimuli. First, two horizontal line segments bordering the scotoma were presented, and as expected, they completed across the gap. Next, when an aligned array of horizontal lines was presented, the horizontal lines did not complete across the gap, and instead patients saw the vertical illusory strip complete across the scotoma.

7. Patients were presented with a checkerboard pattern , both fine (less than 0.3 degree)- and coarse (greater than 1.5 degree)-grained, which were readily filled in. When the checkerboard texture was subjected to counterphase flicker (7.5 Hz flicker; 0.6 check width), B. M. completed the flickering checks. J. R. however, reported that as soon as the pattern was made to flicker, he saw nonflickering stationary checks inside his scotoma, with the result that the margins of his scotoma became "en-

topically" visible. After about 8 seconds, J. R. saw the dynamic checks everywhere, including his scotoma.

8. To determine whether these filling-in effects might be seen in patients with laser-induced paracentral *retinal* scotomata, the tests were repeated on two such patients. Ramachandran found that (a) gaps in bars were not completed, (b) there was no motion or completion of misaligned bars, (c) coarse checkerboard patterns did not complete, (d) fine-grained 2-D random-dot textures were completed. This suggests that many of the completion effects are of cortical origin.

In the lesion studies, the time course for filling in, together with the subjects' reports, indicate that the completion is a visual phenomenon rather than a nonvisual judgment or representation. For example, when their spontaneous reports were tested with comments such as, "You mean you *think* that the checkerboard is uniform everywhere," the patients would respond with emphatic denials like, "Doctor, I don't merely *think* it is there; I *see* that it is there." Insofar as there is nothing in the visual stimulus corresponding to the filled-in perception, it is reasonable to infer, in contrast to Dennett, that the brain is "providing something," not merely "ignoring something." The visual character of the phenomenon also suggests that in looking for the neurobiological mechanism, visual cortex would be a reasonable place to start.

IV. Psychophysical Data: Artificial Scotomata

Ramachandran and Gregory (1991) discovered a species of filling in readily experienced by normal subjects, and conditions for which can easily be set up by anyone. The recipe is simple: adjust the television set to "snow" (twinkling pattern of dots); make a fixation point with a piece of tape, roughly in the middle of the screen; and place a square piece of gray paper, about 1 cm square and roughly isoluminant to the gray of the background, at a distance of about 8 cm from the fixation point (i.e., in peripheral vision). Both eyes may be open, and after about 10 seconds of viewing the fixation point, the square in peripheral vision vanishes completely. Thereafter, one sees a uniformly twinkling screen. Insofar as this paradigm yields filling in that is reminiscent of filling in of the blind spot and cortical scotoma, it can be described as inducing a kind of

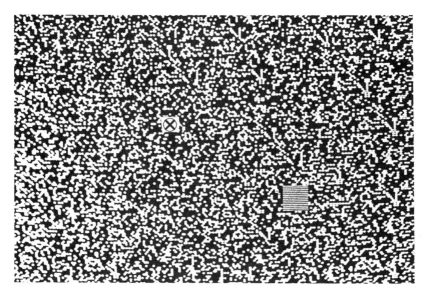

Figure 12.11
Display for artificial scotoma conditions consists of a background texture, a fixation point (the circle), and a small square segment in the peripheral field with a different texture, roughly isoluminant to the background.

artificial blind spot. Hence Ramachandran and Gregory called it an "artificial scotoma" (figure 12.11).

By using a computer to generate visual displays, many different arrangements of background texture and artificial scotomata can be investigated. In exploring the variety of conditions for filling in of an artificial scotoma, Ramachandran and Gregory found a number of striking results, several of which we briefly outline below:

1. Subjects tended to report filling in from outside the gray square to the inside, with a time scale of about 5 to 10 seconds.

2. Once subjects reported filling in to be complete, the background twinkles were then turned off. Subjects now reported that they *continued* to see twinkling in the "scotomic" square for about 3 to 4 seconds after the background twinkles had disappeared.

3. Suppose the background screen is pink and the twinkles are white. The "scotomic" square is, as before, gray, but within the square (which is now computer generated), dots are moving not randomly but coherently, left to right. Subjects report seeing a completely pink screen after about

Figure 12.12
The filling in of the artificial scotoma can be complex. In this condition, subjects report that the text fills in.

5 to 10 seconds, but report that the dots in the square continue to move coherently from left to right. After a few more seconds, however, they report seeing uniformly random twinkles everywhere. Note that the artificial scotoma is in peripheral vision, where resolution is much poorer than in the foveal region (see again figure 12.2). The twinkles that are filled in look just the same as the twinkles elsewhere in the peripheral field.

4. If the screen is covered in text, the peripheral square comes to be filled in with text (figure 12.12).

5. If a smaller square with black borders is inscribed within the region of the gray square, subjects report that the inner area does not fill in with background texture.

Many other experiments in artificial scotomata are now underway in Ramachandran's laboratory, and those few cited here mark only the first pass in exploring a salient and intriguing visual phenomenon. For our purposes here, it is perhaps enough to note that, so far as we can determine, the results from artificial scotoma experiments do not confirm Dennett's hypothesis that, for phenomena such as filling in, "we can already be *quite* sure that the medium of representation is a version of something efficient, like color-by-numbers [which gives a single label to a whole region], not roughly continuous, like bit-mapping" (Dennett, 1991, p. 354).

V. Psychophysics and the Krauskopf Effect

Krauskopf (1963) discovered a remarkable filling-in phenomenon. In his setup, a green disk is superimposed on a larger orange disk. The inner boundary (between green and orange) is stabilized on the retina so that it remains on exactly the same retinal location no matter how the eyes jitter and saccade, but the outer boundary moves across the retina as the eyes jitter and saccade. After a few seconds of the image stabilization, the subject no longer sees a green disk; instead, the entire region is seen as uniformly orange—as filled in with the background color.

Using the Krauskopf image stabilization method to explore further aspects of the filling-in phenomenon, Thomas Piantanida and his colleagues have found more remarkable filling-in results. It is known that adaptation to yellow light alters a subject's sensitivity to a small flickering blue light; more exactly, flicker sensitivity is reduced in the presence of a yellow adapting background. Prima facie this is odd, given that "blue" cones are essentially insensitive to yellow light (it is the "red" and "green" cells that are sensitive to yellow light). Piantanida (1985) asked this question: Is blue flicker sensitivity the same if yellow adaptation is obtained by subjective *filling in of yellow* rather than by actual yellow light illuminating the retina?

To get a perception of yellow in an area where the retina was not actually illuminated with yellow light, Piantanida presented subjects with a yellow bagel, whose inner boundary was stabilized on the retina (using a dual Purkinje eye tracker) and whose outer boundary was not stabilized. The finding was that the yellow background achieved by image stabilization was *as effective* in reducing "blue" cone flicker sensitivity as an actual yellow stimulus. This probably means, therefore, that the reduction in flicker sensitivity as a function of perceived background is a cortical rather than a retinal effect. The most likely hypothesis is that cortical circumstances relevantly like those produced by retinal stimulation with yellow light are produced by yellow filling in, and hence the adaptation effects are comparable.

There is a further and quite stunning result reported by Crane and Piantanida (1983) that is especially relevant here. They presented subjects with a stimulus consisting of a green stripe adjacent to a red stripe, where the borders between them were stabilized, but the outside borders were not stabilized. After a few seconds, the colors began to fill in across the stabilized border. At this point, some observers described what they saw as a new and unnameable color that was somehow a mixture of red and green. Similar results were obtained with yellow and blue. Produced extraretinally, these visual perceptions of hitherto unperceived colors resulted from experimental manipulation of filling-in mechanisms—mechanisms that actively do something, as opposed to simply ignoring something.

Dennett says of the blind spot, "The area is simply neglected" (1991, p. 355). He says that "the brain doesn't have to 'fill in' for the blind spot, since the region in which the blind spot falls is already labeled (e.g., 'plaid' or 'Marilyns' or just 'more of the same')" (p. 355). Part of the trouble with Dennett's approach to the various filling-in phenomena is that he confidently prejudges what the neurobiological data at the cellular level will look like. Reasoning more like a computer engineer who knows a lot about the architectural details of the device in front of him than like a neurobiologist who realizes how much is still to be learned about the brain, Dennett jumps to conclusions about what the brain does not need to do, ought to do, and so forth.

In sections VI and VII below, we discuss neurobiological data that conflict with Dennett's claim that "There are no homunculi, as I have put it, who are supposed to 'care about' information arising from the part of the visual field covered by the blind spot, so when nothing arrives, there is no one to complain" (p. 357). And again: "The brain's motto for handling the blind spot could be: Ask me no questions and I'll tell you no lies" (p. 356). While Dennett's idea may seem to have some engineering plausibility, it is really a bit of a priori neurophysiology gone wrong. Biological solutions, alas, are not easily predicted from engineering considerations. What might, from our limited vantage point, have the earmarks of sound engineering strategy, is, as often as not, out of kilter with the way nature does it.

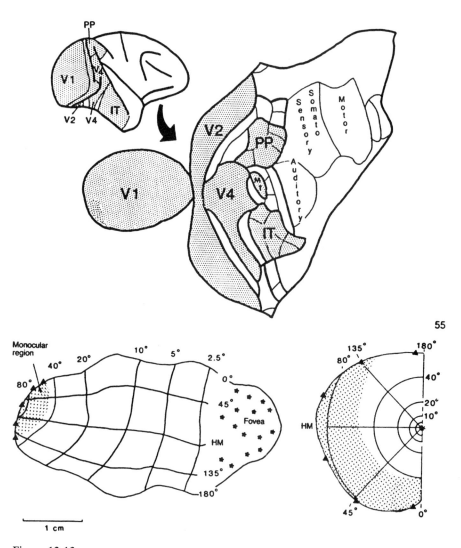

Figure 12.13

(*Above*) visual areas in the cerebral cortex of the macaque, as seen in a lateral view of the right hemisphere, and (arrow) in an unfolded two-dimensional map. The primary visual cortex (V1) is topographically organized. Lines of eccentricity (semicircles in the visual field drawing on lower right) map onto contours that run approximately vertically on the cortical map (*lower left*). Lines of constant polar angle (rays emanating from the center of gaze in the visual field) map onto contours that run approximately horizontally on the cortical map. The foveal representation (asterisks), corresponding to the central 2ϕ radius, occupies slightly more than ten percent of V1. The monocular region (stippled) in the visual field occupies a very small region of the cortical map. (Reproduced with permission from Van Essen and Anderson, 1990.)

VI. The Blind Spot and Cortical Physiology: The Gattass Effect

There are upward of twenty cortical visual areas in each hemisphere of monkeys, and probably at least that many in humans. Many of these areas are retinotopically mapped, in the sense that neighboring cells have neighboring receptive fields, that is, neighboring points in the visual field will be represented by neighboring cells in the cortex. In particular, visual area V1 has been extensively explored (figure 12.13). The receptive field size of V1 cells is about 2 to 3 degrees, and hence is much smaller than the size of the blind spot (about 6×4.5 degrees).

Ricardo Gattass and his colleagues (Fiorani et al., 1990; Gattass et al., 1992; Fiorani et al., 1992) were the first to try to answer the following question: How do V1 cells corresponding to the region of the blind spot for the right eye respond when the left eye is closed and a stimulus is presented to the open right eye (and vice versa)?

For ease of reference hereafter, by "Gattass condition" we denote the setup in which the experimenter records from single cells in V1 in the general area corresponding to the optic disk when the stimulus is presented to the contralateral (opposite side) eye. Call the V1 region corresponding to the optic disk of the contralateral eye, the "optic disk cortex" or ODC. The optic disk is that region of the retina where no transducers exist, corresponding to that part of the visual field where the blind spot resides. Remember that if a cortical region corresponds to the optic disk for the contralateral eye, it will correspond to *normal* retinal area for the ipsilateral (same side) eye. See figure 12.14 for projection patterns.

The seemingly obvious answer to Gattass' question—and the answer Gattass and his colleagues expected—is that the ODC cells will not respond in the monocular condition to stimuli presented in the contralateral blind spot. That is, one would predict that the cells in that region are responsive only to stimuli from the nonblind region of the ipsilateral eye. This is not what they found. Applying standard physiological mapping techniques to monkeys, and using the conventional bars of light as stimuli, they tested the responses of ODC cells (left hemisphere) with the left eye closed. As they moved the bar of light around and recorded from single cells, they found that neurons in the ODC area

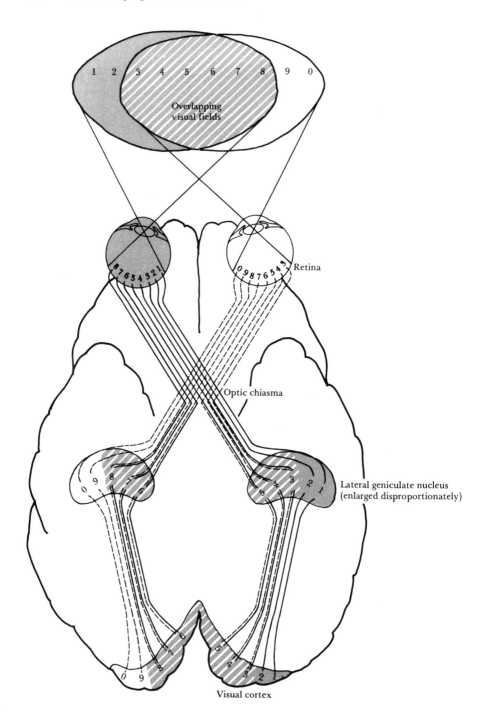

Overlapping
visual fields

Retina

Optic chiasma

Lateral geniculate nucleus
(enlarged disproportionately)

Visual cortex

responded very well. That is, cells corresponding to the blind spot gave consistent responses to a bar of light passing through the blind sector of the visual field. The response data did, however, show that the ODC was somewhat less neatly mapped by contralateral stimuli (i.e., in the blind spot) than by ipsilateral stimuli (i.e., in the nonblind field).

For some cells, an excitatory receptive field—presumably an interpolated receptive field—located *inside* the ODC could be specified. Exploring further, they found that sweeping bars on only one end of the blind spot yielded poor responses or none at all. In other cells, they discovered that the sum of two responses to two bar segments entering either end of the blind spot was comparable to the response for a single non-gappy bar. This indicates that some cells in the Gattass condition exhibit discontinuous receptive fields, presumably via interpolation signals from other neurons with neighboring receptive fields. To study the relevance of neighboring relations, Gattass and his colleagues masked the area immediately surrounding the optic disk during stimulus presentations to the blind spot region of the visual field. They discovered that responses of the ODC neurons were abolished in the masked condition (figures 12.15 and 12.16). Fifteen out of forty-three neurons (mostly from layer 4ca) were found to exhibit interpolation properties across a region of the visual field at least three times the size of the classic receptive field.

VII. Artificial Scotomata and Cortical Physiology: The Gilbert Effect

How do cortical cells respond when their receptive field corresponds to the area of an *artificial* scotoma, such as the kind Ramachandran and Gregory studied? (For ease of reference, we shall hereafter call these

Figure 12.14
Schematic illustration of the projection pathways from the retina to the cortex, showing which parts of the visual field are represented in specific parts of the lateral geniculate nucleus (LGN) and the visual cortex. Note that the left hemifield projects to the right (contralateral), which in turn projects to the right hemisphere. The blind spot of the left eye corresponds approximately to the region coded as 3, which is part of the central region where the fields of the two eyes overlap. By tracking 3 from the visual field, to the retina, to the LGN and the cortex, one can track the pathway for a particular stimulus in the blind region of the left eye. (Reproduced with permission from Lindsay and Norman, 1972.)

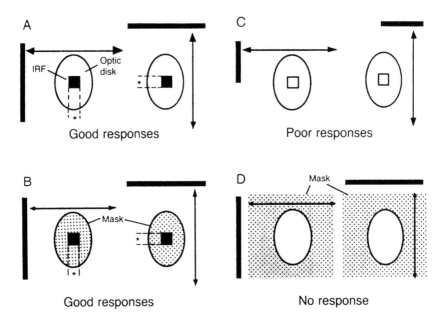

Figure 12.15
Summary of responses of cortical neurons in the optic disk cortical region to bars and masks of varying sizes. IRF: Interpolated receptive field; asterisks indicate locations where stimulation with long bars elicited responses. (After Fiorani et al. 1992.)

cortical neurons "artificial scotoma" or AS cells.) Or when the area from both retinas from which they receive projections is *lesioned*? (hereinafter, we shall call these cortical neurons "retinal lesion" or RL cells.) These questions have been addressed by Charles Gilbert and colleagues at Rockefeller University. Recording from V1 in monkeys, they discovered that the receptive fields of cortical cells surrounding the cortical RL cells expanded in several minutes so that collectively they covered that part of the visual field normally covered by the RL cortical cells (Gilbert and Wiesel, 1992).

A similar result was found in artificial scotoma experiments in cats (Pettet and Gilbert, 1991). The cortical cells in V1 surrounding the AS cortical cells very quickly expanded their receptive fields to include the area normally in the domain of the AS cells. The receptive field expansion was of the order of three- to fivefold. It was observed as soon as tests could be made (2 minutes), and it was reversible, in that once the ex-

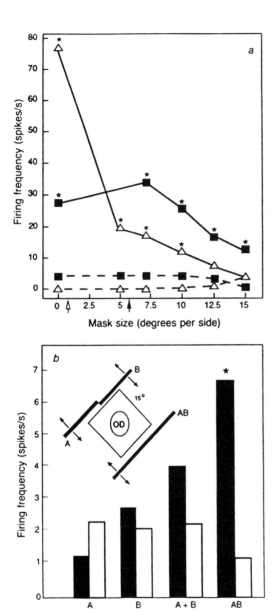

Figure 12.16
(a) Mean response rate of a V1 cell for ten presentations of the stimulus under different masking conditions. Triangles and filled squares linked by continuous lines show response to ipsilateral and contralateral eye, respectively, in paired trials. The lower (*dashed*) lines show the mean spontaneous activity where each eye is opened separately. The size of the ipsilateral classic receptive field is shown below by an outlined arrow, and the diameter of the optic disk (OD) by a filled arrow. (b) Black bars: mean response frequency of the same neuron to stimulation over a mask 15φ per side. Open bars show the mean spontaneous activity in paired trials without stimulation. (Reproduced with permission from Fiorani et al. 1992.)

perimental condition was removed and a standard, nonscotomatic stimulus was presented, normal mapping of cortical cells was restored. Although the neurobiological basis for this modification or interpolation in receptive field properties has not yet been determined, it is conjectured that lateral interactions within the cortex are probably crucial.

The Gattass effect, together with the Gilbert effect, is important evidence that the receptive fields of cortical cells are dynamic and can be modified on very short time scales. What precisely this means in terms of the neurobiological mechanisms of visual experience will require many more experiments. In any case, it is unlikely that the results are irrelevant to determining whether the brain merely ignores the blind spot or whether there is an active process related to filling in. As we try to track down the neurobiology of visual awareness, the discoveries in neuroscience are important clues to the nature of visual processing and to that component of the processing relevant to visual awareness.

Do the results from Gattass et al. and Gilbert et al. mean that, contrary to Dennett's assurances, filling in *is* rendered as a bit-map? No. The choices here are not exhausted by Dennett's alternatives "bit map or color-by-number." We suspect that neither the bit-map metaphor nor the color-by-number metaphor is even remotely adequate to the kind of representation and computation in nervous systems. Indeed, the very lability of a neuron's response properties and receptive field properties means that the bit-map metaphor is misleading. In order to understand more clearly how to interpret the results from Gattass and his colleagues, and from Gilbert and Wiesel, much more needs to be known about interpolation in neural networks and about the interaction of neurons within a mapped region and between adjacent regions. The fact is, very little is known at this point about the detailed nature of neural computation and representation, though we are at a stage where computer models highly constrained by neurobiological and psychophysical data can yield important clues (P. S. Churchland and Sejnowski, 1992).

VIII. Conclusion

In *Consciousness Explained*, Dennett brilliantly and quite properly debunks the idea that the brain contains a Cartesian Theater wherein images and the like are displayed. But the hypothesis that filling in (perceptual completion) may sometimes involve the brain's interpolating ("contributing something rather than ignoring something") certainly need have no truck whatever with Cartesian Theaters, either implicitly or explicitly, either metaphorically or literally, either sotto voce or viva voce. Given the data from psychophysics and neurophysiology, we hypothesize that (a) the brain has mechanisms for interpolation, some of which may operate early in visual processing; (b) brains sometimes visually represent completions, including quite complex completions; and (c) such representation probably involves those interpolation mechanisms.

How did Dennett come to embrace a conclusion so manifestly contrary to the data, some of which were readily available when his book was published? And why does "filling in" play such an important role in *Consciousness Explained*? According to our analysis, the background derives from the background behaviorist ideology that is endemic to Dennett's work from the very beginning—from his first book, *Content and Consciousness* (1969), through *Brainstorms* (1978), *Elbow Room* (1984), *The Intentional Stance* (1987), and *Consciousness Explained* (1991).

Simplified, the heart of Dennett's behaviorism is this: the conceptual framework of the mental does not denote anything real in the brain. The importance of the framework derives not from its description of neural or any other reality; rather, it is an organizing instrument that allows us to do fairly well in explaining and predicting one another's behavior, the literal unreality of qualia, and so forth, notwithstanding. How is it that the framework manages to be a useful instrument, despite the unreality of its categories? Because, according to Dennett, even though there is nothing *really* in the brain that corresponds to visual awareness of red, there is *something or other* in the brain which, luckily enough, allows us to get on pretty well in making sense of people's behavior on the pretense, as it were, that the brain really does have states corresponding to awareness of red. As for filling in, Dennett's rhetorical strategy hoists it as *paradigmatic* of a mental thing that we mistakenly assume to be real.

Dennett's discussions regarding the dubiousness of selected old-time intuitions often fall upon receptive ears because some categories such as "the will" and "the soul" probably do not in fact correspond to anything real, and because neuroscience is bound to teach us many surprising things about the mental, including that some of our fundamental categories can be improved upon. The sweeping behaviorism-instrumentalism, however, does not follow from these observations about the revisability of psychological concepts—nor even from the eliminability by cognitive neuroscience of *some* concepts that turn out to be the psychological counterpart of "phlogiston," "impetus," and "natural place." Thus one may readily concur that qualia cannot be little pictures displayed in the brain's Cartesian Theater, and that the self is not a little person tucked away in the folds of frontal cortex. These debunking treats are, however, just the teaspoon of sugar that makes the medicine go down. And the medicine, make no mistake, is behaviorism. The elixir is *Gilbert Ryle's ghost-be-gone* (Ryle, 1949). Taken regularly, it is supposed to prevent the outbreak of mental realism. Drawing on artificial intelligence's conceptual repertoire of the "virtual machine," Dennett has systematically argued *against* the neural reality, and *for* the mere instrumental utility, of mental categories generally. Dennett's engaging exposition and brilliantly inventive metaphors tend to mask the fact that this less palatable message is indeed the main message (see also McCauley, 1996).

This brief excursion through Dennett's behaviorism and instrumentalism may help explain why he is found defending assorted theses that are highly implausible from a scientific perspective: the brain does not fill in; there is nothing whatever (no "fact of the matter") to distinguish between a misperception and a misrecollection; there is no time before which one is not aware of, say, a sound, and after which one is aware; human consciousness is a virtual machine that comes into being as humans learn to talk to themselves; and so forth (Dennett 1991).

Scientific realism (P. M. Churchland, 1979, 1989), in contrast to Dennett's instrumentalism, proposes that we determine by empirical means—by converging research from experimental psychology, neuropsychology, and neuroscience—what hypotheses are probably true, and hence what categories truly apply to the mind-brain. Some current categories may be largely correct, for example, "visual perception"; some, for example, "memory," "attention," and "consciousness," appear to be subdividing, budding, and regrouping; and some may be replaced entirely by high-level categories that are more empirically adequate. At this stage, it is reasonable to consider sensory experiences to be real states of the brain, states whose neurobiological properties will be discovered as cognitive neuroscience proceeds (P. S. Churchland, 1986, 1988; P. M. Churchland, 1989a).

Perhaps Dennett's main achievement consists in showing the Cartesian dangers waiting to ensnare those who refer to perceptual filling in by means of the expression "filling in." If so, then the achievement is primarily semantic, not empirical. Furthermore, his aim could be satisfied merely by instructing us of the dangers, without requiring also that the very description "filling in" be expunged as untrue of what goes on in the brain. In any case, one might well wonder whether Dennett overestimates the naiveté among scientists. To judge from the literature, those who scientifically study perceptual completion phenomena understand perfectly well that filling in involves no Cartesian Theaters, ghosts, paint, little pictures, putty knives, or homunculi. At the very least, they are no more addled by metaphor than is Dennett when he refers to the brain as "editing multiple drafts." Taken as a linguistic prohibition rather than an empirical hypothesis about the mind-brain, Dennett's thesis that "the brain does not fill in" sound uncomfortably like a quirky edict of the 'word-police.'

Acknowledgments

For helpful discussion at many stages, we thank Paul Churchland, Francis Crick, Peter Dyan, Bo Dahlbom, Ricardo Gattass, Read Montague, Diane Rogers-Ramachandran, Adina Roskies, and Oron Shagrir.

13

Gaps in Penrose's Toilings

Rick Grush and Patricia S. Churchland

Using the Gödel incompleteness result for leverage, Roger Penrose has argued that the mechanism for consciousness involves quantum-gravitational phenomena, acting through microtubules in neurons. We show that this hypothesis is implausible. First, the Gödel result does not imply that human thought is in fact nonalgorithmic. Second, whether or not nonalgorithmic quantum-gravitational phenomena exist, and, if they did, how that could conceivably implicate microtubules, and if microtubules were involved, how that could conceivably implicate consciousness, is entirely speculative. Third, cytoplasmic ions such as calcium and sodium are almost certainly present in the microtubule pore, barring the quantum-mechanical effects Penrose envisages. Finally, physiological evidence indicates that consciousness does not directly depend on microtubule properties in any case, rendering doubtful any theory according to which consciousness is generated in the microtubules.

I. Introduction

Consciousness is almost certainly a property of the physical brain. The major mystery, however, is how neurons achieve such effects as being aware of a toothache or the smell of cinnamon. Neuroscience has not reached the stage where we can satisfactorily answer these questions. Intriguing data and promising research programs do exist (Logothetis and Schall 1989; Llinás and Pare 1993; Llinás and Ribary 1993; Crick 1994; Damasio 1994; Damasio and Damasio 1996; P. M. Churchland 1995; Bogen 1995), but no one would say we pretty much understand the neurobiological mechanisms of awareness.[1] Much more work, both experimental and theoretical, needs to be done. What available data do suggest is that awareness and subjectivity are probably *network* effects, involving many millions of neurons in thalamic and cortical structures. But there are other possibilities. Dualism aside, a different possibility is that consciousness emerges from quantum-mechanical goings-on in sub-neuronal structures.

Quite a lot is known about how single neurons work. The biophysics of the synapse, the neuronal membrane, neuron-to-neuron interactions, enzyme-gene interactions, and organelle behavior (e.g., mitochondria, microtubules), is known in impressive, though not complete, detail.[2] Given what is known, "very remote" is the label typically stamped on the possibility that quantum-mechanical effects play any significant explanatory role in neuronal function.[3] "Very remote" is not equivalent to "certainly not," of course. The possibility that quantum-mechanical effects give rise to conscious awareness remains alive, especially in certain quarters of physics and mathematics. An otherworldly, gaze-averting fondness for Platonism in mathematics, twinned to a fascination for the counterintuitive aspects of quantum physics, can foster the hunch that something really uncanny—and completely unkenned—is going on in the brain. Hoisting its status from "campfire possibility" to "scientific possibility" is problematic, however, given that quantum-level effects are generally agreed to be washed out at the neuronal level. Roger Penrose, however, has gallantly taken up the challenge in his widely discussed book, *The Emperor's New Mind* (Penrose 1989, henceforth *Emperor*) and in its successor, *Shadows of the Mind* (Penrose 1994b, henceforth *Shadows*).

The crux of the Penrose idea is that quantum-mechanical effects exist at the *subneuronal* level—the level of cell organelles, in particular, micro-tubules (figure 13.1), whose pore diameter of about 14 nm, as well as other physical properties, makes them candidates for the possibility of harnessing quantum-level effects. This is the tactic to avoid the afore-mentioned "washed-out" objection. Why expect a quantum-level effect *anywhere* in the brain? Because, *avers* Penrose, certain cognitive pro-cesses—including those responsible for mathematical knowledge—are nonalgorithmic (in a sense to be discussed below), while all classical-level biochemical processes are algorithmic. The central motivation under-pinning Penrose's whole argument is therefore a problem in the *epis-temology of mathematics*. It is the problem of how we understand mathematics if understanding does not *consist* in following a rule, but in-volves understanding the meaning of mathematical concepts (see below).

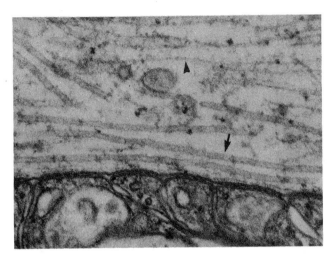

Figure 13.1
Electron micrograph of a longitudinally oriented ultrathin section (<500 angstroms) through a myelinated axon near a node of Ranvier in rat optic nerve. The preparation is stained with magnesium uranyl acetate and lead citrate to highlight cytoskeletal structures and membranes. Microtubules are clearly delineated (arrow), as are the smaller neurofilaments (arrowhead). (This micrograph was kindly provided by Mark Ellisman at University of California, San Diego.)

This is a rather more arcane starting point than, say, one's awareness of a toothache or the sleeping-dreaming-wakefulness cycle, which are pretty robust phenomena with a nontrivial log of well-researched data from psychology and neuroscience.[4]

In what follows we present a compact version of Penrose's argument as we understand it from *Emperor* and *Shadows*. Support for the quantum-consciousness connection is drawn chiefly from three sources: (1) Gödel's incompleteness result and the fact that mathematical understanding exists; (2) the properties of microtubules, long protein structures found in *all* cells, including neurons; and (3) heretofore unrecognized physical processes, perhaps exemplified in a kind of physical structure known as a "quasicrystal." Bringing these three together in such a way as to make a case for the role of quantum-level processes in consciousness is the task Penrose sets himself. Our task will be to analyze and evaluate the argument.

To avoid standing in shadowy places we wish to state at the outset that, in our view, the argument consists of merest possibility piled on merest possibility teetering upon a tippy foundation of "might-be-for-all-we-know's." It also rests on some highly dubious assumptions about the nature of mathematical knowledge. Our assessment is not that the Penrose hypothesis is demonstrably false, in the way that molecular biologists can confidently say that hereditary material is not a protein; it is DNA. Neurobiology is simply not far enough along to rule out the Penrose possibility by virtue of having a well-established, well-tested, neurobiological explanation in hand. Rather, we judge it to be completely unconvincing and probably false.

II.   Compact Version of the Penrose Argument[5]

Part A: Nonalgorithmicity of human conscious thought

A1 Human thought, at least in some instances, is sound[6] yet nonalgorithmic (i.e. noncomputational). (Hypothesis, based on the Gödel result.)

A2 In these instances, the human thinker is aware of or conscious of the contents of these thoughts.

A3 The only recognized instances of nonalgorithmic processes in the universe are perhaps certain kinds of randomness; for example, the reduction of the quantum-mechanical state vector. (Based on accepted physical theories.)[7]

A4 Randomness is not promising as the source of the nonalgorithmicity needed to account for premise A1. (Otherwise, mathematical understanding would be magical.)

Therefore:

A5 Conscious human thought, at least in some cases, perhaps in all cases, relies on principles which are beyond current physical understanding, though not in principle beyond any (e.g., some future) scientific physical understanding. (Via A1–A4.)

Part B: Inadequacy of current physical theory, and how to fix it

B1 There is no current adequate theory concerning the "collapse" of the quantum-mechanical wave funtion, but an additional theory of *quantum gravity* might be useful to this end.

B2 A more adequate theory of wave-function collapse (a part, perhaps, of a quantum gravity theory) could incorporate nonalgorithmic, yet nonrandom, processes. (Penrose hypothesis.)

B3 The existence of quasicrystals is evidence for some such currently unrecognized, nonalgorithmic physical process.

Therefore:

B4 Future theories of physics, in particular quantum gravity, can be expected to incorporate nonalgorithmic processes. (Via B1–B3.)

Part C: Microtubules as the means of harnessing quantum gravity

C1 Microtubules have properties that make certain quantum-mechanical phenomena (e.g., superradiance) possible. (Hameroff-Penrose hypothesis.)

C2 These nonalgorithmic nonrandom processes will be sufficient, in some sense, to account for A5. (Penrose hypothesis.)

C3 Microtubules play a key role in neuronal functioning.

C4 Neurons play a key role in cognition and consciousness.

C5 Microtubules play a key role in cognition and consciousness (by C3, C4, and transitivity.)

Therefore:

C6 Microtubules, because they have one foot in quantum mechanics and the other in conscious thought, provide a window for nonalgorithmicity in human cognition.

Therefore:

D *Quantum gravity, or something similar, via microtubules, must play a key role in consciousness and cognition.*

Briefly, our analysis of this argument indicates that A1 is most likely false, and section III below provides reasons for denying it. This undercuts the case for A5, and hence part A. B3 is almost certainly false (this is the subject of section IV), and given its falsity, B2 is entirely speculative as well. This undercuts the case for B4, and hence the conclusion of part B is exposed as entirely speculative. C1 is quite speculative, C2 is no more than a guess, and C5 is simply a bad inference (these are discussed in section V), hence part C looks tenuous. In short, it appears to us that even if D did happen to be true, the argument embodied in A, B, and C provides no reason to believe that it is. In section VI we provide independent reasons for thinking that D is probably false.

III. Are There Instances of Conscious Human Reasoning That Are Sound and Nonalgorithmic?

Insight, Pattern Recognition, and Artificial Neural Networks

The Gödel result forms the springboard of the reasoning underlying Penrose's premise A1, and we restate his argument below. As a preliminary, note that by "nonalgorithmic" is meant "noncomputable."[8] This implies that the performance of the system could not be produced by any algorithmic procedure; more, it could not be *approximated* by an algorithmic procedure.[9] The behavior of a river eddy is weakly nonalgorithmic insofar as it is a complex system and its states are continuous. It could, however, be *approximated* by an algorithm, *to any desired degree of accuracy*, and given Penrose's conventions this entails that its behavior is algorithmic. "Nonalgorithmic," in the sense Penrose quite reasonably intends, is therefore a *very* strong constraint, so strong, in fact, that whether there exist any physical systems in the real world whose behavior is noncomputable in this strong sense remains very much an open question. Penrose conjectures[10] that quasicrystals may be such phenomena. As for consciousness, the Penrose hypothesis is that, given human mathematical performance, we can tell that the brain must be such a (deeply) noncomputable system.

Here is Penrose's own summary of the argument:

> It is a kind of *reductio ad absurdum* argument, in which I try to show what would happen if we tried to construct robots with the kind of ability to understand that we have. Because the Gödel argument is basically about understanding; it tells us how to move from one formal system to a system outside that, from the understanding of what the system is trying to say. It is concerned with the question of the *meanings* of the symbols, which is a dimension that a computational system does not have; a computational system just has the rules which it follows. What one can do in mathematics is, by understanding the meanings of the symbols, one can go beyond the formal rules, and see what new rules must apply from those things, and one does this by understanding their meanings. (Penrose 1994a, p. 19)

Granted that some instances of understanding and extending understanding do not involve *explicit* rule following, is there any framework for approaching such cognition? Indeed there is, and famously so. Artificial neural nets (ANNs) are capable of learning complex pattern recognition tasks as well as sensorimotor integration tasks (cf. P. S. Churchland and Sejnowski 1992; P. M. Churchland 1995; Jordan 1989). Once the synaptic weights have been set, typically by training on a range of cases, networks can perform very well on new cases, even giving "good" answers in cases that are nonstandard or missing bits or presented in unusual conditions. Given recurrent connections between units, ANNs can recognize sequences, for example, sequences of sounds. Training a network is not programming with an explicit algorithm. The only algorithms in the neighborhood are the relatively simple ones used to adjust the weights, in reinforcement learning or via a Hebbian learning rule, for example. In any case the ANN has no *explicit* rules that govern its performance, any more than a child does when it successfully extends "dog" beyond the family retriever to the neighbor's poodle and grandma's great dane. The same applies to concepts such as "chair," "cold front," "promising student," "fair," "reasonable," and so forth.

Pattern recognition has been argued (cf. P. M. Churchland 1995) to be the key cognitive function of nervous systems, underlying not merely capacities such as recognizing a dog or a chair but also, in the cognoscenti, recognizing a chess configuration and a theorem in the predicate calculus. In logic or mathematics, insight-cum-recognition can be followed up with a proof to determine whether one's insight was correct. On the other hand, for other highly complex patterns such as instances of injustice or insanity, for example, verifying insight may involve nothing so straightforward as application of a proof procedure. The general point, however, is that what gets called "insight" and "intuition" could very well be complex pattern recognition performed by recurrent neural networks.

The ANN processes are analog and parallel; the machine is flexible and plastic (cf. Mead 1989). These are very striking capacities and they are what make ANNs so exciting to robotics, artificial vision, and so forth, and what makes them relevant to real nervous systems. "Computing without rules" was indeed the popular watchword in the early stages of connectionist research (cf. P. S. Churchland and Sejnowski 1992; P. M. Churchland 1995). That ANNs can learn, rather than be programmed, that they have analog properties, that they are flexible, fault tolerant, and can give good answers to degraded inputs are, inter alia, what make ANNs far more suitable and powerful than classical programming techniques for many problems in the simulation of nervous system capacities. But uncanny they are not. Are their input-output functions *non*computable in the weak sense of not being instances of explicit rule-following or discrete-state transitions? Yes. Can the behavior of neural nets (artificial and otherwise) be *approximated by an algorithm*? So far as anyone knows, yes. This may, certainly, be a strained and semifictional sense of "computable" if no algorithm can execute the function in real time. Nevertheless, the "approximatability" does mean that they fail to have the property Penrose is after, namely, being non-computable *and* nonapproximatable. That is, they *are indeed computable and algorithmic, in the sense Penrose intends.* Now *if* Penrose is right in supposing human thought cannot even be approximated by an algorithm, then the success of ANNs is not, by itself, enough to subvert Penrose. At the risk of repeating ourselves, we do emphasize that it is not known whether *any* physical processes exist that are strongly non-computable in the sense Penrose seeks. (See also section IV.) *Even if they are not counterexamples to Penrose's hypothesis,* the success of ANNs teaches us that phenomena that appear intractable to conventional programming on a classical machine might very well be managed elegantly by a nonclassical, analog device.

What is Penrose's argument for premise A1?

A1a In order to ascertain mathematical truth, human mathematicians are not using a knowably sound algorithm.[11]

A1b The brain procedure that does underlie this "ascertaining mathematical truth" is sound.

A1c If human mathematicians were using a sound *algorithm*, this algorithm would be knowable.

A1d Therefore, human mathematicians do not use an algorithm to ascertain mathematical truth.

A1e The understanding mathematicians employ is not different in kind from everyday human understanding and conscious thought.

Therefore, premise A1:

Human thought, at least in some instances, *perhaps in all*, is sound, yet nonalgorithmic.

Critical analysis of Penrose's argument for premise A1

Penrose's arguments in favor of A1a and A1c are where most of the technical machinery is brought to bear. It may therefore be a relief to the reader that we propose, for convenience of strategy, to grant both of these premises, and focus rather on A1b.

Our point is this: *even if* humans are using some sort of algorithm, *and* that algorithm is knowable, A1a presents a problem *only if we assume that this algorithm is sound.* The alternative is supposed to be not worth considering because an unsound procedure would license entailment to anything, and we can be sure that (p & ~ p) is not true. Matters are not quite so simple, however, because these are questions about human knowledge, not about what eternal immutable truths really are on display in Plato's heaven. By definition, Plato's realm contains only truths. What is in the human mind-brain is a matter not of definition but of empirical fact. Our only access to Plato's realm is through our brains, and our brains have to use cognitive procedures to figure things out. Were our knowledge system to contain an inferentially remote falsehood, some far-flung, plausible, but false proposition, we might have a hard time deploying the cognitive machinery to force it to the surface or to recognize it to be false. It is conceivable that one's mathematical understanding sequesters somewhere a false, but practically isolated, proposition masquerading as a truth. Thus we have to consider this possibility: humans could be using a cognitive procedure(s) which is unsound[12] but *benignly* so—perhaps because it includes the axiom of choice (explained below)—or perhaps because it includes the negation of the axiom of choice, or for some other reason altogether.[13]

To make premise A1 plausible Penrose must do three things: first, identify some range of phenomena—some cognitive procedures, or set of insights or whatever—which are uncontroversially sound and which are not known to be algorithmic. Let us call such a procedure (*or insight*) an S-procedure. Second, he must then invoke A1a to claim that in fact S-procedures cannot be supported by a knowable algorithm or approximated by a knowable algorithm. Third, he must argue for a presumed counterfactual: if S-procedures were supported by an algorithm, this algorithm *would in principle be knowable.*

How successful is Penrose in satisfying the first of these three conditions? Not very, for the simple reason that there do not seem to be any S-procedures. Note that anything which is knowably algorithmic cannot be an S-procedure, and so this rules out inference rules like *modus ponens*,[14] anything formalizable in predicate logic or Zermelo-Fraenkel axiomatic set theory (ZF), and the like. As we shall see, when these are excluded there is reason to doubt that any procedures for mathematical deliberation are sound.

Mathematical thought, at least in some instances, is Penrose's prime candidate for a sound, noncomputable S-procedure. Errors in workaday human cognition are legion, belying any suggestion that sound procedures might be operative in nonmathematical reasoning, and Penrose clearly does not want to deny this (cf. Penrose 1994b). Is the case for mathematical thought better? Even in the domain of mathematics, mathematicians do make errors, errors that mathematicians themselves confess to be errors. Such errors are likely to be inobvious, and it can take months to determine whether a putative proof of, for example, Fermat's Last Theorem, is free of errors. To avoid impugning the underlying procedures, Penrose adopts the equivalent of a performance-competence distinction. Granted, the argument goes, mathematicians make mistakes, but these mistakes are merely performance mistakes resulting from the misapplication of an *underlying sound competence*.

In linguistics, where Chomsky made famous the performance-competence distinction, many difficulties dog the task of rendering it precise. Crudely, one problem is that there does not appear to be any principled way to distinguish between these two cases: (1) the sentence Q really is grammatically correct but the native speakers have limitations on memory, attention, and so forth, and hence they conflict in their judgments; (2) Q is not really grammatical because native speakers conflict in their judgments. The trouble arises when trying to adjudicate between competing theories of syntax, since the performance-competence distinction can always be invoked to insulate aspects of a formal syntactic theory from empirical disconfirmation. Restricting application of the distinction to unproblematic cases helps enormously (cf. Bates and MacWhinney 1989). Thus it is important to identify sentences that both exhibit the relevant properties but are simple enough so that judgment discrepancies cannot fairly be attributed to cases where the distinction does not obviously subvert experimental testing.

Comparably, to protect himself from begging any questions, Penrose must identify some set of mathematical capacities or abilities (our S-procedures) that are not only sound but are simple enough, or short enough, such that performance errors are minimized or eliminated altogether. The secondary assumption is that performance on these tasks will result from deployment of the underlying sound procedures which support more complex and lengthy episodes of mathematical reasoning. So circumscribed, this set of capacities and abilities seems to be what

Penrose intends by the phrase, "the perception of unassailable mathematical truth" (Penrose 1994b, p. 130). The danger in failing thus to circumscribe is that one may presume the actual truth of what is merely believed-to-be-true, and in consequence postulate capacities the brain does not actually have. These capacities and abilities and their underlying brain procedures are now our S-procedure candidates (or simply, S-candidates). Do we know *they* are sound?

Trying to delimit instances of "the perception of unassailable mathematical truth" uncovers deep and troubling issues in the epistemology of mathematics generally. First, and most notoriously, what counts as unassailable in mathematics differs from century to century and from mathematician to mathematician. The brilliant nineteenth-century mathematician Cauchy, for example, denied the existence of infinite sets. Infinite sets, he reasoned (cf. Boyer 1959, p. 296) (and he was not alone), would have proper subsets with which they could be put into one-to-one correspondence. His mathematical intuitions led him to conclude that this would be a contradiction, and hence that the existence of such sets should be rejected as impossible. Thanks to Cantor it can be shown that there is no contradiction, however much our intuitions bid us believe otherwise. The statement that Cauchy "clearly perceived" as contradictory is now taken as a right and proper—an unassailable, noncontradictory, teach-to-undergraduates—*definition* of an infinite set. Why not view this as a development in mathematical understanding, not unlike progress in physics, chemistry, and biology?(cf. Bloor 1976, pp. 131–56; Boyer 1959).

Discrepancies in judgment (differences of opinion) are not merely a thing of the hoary old past, but exist today. One instance concerns the axiomatic status of the so-called axiom of choice, which is quite easy to state and understand: for any collection of nonempty sets there exists another set that contains exactly one element from each set in the collection. Thus, as in the case of Cauchy's insight, when careful, sober, mathematical intuitions fail to coincide about the truth of the axiom of choice, the failure does not seem to be explainable on grounds of performance errors. Sound[15] procedures (to a first-approximation, truth-producing procedures) cannot yield *both* a given result (S is true) and that result's denial (S is false), for if they do they simply are not

truth-producing. Nevertheless, some mathematicians' mathematical intuitions lead them to embrace the axiom of choice, while others' lead them
to deny it.[16] Some mathematicians, typically Platonists, have "perceived"
the unassailable truth of propositions about infinite sets, while constructivists "perceive" the contradictory nature of transfinite sets. For
constructivists the law of the excluded middle ($p \lor \sim p$) is not universally
true and hence is not a law; for apriorists, it is—and so on.[17]

Penrose has a problem for his assumption regarding the "soundness"
of human mathematical capacities when the careful, reflective performance of mathematicians on relatively simple statements, such as
($p \lor \sim p$), the axiom of choice, and the existence of infinite sets, is dis-
crepant. He has essentially three options: (1) He could claim that some of
the mathematicians (which ones—the constructivists?) are making performance errors in these and similar cases, care and IQ notwithstanding.
This is unconvincing because the examples do not make heavy demands
on attention and understanding, compared to many other mathematical
statements. (2) He could claim that *some* mathematicians do lack
underlying sound procedures (competence), while others luckily have
them. This is not an attractive option either, because those who allegedly
depend on an unsound procedure (from a Platonist's point of view that
might be Cauchy or Dummett, for example) do in fact make significant
insightful contributions to mathematics. At the very least, it is safe to say
that they understand Gödel's theorem. Now if some mathematicians
(e.g., the constructivists and intuitionists) can do brilliant mathematics
while having unsound mathematical understanding, how can we be sure
that this does not hold generally? (3) He could claim that these are not
good examples of what he has in mind as S-candidates. This looks em-
barrassingly ad hoc, especially when something like the truth of an old
saw like ($p \lor \sim p$) can be reasonably assailed, albeit with complicated
background argument. Moreover, if *these* examples will not do, if anything knowably algorithmic including simple inferences, such as *modus
ponens* or anything else formalizable in first-order logic or ZF will not
do, what will?

Disappointingly, Penrose fails to provide any actual examples of
background mathematical understanding which can be known to be
sound. In fact, *Shadows* is rife with admissions of the form, "... as

mathematicians gain in experience, their viewpoints may well shift with regard to what they take to be unassailably true—if indeed they ever take *anything* to be unassailably true" (Penrose 1994b, p. 193). Given such admissions, why does Penrose still cling to the belief that mathematical performance is backed by truly sound procedures as opposed to usually reliable, or heuristically useful, procedures?

His core argument is: "It would be an unreasonable mathematical standpoint that allows for a disbelief in the very basis of its unassailable belief system!" (Penrose 1994b, p. 131). That is, if a mathematician (or anybody else) has unassailable beliefs, then that person must believe that the procedures which support or result in those beliefs are sound. But does "A is unassailable" mean "A is certainly true" or does it mean "one is convinced that A is true?" Is (p v ~ p) really unassailable for a Platonist, or is it rather that she is convinced that it is true while recognizing that some of her esteemed intuitionist colleagues do not take it to be true? She also knows full well that being utterly convinced that A is true is not a divine guarantee of the truth of A. This matters, because if there is any doubt at all, even a tiny doubt, that any of her beliefs really are true, then the inference to the soundness of their source is blocked. This does not mean she thinks that the underlying procedures must be hopelessly flawed, but only that there are some puzzling propositions where the reasonable person realizes there can be a difference of opinion.

Now it would seem a perfectly reasonable view, one often adopted by cautious, reflective humans, that some sources of information should be taken to be generally reliable, yet not entirely infallible, and that any of its entailments can be adopted with *very high confidence*, but not with the complete certainty a stroll in Plato's heaven might provide. Bus schedules, phone books, newspapers, college textbooks, mathematics textbooks, scholarly publications, eyewitness testimony, expert opinions, etc., etc., are all *known to be flawed from time to time, and hence known to be unsound.* Perhaps the *un*reasonable position is the one with standards so high as to *reject* any sources of information that might be flawed. On the contrary, it seems reasonable to admit the fallibility and retain some (perhaps quite high) measure of confidence in them.

Although respected mathematicians have undergone changes of mind, even on core foundational issues, Penrose's Platonism leads him to say,

"... it is an unreasonable mathematical standpoint that allows for a disbelief in the very basis of its unassailable belief system" (1994b, p. 131). Note, finally, that "M does not believe that A is unassailably true" does *not* entail "M *dis*believes A." It might merely mean that M is not certain, even though M takes A to be highly likely, and in daily life M acts as though it were unassailable. For example, consider the axiom of choice. One may be convinced of its truth, while not being prepared to stake one's life on it as an unassailable truth.

To make the point a bit more strongly, the inference from "I really believe that A is true," or "I don't see how A could *possibly* be false," to "A *is* unassailably true" is an inference rule known to be unsound. To take but one example, Kant thought it a necessary truth that Euclidean geometry described physical space. That very rule *has*, in fact, led to falsehoods. Now either our mathematician does have beliefs that she takes to be absolutely unassailable, in which case she is unsound, because such a belief could only be the result of the unsound inference rule (or something similar) specified three sentences back, or the mathematician has beliefs held only with great confidence, in which case her inference to the soundness (as opposed to the reliability) of the source of those beliefs is not licensed.[18]

Are there any alternatives to a Platonist ontology of mathematical objects (abstract, immutable objects—truths, numbers, etc.) and its usual companion, an a priori epistemology of mathematics (grasping with the intellect the absolute and immutable truths in Plato's heaven)? Indeed there are (cf. Heyting 1956; Lakatos 1976; Benacerraf and Putnam 1983; Dummett 1991; Quine 1970; Kitcher 1984b). A major motivation for seeking a more satisfactory epistemology is just this: What are supposed to be the nature of the interactions between the Platonic realm and the thinker's *brain*? If the denizens of the Platonic realm cannot causally interact with anything, let alone human brains, how on earth can mathematical understanding be acquired by the human brain? Plato's own answer—that we do not learn, we only remember our soul's prebirth observations of truths in the realm—is less than satisfactory.

Even supposing we retrofit Plato's account with supports from evolutionary biology, the idea still founders. Evolution may have wired-in a variety of capacities, but in the life of primates and early hominids there was no evolutionary pressure to acquire fancy mathematical knowledge (e.g., the infinitesimal calculus), and some of the mathematics surely had to be discovered by some and then learned by others. Doubtless the struggle for survival meant that skills in planning, preparing, anticipating, communicating, and so forth would have had great value, and brain structures subserving such skills may well be deployable for culturally dependent skills such as reading, writing, and mathematics. It is harder to see, however, why all-up *soundness*, as opposed to reliability, should be selected for. (Note, too, that even if mathematical capacities are hardwired in, this is no guarantee of the soundness of mathematical understanding.) Evolution is a satisfier, not an optimizer, and "approximately accurate" or "accurate for most of the likely cases" is typically good enough.[19] How humans come to have the conceptual and cognitive resources to develop formal systems, proof theory, and mathematical certainty is a puzzle—though not, perhaps, more intractable than how we have the resources to read and write, to compose and play music, to skate, hang-glide, and perform eye surgery. The idea, therefore, that mathematical capacity is an independent faculty of pure reason, whose exercise yields mathematical (or any other absolutely certain) knowledge by virtue of intuitive grasping of propositions and objects in Plato's realm, is wanting in biological plausibility.

Cognitive models of higher cognitive processes in general, and mathematical cognition in particular, are not as far advanced as modeling of sensory processes and modeling of single neurons. Suffice it to say that the epistemology of mathematics has not kept pace with philosophical developments in other domains. Although the existence of the epistemological problems is well recognized among philosophers of mathematics, it is often of marginal interest to mathematicians themselves. One of the outstanding exceptions is the recent work by Philip Kitcher (1984b; also, see P. M. Churchland 1995) who does make a splendid attempt to bring the epistemology of mathematics up to date.

Platonism is surely a kind of convenient myth, rather like the way in which frictionless planes and ideal gases are convenient myths, or perhaps even as the "spirit of Christmas" and "Zeitgeist" are convenient myths. As such, however, it cannot support grand metaphysical theories, such as that espoused by Penrose (figure 13.2). Nor can it provide much

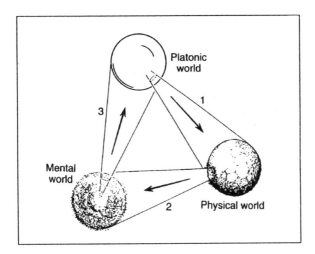

Figure 13.2
Penrose's Three Worlds. The drawing schematically illustrates the idea that the physical world can be thought of as a projection from part of the Platonic world of eternal Truths, that the mental world arises from part of the physical world (presumably the brain), and that the Platonic world is "grasped" somehow during mental activities. (From Penrose 1994b, courtesy of Oxford University Press.)

in the way of significant constraints on the cognitive neurobiology of understanding and consciousness. When the "just so" story is taken literally and used to constrain theories about natural phenomena, it positively gets in the way.[20]

IV. Quasicrystals: Arguments Against B3

A consequence of Penrose's Gödel-inspired arguments for strong (no-algorithm-can-even-approximate) noncomputability in the mind-brain is that current theories in physics are fundamentally incomplete. In Penrose's view they ought to be augmented by a theory of quantum gravity. One might, however, prefer to *tollens* here rather than to *ponens*. In other words, one's confidence in current physics is a prima facie reason for denying the correctness of these Gödel-inspired arguments. The considerations given in the previous section mean that this option is not unattractive. From Penrose's perspective, therefore, it is important to have hard evidence for the existence of such postulated nonalgorithmic processes apart from the contentious case at hand, namely, the mind-brain. There are sections in *Emperor* which could be construed as attempting to provide such evidence.[21]

The reasoning behind premise B3 we reconstruct as follows:

B3a Because there exist sets of tiles which tile the plane only non-periodically, the question of whether a given set of tiles will tile the infinite Euclidean plane is not decidable (algorithmic).

B3b Some of these nonperiodic sets tile the plane with fivefold symmetry.

B3c There exist "quasicrystals" whose lattice structure exhibits a similar fivefold symmetry.

B3d So the growth of these crystals depends on nonalgorithmic processes (maybe).

Therefore, premise B3:

The existence of quasicrystals is evidence for some such currently unrecognized, nonalgorithmic physical process.

The argument is unconvincing. The chief problem is that B3d and hence B3 simply do not follow from B3a–c. First, even if the analogy between the structure of quasicrystals and the nonperiodic tilings were close, the "problems" whose computability is at issue in each case are different. In the case of the tiling problem, the undecidable feature is not how to put the tiles together in order to tile some region (putting the tiles together may well be algorithmic), but whether or not, given a set of tiles and perhaps some specified way of putting them together, these tiles can cover the entire infinite Euclidean plane without gaps or overlaps. Second, the analogy simply does not hold. The reason is that *quasicrystals are in fact finite*, unlike the infinite Euclidean plane, and hence their growth undoubtedly is computable. Indeed, algorithms have been proposed (cf. Onada et al. 1988; Sasajima et al. 1994) for the growth of just such crystals (as Penrose himself notes!) (Penrose 1989, p. 449, n. 7). Although the information required to determine the appropriate arrangement might not be locally available to individual atoms of the lattice, that is not a problem as far as algorithmicity goes.

Without this premise, the whole of part B of the Penrose argument—that there are in fact nonalgorithmic (in the strong sense characterized earlier, in part A) processes in the universe—amounts to no more than unsupported speculation. Now it might be wondered whether we are uncharitably pillorying an argument that Penrose himself no longer favors or deploys in *Shadows*. However that may be, the fact is that *the speculation that such processes really do exist* continues to be a crucial underpinning of the complex structure of the overarching argument. Naturally enough, identifying this claim as speculative does *not* entail that it is actually false, and we are prepared to admit that, despite the absence of evidence, this speculation could turn out to be correct. Our point here is practical and simple: because investment of research time and energy is often made with the background probabilities in mind, it is important to recognize a bald speculation as a bald speculation. Forewarned, one might nevertheless decide to throw in one's lot with the speculation anyhow.

V.   Are Microtubules the Generators of Consciousness?

We come now to the specific hypothesis about how quantum gravity and consciousness are parts of the same mystery. As the idea that microtubules are the key originated with and is mainly articulated by Stuart Hameroff, later to be adopted by Penrose, we focus first on the story as it comes from Hameroff (Hameroff 1994; Hameroff, Rasmussen, and Manson 1989; Hameroff and Watt 1982; Hameroff et al. 1992; Jibu et al. 1994).

Here is Hameroff's summary statement (1994) of the conjecture:

To summarize, cytoskeletal microtubules are likely candidates for quantum coherence relevant to consciousness because:

• Microtubule individual subunit (tubulin) conformation may be coupled to quantum-level events (electronic movement, dipole, phonon) in hydrophobic protein regions.

• Microtubule crystalline lattice structure, symmetry, cylindrical configuration, and parallel alignment promote long-range cooperativity and order.

• Hollow microtubule interiors appear capable of water-ordering, waveguide super-radiance and self-induced transparency. (p. 105)

First, we note that all body cells have microtubules, where a major function is to support cell division. In neurons, one of their known functions is transport, on their outside surface, of molecules such as neurotransmitters and various proteins between the cell body and the axon, and between the cell body and the dendrites (figure 13.3). Now

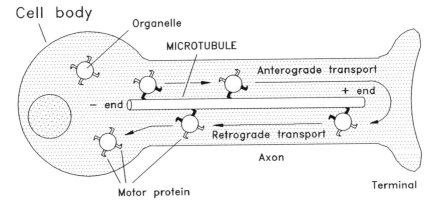

Figure 13.3
Very schematic drawing of a neuron, showing the microtubule's role as a structure along which organelles get transported from the cell body to the terminal and back. (Adapted from Hall 1992.)

it is generally believed that some general anesthetics (hydrophobic ones) alter the neuronal membrane receptors and protein channels, with an effect on protein water-binding. Hameroff builds on these data by arguing that the protein constituting the microtubules (tubulin) might also have *its* water-binding properties affected. *If* it did, and *if* tubulin structures did have the quantum-mechanical properties of "super-radiance"[22] and "self-induced transparency," then, the argument goes, the loss of consciousness under hydrophobic anesthesia might be attributable to these changes in the microtubules. Briefly, here are some reservations.

The Anesthesia-Microtubule Connection

1. There is no direct evidence that changes in microtubules in neurons are responsible for the phenomenological effects of general anesthetics. What the most recent data do indicate is that, at surgical concentrations, ligand-gated ion channels (proteins) in the neuronal membrane are the main sites of anesthetic effects. Relative to the quantum effects envisaged above for microtubules, these are *large* effects. In their review article in *Nature* (1994), Franks and Lieb state that, among possible receptor targets, $GABA_A$ (γ-aminobutyric acid) receptor protein has been established by electrophysiological studies to be a major target. The general anesthetics that potentiate the GABA receptor protein include inhalational

agents such as halothane, enflurane, and isoflurane, as well as intra-
venous anesthetics such as pentobarbitol, propofol, and alphaxalone.
GABA is the major inhibitory neurotransmitter in the brain, and potentiation of the GABA receptor probably upregulates inhibition, which
effectively overrides excitation. This is consistent with the finding that
anesthetic interactions with the GABA receptor protein extend its open
time. The other receptor that has been shown to be a target is the excitatory voltage-dependent NMDA (N = methyl D = aspartate) receptor. It
is inhibited by the agent ketamine.[23] To repeat, these effects on receptors
are large effects in the millivolt range.

2. Even if disruption of microtubule function were consistently cor-
related with general anesthetics, there is no reason to suppose that
"normal" microtubule functioning is anything more than a necessary
background condition—one necessary condition among hosts of others
(e.g., availability of oxygen, adenosine triphosphate, glucose, etc.).

The Microtubule-Superradiance-Consciousness Connection

3. There is no evidence[24] that quantum coherence involving superradiance (or anything else, for that matter) occurs in microtubules. At
best, what Hameroff has done is to show that it might be possible. This
should most definitely be distinguished from providing *evidence* that it is
actual.

4. It is highly unlikely that the pore of the tubulin tube contains
nothing but pure water, since there is no known mechanism for keeping
out common cytoplasmic ions such as calcium and sodium. This is a
major problem for the hypothesis because impurities are an obstacle to
the postulated long-range cooperativity, especially superradiance. It is
therefore highly speculative that quantum coherence involving superradiance occurs in microtubules.

5. An ancient and still common palliative for the disease known as
gout is the drug colchicine. This was introduced to American medical
practice by Benjamin Franklin. For our purposes, colchicine has the
highly interesting property that, inter alia, it disrupts microtubules by
attaching to the "add-on" end and preventing repolymerization repairs.
After a period of colchicine treatment for gout, therefore, the microtubules show considerable depolymerization.[25] This is a major monkey

wrench for superradiance,[26] a bit like the way in which breaks in fibers disrupt fiberoptic transmission. The capacity of the microtubule to support the self-focusing soliton wave (Jibu et al. 1944) (which "transmits" the superradiance effect down the length of the tube) depends crucially on the characteristics and the uniformity of the wave-guide, which in this case is just the interior of the microtubule. So any disruption as radical as depolymerization of the tubule prevents any quantum phenomena of the sort at issue. If Hameroff and Penrose are right, then microtubule depolymerization ought to block superradiance and hence significantly impair consciousness. Does it impair consciousness? Not that anyone has noticed, and loss of awareness is a major thing not to notice. It is known, however, that prolonged use can cause paralysis, beginning with the lower extremities. The colchicine data are surely an embarrassment for the Hameroff hypothesis.

6. Hameroff envisages consciousness as involving a unity across diverse brain regions. Even if the interesting quantum events did occur in a single tubule, to play a role in consciousness the effect must be transmitted from one tubule to its microtubule neighbor within the cell. If big transmitter molecules are in the vicinity, making their usual way to and from the synapse, the prediction is that this would seriously inhibit the spread of the quantum coherence. The next-stage-up problem has the same form: to play a role in consciousness the effect must be transmitted from one *neuron* to other neurons. The problem with this step is that the principal neuromembrane effects involving voltage change are big—on the order of tens of microvolts—and it is a fair prediction that these effects would wipe out the nanoeffects from the microtubules.[27] This is not to say it cannot be done, but no one has the slightest evidence that it is done, nor the slightest idea how it might be done.

7. Given the Hameroff hypothesis, one might predict that disruption of microtubule function underlies other, more routine, changes in the state of awareness, such as the daily shift from being awake to being in deep sleep. This shift is generally regarded as a major change, from being conscious of events to not being conscious of them (see Llinás and Ribary 1993; Flanagan 1996). There is no reason to suppose that microtubules alter function concordant with these state changes, for example, by ceasing their water-ordering, wave-guided superradiancing and

self-induced transparency. What we do know is that certain neurons do change in very specific ways with changes in sleep and wakefulness—in thalamic and brain-stem structures in particular (cf. Steriade, McCormick, and Sejnowski 1993).

Penrose's preferred role for microtubules differs a bit from that of Hameroff. He sees them as altering neuronal signaling via modifying presynaptic efficacy. The idea seems to be this: If the tubules can do this, then perhaps they can shape specific patterns of activation in the brain, and these particular patterns are what support consciousness. So what microtubules must do is somehow to encode the information derived from sensory structures, process it, and then modify the firing of neurons in such a way as to support the consciousness of the stimulus, and perhaps a purposeful response as well. How plausible is this?

Here are some reservations specific to the Penrose version of the microtubule story.

1. Microtubules are seldom seen in close proximity to the business end of the synaptic complex. Generally, they appear to end about a micron from the synaptic complex, which means, for the kind of effect that Penrose is talking about, the distance may as well be meters (see Peters, Palay, and Webster 1978).

2. How is the microtubule supposed to communicate with the synapse to have the Penrose effect? What precisely is supposed to be the effect on the neuronal membrane, and how is it achieved? Penrose does not give us a clue. The release of transmitter vesicles, for example, does not have any characteristic association with microtubules, so far as is known.

3. Suppose Penrose has in mind that the alleged quantum goings-on in the microtubules modify neurotransmitter release. Is this reasonable? Not very. What is known is that release of a vesicle of neurotransmitter, when a spike reaches the axon terminal, is highly dependent on calcium channels and on the phosphorylation rate of membrane proteins. Neuromodulators (e.g., norepinephrine, any of the various neuropeptides, caffeine, etc.) can affect calcium channels and hence affect neurotransmitter release. Caffeine, for example, works by blocking the receptor adenosine, which acts as a second messenger to downregulate the neuron. These are very big effects in the world of neurons. Even if microtubules did display the quantum goings-on, the effects would seem to be trivial relative to the effects of the neuromodulators (see Stevens and Wang 1994).

4. The encoding problem, for microtubules, is ignored by Penrose. If microtubules are to perform their Penrosian function they must be able to *get* the information that they then (nonalgorithmically) process. Neurons depend, for *their* signals, mostly on neurotransmitters and neuromodulators which alter the neuronal membrane's permeability to various ions. Is the idea that microtubules can use *these* ion concentrations as sources of information? Maybe, but this seems to conflict with the requirement that microtubules be insulated from their ionic environment in order to support quantum coherence, and so on.[28] Even if that can be resolved, how is this supposed to work?

Even with generous conjecture-granting, Penrose is still not out of the woods. As Hameroff in (3) above has problems about getting a global effect out of a highly local effect, so of course does Penrose. How is it that microtubule clusters in different neurons coordinate their activity to shape the overall patterns of neural activity which support consciousness? For surely changes in a single neuron will not cause the generation or loss of consciousness. No answer. Are microtubules able to support some form of long-range quantum coherence or entanglement? No answer. Quantum entanglement we assume is ruled out, because it would require that the insulated interiors or surfaces of the microtubules interact in some way, and since they will be in separate neurons across wide stretches of the brain it is not clear how this could happen. Finally, how realistic is it to predict a quantum-coherent state between the spatially separated microtubules (or their contents)? Penrose correctly assesses the prospects when he remarks (in *Shadows*) "Such a feat would be a remarkable one—almost an incredible one—for Nature to achieve by biological means" (p. 373).

VI. Conclusions

Let's take stock of where we are. The first part of the Penrose argument (part A) is in trouble. There is reason to doubt that human cognition or consciousness must take advantage of nonalgorithmic processes since unsound, albeit reliable, algorithmic processes escape Gödel's net. Second, part B of the argument is entirely speculative—there is no evidence at all (including quasicrystals) that there are any (strongly) nonalgorithmic processes anywhere in the universe. Indeed, even if Penrose's quantum gravity hunch were correct (another big "if"), it need not incorporate any nonalgorithmic processes. Finally, the prospects for part C look grim. There is no experimental evidence that microtubules do support interesting quantum phenomena, and, save in the unlikely event that the water in and around them is pure, it is doubtful that they do. Water purity is not the only problem: other highly speculative conditions would also have to obtain. Even if they can support such phenomena, long-range coherence seems quite far-fetched. Furthermore, because microtubules can depolymerize without noticeable effect on consciousness, it seems unlikely that they support conscious thought.

Consciousness is a problem, but it must be remembered that we are still in the very early stages of understanding the nervous system. Many fundamental questions about basic phenomena—such as the role of recurrent projections, the nature of representation in sensory systems, whether sensory systems are hierarchically organized, precisely how memory is stored and retrieved, how sensorimotor integration works, what sleep and dreaming are all about—have not yet been satisfactorily answered. Is the problem of consciousness utterly different from all these other problems? Perhaps, but qua mystery, it does not come with its degree or depth or style of mysteriousness pinned to its shirt. Sometimes the problems that appear to be the really tough ones, such as the composition of the stars, turn out to be easier to solve than seemingly minor puzzles, such as the precession of the perihelion of Mercury. Undoubtedly, many surprises await us, and for all we know some of them may involve surprises for (or from) physics. Nevertheless, before making a heavy research investment in a precarious and far-fetched hypothesis, it would be nice to have something solid to go on. This may be a matter of taste, however.

Despite the rather breathtaking flimsiness of the consciousness-quantum connection, the idea has enjoyed a surprisingly warm reception, at least outside neuroscience. One cannot help groping about for some explanation for this rather odd fact. Is it not even *more* reductionist than explaining consciousness in terms of the properties of networks of neurons? Emotionally, it seems, the two reductionist strategies arouse quite different feelings. After some interviewing, in an admittedly haphazard fashion, we found the following story gathering credence.

Some people who, intellectually, are materialists, nevertheless have strong dualist hankerings—especially hankerings about life after death. They have a negative "gut" reaction to the idea that neurons—cells that you can see under a microscope and probe with electrodes, brains you can hold in one hand and that rapidly rot without oxygen supply—are the source of subjectivity and the "me-ness of me." The crucial feature of neurons that makes them capable of processing and storing information is just ions passing back and forth across neuronal membranes through protein channels. That seems, stacked against the "me-ness of me," to be disappointingly humdrum—even if there are lots of ions and lots of neurons and lots of really complicated protein channels.

Quantum physics, on the other hand, seems more resonant with those residual dualist hankerings, perhaps by holding out the possibility that scientific realism and objectivity melt away in that domain, or that even thoughts and feelings are, in the end, the fundamental properties of the universe (Bennett, Hoffman, and Prakash 1989). Explanation of something as special as what makes me *me* should really involve, the feeling goes, something more "deep" and mysterious and "otherworldly" than mere neurons. Perhaps what is comforting about quantum physics is that it can be invoked to "explain" a mysterious phenomenon without removing much of the mystery, quantum-mechanical explanations being highly mysterious themselves.

Now we are *not* for a moment suggesting that anything like this is behind Penrose's work, and whether our general diagnosis is right or wrong has no bearing whatever on the strengths and weaknesses of his arguments. It may, however, explain why the very possibility of a quantum-physical explanation is often greeted warmly, whereas an explanation in terms of neurons may be considered "scary," "degrading," and even "inconceivable." But why should it be less scary, reductionist, or counterintuitive that "me-ness" emerges from the collapse of a wave function than from neural activity?

Nothing we have said in this paper demonstrates the falsity of the quantum-consciousness connection. Our view is just that it is no better supported than any one of a gazillion caterpiller-with-hookah hypotheses.

14

Feeling Reasons

Patricia S. Churchland

Introduction: The Social Significance of Agent Autonomy and Responsibility

Much of human social life depends on the notion that agents have control over their actions and are responsible for their choices. We assume that it is sensible to punish and reward behavior so long as the person was in control and chose knowingly and intentionally. Without the assumptions of agent control and responsibility, human social commerce is hardly conceivable. As members of a social species, we recognize cooperation, loyalty, and reciprocation as prominent features of the social environment, and we react with hostility when group members disappoint socially salient expectations. Inflicting disutilities on the socially renegade and rewarding civic virtue helps restore the standards. In other social species, too, social unreliability, such as failures to reciprocate grooming or food-sharing, provokes a reaction likely to cost the renegade animal or his kin, sooner or later. For example, de Waal (1982) observed that chimpanzees who renege on a supportive coalition when loyalty is needed will later suffer retaliation. In social mammals at least, mechanisms for keeping the social order seem to be part of what evolution bequeathed to brain circuitry (Clutton-Brock and Parker 1995). The stability of the social-expectation baseline is sufficiently important to survival that individuals are prepared to incur some cost in enforcing those expectations. Just as an anubis baboon learns that tasty scorpions are to be found under rocks but cannot just be picked up, so it learns that failure to reciprocate grooming when it is duly expected may yield a smart slap. Much of behavior is guided by the expectation of certain consequences—not only what will happen in the physical world but including also what will happen in the social world (Cheney and Seyfarth 1990; de Waal 1989).

What is it—for us or baboons or chimpanzees—to have control over one's behavior? Are we really responsible for our choices and decisions? Will neuroscientific understanding of the neuronal mechanisms for decision making change how we think about these fundamental features of social commerce? These are some of the questions I wish to consider in this essay.

Are We Responsible and In Control if Our Choices and Actions Are Caused?

A venerable tradition bases the conditions for free will and control on a contrast between being caused to do something and not being so caused. For example, if someone pushes me from behind and I bump into you, then my bumping you was caused by the push; I did not choose to bump you. Examples conforming to this prototype have given credence to the idea that in order for a choice to be free, it must be uncaused. That is, it is supposed that a free choice is made when, without prior cause and without prior constraints, a decision comes into being and an action results. This contracausal construal of free choice is known as libertarianism (see Campbell 1957). Is it plausible?

As David Hume pointed out in 1739, the answer is surely no. Hume argued that our choices and decisions are in fact caused by other events in the mind: desires, beliefs, preferences, feelings, and so forth. Neither do the precipitating events, whether described as mental or neuronal, need to be conscious. He also made the much deeper and more penetrating observation that agents are not considered responsible for the choices they made unless they are caused by their desires, intentions, and so forth. Randomness, pure chance, and utter unpredictability are not preconditions for control. Hume puts the issue with memorable compactness:

... where [actions] proceed not from some cause in the characters and dispositions of the person, who perform'd them, they infix not themselves upon him, and can neither redound to his honor if good, nor infamy, if evil. (p. 411)

Logic reveals, Hume argued, that responsibility is actually inconsistent with libertarianism (uncaused choice). Someone may choose to climb onto his roof because he does not want rain to come into his house, he wants to fix the loose shingles, and he believes that he needs to get up on the roof to do that. His desires, intentions, and beliefs are part of the causal antecedents resulting in his choice. If, without any determining desire and belief, he simply went up onto the roof—as it were, for no reason—his sanity and hence his control is seriously in doubt (a roof is a dangerous place). More generally, a choice undetermined by anything the agent believes, intends, or desires is actually the kind of thing we consider out of the agent's control and not the sort of thing for which we hold someone responsible. Furthermore, desires or beliefs, were *they* uncaused rather than caused by other stable features of the person's character and temperament, are likewise inappropriate preconditions for responsible choice (see also Hobart 1934).

Neither Hume's argument that choices are internally caused nor his argument showing that libertarianism is absurd has ever been convincingly refuted (for disagreements with Hume, see Kenny 1989). Note, moreover, that his arguments hold whether or not one thinks of the mind as a separate Cartesian substance or as a pattern of activity of the physical brain, whether one thinks of the etiologically relevant states as conscious or unconscious. If anything in philosophy could count as a result, Hume's argument on free will does. Nonetheless, the idea that randomness in the physical world is somehow the key to what makes free choice free remains appealing to those inclined to believe that free choice must be uncaused choice. The appeal of quantum mechanics, chaos, and so forth as a "solution" to the problem of free will and responsibility generally derives from an intuition innocent of exposure to Hume's result.

If all behavior is caused, what is the difference between voluntary and involuntary actions? When, if ever, is an agent responsible? Many possibilities have been explored in attempts to explain how the notions of control and responsibility can make sense in the context of causation, of determinism. To begin with, it is clear that the distinction between internal and external causes will not suffice to distinguish the voluntary from the involuntary. A patient with Huntington's disease cannot prevent himself from making choreiform movements; a sleepwalker may unplug the phone or kick the dog; a phobic patient may have an over-whelming urge to wash her hands. The cause of the behavior in each of these cases is internal, in the subject's brain. Yet the behavior is considered to be out of the agent's control.

Another strategy is to base the distinction on felt differences in inner experience between those actions we choose to do and those over which we feel we have no control. Thus it allegedly feels different when we evince a cry as a startle response to a mouse leaping out of the compost heap, and when we cry out to get someone's attention. Is introspection a reliable guide to responsibility? Can introspection distinguish those internal causes for which we are responsible from those for which we are not? (See also Crick 1994.) Probably not. There are undoubtedly many cases where introspection is no guide at all. Phobic patients, obsessive-compulsive patients, and those with Tourette syndrome are obvious examples that muddy the waters. The various kinds of addictions present further difficulties. A contented smoker typically feels that the desire for a cigarette is indeed his, and that his reaching for a cigarette feels as free as his reaching to turn on the television. Not so the smoker who is trying to quit the habit. The increase in intensity of sexual interest and desire at puberty is surely the result of hormonal changes in the brain, not something over which one has much control. Yet engaging in certain activities, such as ogling the opposite sex, feels as free as tying one's shoes. More problematic, perhaps, are the many examples from everyday life where one may suppose that the decision was entirely one's own, only to discover that subtle manipulation of desires had in fact been the decisive factor. According to the fashion standards of the day, one finds certain clothes beautiful, others frumpy, and the choice of wardrobe seems, introspectively, as free as any choice. There is no escaping, however, the fact that what is in fashion has a huge effect on what we find beautiful in clothes, and this affects not only choice in clothes but also such things as aesthetic judgment regarding the plumpness or slenderness of the female body.

Social psychologists have produced dozens of examples that further muddy the waters, but a simple one will convey the point. On a table in a shopping mall, experimenters placed ten pairs of identical panty hose, and asked shoppers to select a pair, and then briefly explain their choice.

After selection, the choosers referred to color, denier, sheerness, and so forth, as their rationale. In fact, there was a huge "position effect": shoppers tended to pick the pantyhose in the rightmost positions on the table and, in fact, the pantyhose were identical and differed not at all in color, sheerness, and so on. None of the subjects considered position to be a factor; none of them referred to it as a basis for choice, yet it clearly was so. Other examples of priming, subliminal perception, emotional manipulation, and so on, reveal introspection to be a highly unreliable guide.

In a different attack on the problem, philosophers have explored the idea that if the choice was free, the agent could have chosen to do otherwise, that in some sense the agent had the power to do something else (see Taylor 1974; Kenny 1989). The weakness in the strategy shows up when we ask further, "What exactly does that mean?" If all behavior has antecedent causes, then "could have done otherwise" seems to boil down to "would have done otherwise if antecedent conditions had been different." Accepting this equivalence means the criterion is too weak to distinguish between the shouted insults of a person with Tourette syndrome, whose tics include random and undirected outbursts ("idiot, idiot, idiot"), and those of a member of Parliament responding to an honorable member's proposal ("idiot, idiot, idiot"). In both cases, had some of the antecedent conditions been different, obviously the results would have been different. Nevertheless, we hold the parliamentarian responsible, but not the person with Tourette syndrome.

In our legal as well as our daily practice, the pattern is to accept certain prototypical conditions as excusing a person from responsibility, but to assume him responsible unless a specific exculpatory condition obtains. In other words, responsibility is the default condition; excuse from and mitigation of responsibility has to be established. The set of conditions regarded as exculpatory can be modified as we learn more about behavior and its etiology. Thus, a child Touretter might have been smacked for his ticcing outbursts in public, until it is understood that the tics are not within his control and that punishment is totally inefficacious.

Aristotle (400 B.C./1995) was the first to articulate this strategy, and the core of his ideas on this matter is still reflected in much of human practice, including current legal practice. In his systematic and profoundly sensible way, Aristotle pointed out that it is a necessary condition that the cause be internal to the agent, but in addition, he characterized as involuntary the actions produced by coercion and actions produced in certain kinds of ignorance. As Aristotle well knew, however, no simple rule demarcates cases here. Clearly, some ignorance is not considered excusable when it may fairly be judged that the agent should have known. Additionally, in some cases of coercion, the agent is expected to resist the pressure, given the nature of the situation. As Aristotle illustrates in his own discussion of such complexities, we seem to proceed to deal with these cases by judging their similarity to uncontroversial and well-worn prototypes. This run-of-the-mill cognitive strategy is reflected in the fundamental role that precedent law is accorded in determining subsequent judgments (see more extended explanations in P. M. Churchland 1995).

It is unlikely that there exists a sharp distinction between the voluntary and the involuntary—between being in control and being out of control—either in terms of behavioral conditions or in terms of the underlying neurobiology. The differences are differences in degree, not a clean bifurcation specified by necessary and sufficient conditions. An agent's decision to change television channels may be more in his control than his decision to pay for his child's college tuition, which may be more in control than his decision to marry his wife, which may be more in control than his decision to turn off the alarm clock. Some desires or fears may be very powerful, others less so, and we may have more self-control in some circumstances than in others. Hormonal changes, for example in puberty, make certain behavior patterns highly likely, and in general, the neurochemical milieu can have a powerful effect on the strength of desires, urges, drives, and feelings.

As I shall suggest below, however, at opposite ends of the self-control spectrum are prototypical cases that differ sufficiently in behavioral and internal features to provide a foundation for a basic, if somewhat rough-hewn, distinction between being in control and not, between being responsible and not. It will also be apparent as we reflect on the spectrum's end points that there are many parameters relevant to being in control. In our current state of neurobiological and behavioral knowledge, we do not know how to specify all those parameters. Nevertheless, we do know that activity patterns in certain brain structures, including the amygdala, hypothalamus, somatosensory cortices, and ventromedial frontal cortex are important, and that levels of alleged neuromodulators, such as serotonin, dopamine, and norepinephrine, as well as hormones, play a critical role. Ultimately, as I shall explore later, a range of optimal values may be specifiable, and therewith, a contrasting range that is clearly suboptimal.

Are We More In Control and More Responsible to the Degree That Emotions Play a Lesser Role and Reason Plays a Greater Role?

A view with deep historical roots assumes that, in matters of practical decision, reason and emotion are in opposition. To be in control, on this view, is to be maximally rational. To that end, one must maximize suppression of emotions, feelings, and inclinations. Emotion is considered the enemy of morality, and consequently moral judgment must be based on reason detached from emotion.

Immanuel Kant is the philosopher best known for adopting this view. In his moral philosophy, Kant saw human agents as attaining virtue only if they succeed in downplaying feeling and inclination and giving reason complete control.[1] He says: "The rule and direction for knowing how you go about [making a decision],[2] without becoming unworthy of it, lies entirely in your reason" (Kant 1797/1964). In Kant's view, we would be perfectly rational save for the inclinations, feelings, and desires based in our bodies. The perfect moral agent, Kant seems to suggest, is one whose decisions are perfectly rational and are detached entirely from emotion and feeling.[3] (DeSousa calls such an agent a "Kantian monster"; DeSousa 1990, p. 14). The kinds of cases that inspire Kant's veneration of reason and his suspicion of the passions are the familiar "heart-over-head" blunders where the impassioned do-gooder makes things worse, when the long-term consequences were neglected while immediate need was responded to, when the fool does not look before he leaps. A powerful rationalist assumption underlies the great bulk of ethical theory in the latter half of this century. For example, the Kantian framework permeates the work of Nagel (1970), Rawls (1971), Gewirth (1978), and Donagan (1977).

Understanding the consequences of a plan, both its long- and short-term consequences, is obviously important, but is Kant right in assuming that feeling is the enemy of virtue, that moral education requires learning to disregard the bidding of inclination? Would we be more virtuous, or more educable morally, were we without passions, feelings, and inclinations?

Not according to Hume, against whom Kant was probably reacting. Hume asserted that "reason alone can never be a motive to any action of the will; and secondly, it can never oppose passion in the direction of the will" (p. 413). As he later explains: "T'is from the prospect of pain or pleasure that the aversion or propensity arises towards any object. And these emotions extend themselves to the causes and effects of that object, as they are pointed out to us by reason and experience" (p. 414). As Hume understands it, reason is responsible for delineating the various consequences of a plan, and thus reason and imagination work together to anticipate problems and payoffs. But feelings, informed by experience, are generated by the mind-brain in response to anticipations, and incline an agent toward or against a plan.

Common culture also finds something not quite right in the image of nonfeeling, nonemotional rationality. In the highly popular television series, *Star Trek*,[4] three of the main characters are portrayed as capable of distinct degrees of emotional response. The pointy-eared semialien, Mr. Spock, is typified by the absence of emotion. In trying circumstances, his head is cool, his approach is calm. He faces catastrophe and narrow escape with easy-handed equanimity. He is puzzled by the humans' propensity to anger, fear, love, and sorrow, and correspondingly fails to predict their appearance. Interestingly, Mr. Spock's cold reason sometimes results in bizarre decisions, even if they have a curious kind of "logic" to them.[5] By contrast, Dr. McCoy is found closer to the other end of the spectrum. Individual human suffering inspires him to risk much, to ignore future costs, or to fly off the handle, often to Mr. Spock's taciturn evaluation, "but that's illogical." The proper balance between reason and emotion is more nearly epitomized by the legendary and beloved Captain Kirk. By and large, his judgment is wise. He can make tough decisions when necessary, he can be merciful or courageous or angry when appropriate. He is more nearly the ideal Aristotle identifies as the practically wise man.[6]

Neurophysiological studies are highly pertinent to the question of the significance of feeling in wise decision making. Research by the Damasios and their colleagues on a number of patients with brain damage shows that, when deliberation is cut off from feelings, decisions are likely to be poor. Consider the patient S. M. whose amygdala has been destroyed and who lacks normal feelings of fear. She does not process danger signals normally, does not recognize feelings of fear in herself, and does not evince normal facial expressions in fearful circumstances. S. M. does have a concept of fear of sorts, and she can tell when a human face shows a fear response. In complex circumstances, with no access to gut feelings of unease and fear, she is as likely as not to make a decision that normally wired people could easily see to be contrary to her interest. Whereas a normal subject would say he has an uneasy feeling about someone who is in fact predatory, S. M. generates no such feelings. In a rather more complex way, the point is dramatically illustrated by the patient E. V. R., who first came to the Damasios laboratory at the University of Iowa College of Medicine more than a decade ago.

A brain tumor in the ventromedial region of E. V. R.'s frontal lobes had been surgically removed earlier, leaving him with bilateral lesions. Following his surgery, E. V. R. enjoyed good recovery and seemed very normal, at least superficially. For example, he scored as well on standard IQ tests as he had before the surgery (about 140). He was knowledgeable, answered questions appropriately, and so far as mentation was concerned, seemed unscathed by the loss of brain tissue. E. V. R. himself voiced no complaints. In his day-to-day life, however, a very different picture began to emerge. Once a steady, resourceful, and efficient accountant, he now made a mess of his tasks, came in late, failed to finish easy jobs, and so forth. Once a reliable and loving family man, his personal life became a shambles. Because he scored well on IQ tests and because he was knowledgeable and bright, E. V. R.'s problems seemed to his physician more likely to be psychiatric than neurological. As we now know, this diagnosis turned out to be entirely wrong.

The case of E. V. R. is by no means unique, and there are a number of patients with similar lesions and comparable behavioral profiles. After studying E. V. R. for some time, and comparing him with other cases with similar damage, the Damasios and their colleagues began to devise new tests to determine which of E. V. R.'s emotional responses were not in the normal range. For example, shown horrifying or disgusting pictures, his galvanic skin response (GSR)[7] was flat. Normals, in contrast, showed a huge response while viewing such pictures. On the other hand, he could feel fear or pleasure in uncomplicated, more basic, situations. During the following years, new and more revealing tests were devised to try and probe more precisely the relation between reasoning logically on the one hand, and acting in accordance with reason on the other. For there was no doubt that E. V. R. could evince the correct answer to questions concerning what would be the best action to take (e.g., defer a small gratification now for a larger reward later), but his own behavior often conflicted with his stated convictions (e.g., he would seize the small reward now, missing out on the larger reward later; Saver and Damasio 1991).

Antoine Bechara, working with the Damasios, developed a particularly revealing test. In this test, the subject is presented with four decks of cards and told that his task is to make as much profit as possible, given an initial loan of money. Subjects are told to turn over the cards, one at a time, from any of the four decks. They are not told how many cards can be played (a series of 100) or what the payoffs are from each of the four decks. One has to discover everything by trial and error. After turning over each card, the subjects are rewarded with an amount of money, and on some cards they may be penalized and be required to pay out money. Behind the scenes, the experimenter designates two decks, C and D, to be low-paying ($50) and to contain some moderate penalty cards; two other decks, A and B, pay large amounts ($100), but contain very high penalty cards. Things are rigged so that players incur a net loss if they play mostly A and B, but do well if they play mostly the C and D decks. Subjects cannot calculate exactly their losses and gains, because there is too much mentally to keep track of. Instead, subjects must generate a sense of what strategy will work to their advantage.

During the game, normal controls come fairly quickly to stick mainly with the low-paying but low-penalty decks (C and D) and make a profit. What is striking is that subjects such as E. V. R. (ventromedial frontal damage) tend to end with a loss because they choose mainly the high-paying decks despite the profit-eating penalty cards. Subjects with brain damage to regions other than the ventromedial behave like controls. As Bechara et al. (1994) note, even after repeated testing on the task as long as a month later or as soon as twenty-four hours later, E. V. R. continued to play the losing decks heavily. When queried at the end of the trial, he verbally reported that A and B were losing decks. To put it rather paradoxically, rationally E. V. R. does indeed know what the best long-term strategy is, but in exercising choice in actual action, he goes for short-run gain, incurring long-run loss. Is E. V. R. merely showing frontal perseveration? No, because he does score normally on the Wisconsin card-sorting task, in contrast to perseverative patients. In any case, he does sometimes try other decks. To make matters more difficult for the Kantian ideal, his judgments of recency and frequency are flawless, his knowledge base and short-term memory are intact (Bechara at al. 1994). Moreover, E. V. R. can articulate the future consequences of alternative actions well enough, so the problem cannot be lack of understanding of what might happen. In sum, what seems chiefly to be amiss here is not E. V. R.'s capacity to reason; rather, it is the inability of emotions to affect his reason and decision making.

That his "pure reasoning," displayed verbally, and his "practical decision making," displayed in choice, were so at odds suggested to the Damasios that the real problem lay with E. V. R.'s lack of emotional responsivity to situations that involved some understanding of the meaning and implication of the events. This is consistent with his lack of GSR while viewing emotionally charged photographs. That is, although E. V. R. would react normally to simple conditions such as a loud noise or a threat of attack, he failed to respond in more complex situations whose significance might involve more subtle or culturally mediated features, such as the social consequences of failure to complete jobs, or the future consequences of a sudden marriage to a prostitute, or profit-making in the Bechara gambling task. E. V. R. and similar subjects seems to have a kind of insensitivity to the significance of future consequences, whether they are rewarding, as in the gambling task, or punishing, as in a reverse gambling task. This insensitivity seems best understood in terms of the failure to provide a "value mark," via somatic states, to the various options (Bechara et al. 1994; Damasio 1994; Adolphs et al. 1996).

Further results came from the analysis of skin conductance data taken by a galvanometer placed on the arm of each subject during the gambling task (Damasio et al. 1991). In the gambling task, neither the controls nor the frontal patients showed a skin response to card selections in the first few plays of the game (selections 1–10). At about the tenth selection, however, controls began to exhibit a skin response immediately prior to beginning to reach for the "bad" decks. When queried at this stage about how they were making their choices, controls (and frontal patients) said they had no idea whatever, they were just exploring. But about selection 20, controls continued to show a consistent skin response just before reaching for the "bad" decks. In their verbal reports, controls said that they still did not know what was the best strategy, but that they had a feeling that maybe decks A and B were "funny." By selection 50, controls typically could articulate, and follow, the winning strategy. Frontal patients never did show a skin response in reaching for any deck. What is so striking here is that in controls, good choice seemed in some measure biased by the feeling even before subjects were aware of the feeling, and well before they could articulate the winning strategy. That many of our daily choices are likewise biased without our being aware of the feeling seems altogether likely.[8]

The significance for choice of feeling, and of unaware biasing by feeling, has implications for the economists' favored model of "rational choice." According to this model, the ideally rational (wise) agent begins deliberation by laying out all the alternatives, calculating the expected utility for each alternative based on the probability of each outcome multiplied by the value of (goodies accruing to) each outcome. He ends by choosing the alternative with the highest expected utility score. In light of the data just considered, this model seems highly unsatisfactory. At best, it probably applies to a small range of highly quantifiable problems, but even then comes into play after "cognition cum feeling" brings to awareness the restricted set of "feels-reasonable" alternatives. At any rate, the economists' model is unlikely to come even close to giving the whole story of rational choice.

A major idea in the Damasios' work on decision making is that representation of changes in body state, comprising visceral feeling as well as musculoskeletal signals (both external "touch" sensations and sympathetic changes in skin), play an essential role in biasing choice.[9] Body-state representation systematically integrates diverse changes in information originating in the sympathetic system. As future plans and possible plans develop, the imagination generates representations of plan sequelae, and to these, as well as to perceptually driven representations, visceral responses are generated, via mediation of the amygdala and hypothalamus. Somewhat more elaborately, therefore, the Damasios envisage a complex to-ing and fro-ing of signals between thalamocortical states and changes in the body itself as being the crucial pathways for self-representation and for sensible decision making.

The connection between this hypothesis and the case of E. V. R. and others with similar (ventromedial frontal) lesions is obvious. The point is not that E. V. R.-type patients feel nothing at all. Rather, it is that in those situations requiring imaginative elaboration of the consequences of an option, feelings are not generated in response to the imagined scenario. This is because the ventromedial frontal region needed for integration of body-state representation and fancy "scenario-spinning" is disconnected from the person's "gut feelings." Normally, neurons in ventromedial frontal cortex would project to and from areas such as the amygdala and hypothalamus that contain neurons carrying body-state signals. In patients with destruction of ventromedial cortex, those pathways are disrupted.

It is this set of complex responses, involving future-consequences recognition, visceral changes, and feelings, that the Damasios see as inclining the person to one decision rather than another. That is, in the context of acquired cognitive-cum-emotional understanding about the world, neuronal activity in these pathways biases sensible decisions, and biases them in "rational" directions. Moreover, the biasing can begin before subjects are aware of it, and before they can articulate their inclinations, even though a particular decision may seem, introspectively, to be the outcome solely of conscious deliberation. Their hypothesis is that when E. V. R. is confronted with a question (Should I finish this job or watch the football game? Should I choose from deck A or deck C?), his brain's body-state representation contains nothing about changes in the viscera, and hence he is missing important biasing cues that something is foolish or unwise or problematic. His frontal lobes, needed for a complex decision, have no access to information about the valence of a complex situation or plan or idea. Therefore, some of E. V. R.'s behavior turns out to be foolish and unreasonable (for a comprehensive account, see Damasio 1994).

Are There Significant Neurobiological Differences Between "In Control" Agents and "Out of Control" Agents?

I am assuming that there is a real difference in what we may loosely call "life success" between agents whose behavior is generally at the "in control" end of the spectrum—agents typified by the fictional Captain Kirk—and on the other hand, agents whose behavior is often at the "out of control" end of the spectrum, typified by the obsessive-compulsive subject. To a first approximation, the behavior of the "in controls" is more conducive to their interests, short and long term, and they generally make sensible, reasonable, and wise decisions about both short- and long-term plans. Undoubtedly, the relevant behavioral differences cannot be simply reduced to a formula for "reproductive fitness" or even "inclusive fitness," yet they are almost certainly deeply related to properties to which natural selection is sensitive. Are there likely to be prototypical neurobiological differences that correlate with these behavioral differences, vaguely specified though they are? Is it possible to provide an outline of the neurobiology prototypes at either end of our "in control"/ "out of control" spectrum, based on empirical data so far?

In a rather crude, semispeculative, and somewhat metaphorical way, yes. Having made all those hedges, let me now be a bit bolder. To begin with, converging data from neuropsychological research, animal studies, and anatomy implicate certain brain structures as especially crucial in emotional response. Assuming that the Damasio hypothesis is largely correct, these structures are presumably essential for "in control" behavior. So far, the list of structures includes the amygdala, somatosensory cortical areas I and II, insula, hypothalamus, anterior cingulate cortex, basal ganglia, and ventromedial frontal region of cortex. That there is more than one area indicates that "control," in this vague sense, is probably a distributed function in which a number of structures participate. Notably, the aforementioned structures also heavily project to and from each other. We also know that the connectivity between these regions is essential to normal functioning, as evidenced by subjects such as E. V. R., S. M., and others. Given the data, therefore, it may be expected that certain dynamical properties of the neural networks in these regions probably characterize functioning in the normal range. How might we begin to specify the dynamical properties typical of the normal range?

The brain is a complex dynamical system. If we consider the brain's neurons as defining the axes of a multidimensional state space, patterns of neuronal activity can be represented as points in that state space, and sequences of neuronal activity as trajectories in that state space. Additionally, trajectories can be linked to make sequences of such trajectories. Planning for a future contingency, for example, how to portage around some heavy rapids or how to convince a jury of Simpson's guilt, involves putting together a long and complex sequence of trajectories, first in imagination and then later in behavior. Given available data, it seems reasonable to assume that the "well-tempered" brain of a person who is typically wise, sensible, and reasonable embodies a kind of stable landscape in that state space. This means, among other things, that trajectories, appropriate to the sensory environment, through that state space, are highly stable to small perturbations. On the other hand, when the structures are damaged by lesions or by highly abnormal changes in neurochemical milieu, the landscape of the state space changes, and the trajectories become unstable and bizarre. To use a related analogy, the limit cycle characterizing the stable path in neuronal activation space can suddenly be replaced by very different, and behaviorally inappropriate, limit cycles.

Certain general features of the "neuronal landscape" may be particularly dependent on the neurochemicals of the widely projecting axonal systems, such as those involving serotonin, dopamine, or norepinephrine (figure 14.1). When the concentrations of these chemicals change by a certain threshold amount, they may quite radically change the terrain of the landscape, for example by flattening it to make trajectories more susceptible to perturbations, or digging deep grooves that are hard to get out of even when the environment calls for a different trajectory. The widely projecting systems appear to play a role in modulating the responses of neurons, for example by changing the gain or by

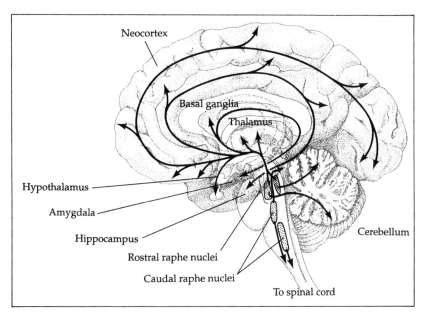

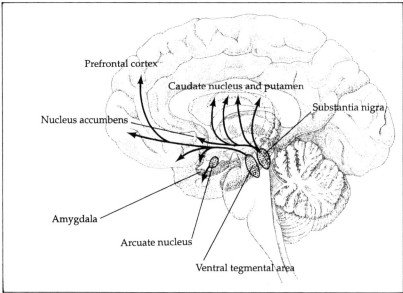

Figure 14.1
(A) A schematic illustration of the projection patterns of neurons containing serotonin (5-HT) whose cell bodies are located in the chain of raphe nuclei lying along the midline of the brain stem. Within each region receiving a projection, there are many axon terminals. (B) A schematic illustration of the projection pattern of neurons containing dopamine whose cell bodies are located in nuclei of the hypothalamus. (With permission from Nicholls, Martin, and Wallace 1992.)

down-regulating responsivity to neurotransmitters such as glutamate. They appear to play a crucial role in sleep and dreaming, in attention, and in mood, and they are found in brain-stem structures that project diffusely to cortical and subcortical structures. We do not, however, understand in detail the interactions between these systems, nor exactly how changing their concentrations changes the neuronal activation landscape.

What is known at the behavioral level is that obsessive-compulsive disorder (OCD), for example, is very treatable by serotonin agonists such as fluoxetine (Prozac); patients gain control over their phobias and their compulsive behavior. It is well-known that many cases of medical depression respond extremely well to drugs that enhance serotonin or norepinephrine, giving patients control over their anger and lassitude. Tourette syndrome is much more controlled when patients are given serotonin agonists. Each of these interventions can be seen, in keeping with the favored metaphor, as establishing or reestablishing general features in the neuronal activation landscape that make it stable against noise and perturbation, while allowing exploration and innovation without wild deviation from the stable trajectories.

Research from basic neuroscience as well as from lesion studies and scan studies will be needed to transform this speculative outline into a substantial, detailed, testable account of the general features of the landscape that are typical of "in control" subjects. These dynamical-system properties may be quite abstract, for "in control" individuals may differ in temperament and in cognitive strategies (see Kagan 1994). As Aristotle might have put it, there are different ways to harmonize the soul. Nevertheless, the prediction is that, at the very least, some such general features are specifiable. It is relatively easy to see that dynamical-system properties do distinguish between brains that perform certain tasks, such as walking well or poorly. What I am proposing here is that more abstract skills that are characterizable behaviorally, such as being a successful shepherd dog or a competent lead sled dog, can also be specified in terms of dynamical-system properties, dependent as they are on neural networks and neurochemical concentrations. My hunch is that human skills in planning, preparing, and cooperating can likewise be specified, not now, not next year, but in the fullness of time as neuroscience and experimental psychology develop and flourish.

Learning What Is Rational and What Is Not

Aristotle would have us add here the point that there is an important relation between self-control and habit formation. A substantial part of learning to cope with the world, to defer gratification, to show anger and compassion appropriately, and to have courage when necessary involves acquiring appropriate decision-making habits. In the metaphor of dynamical systems, this is interpreted as sculpting the terrain of the neuronal state space so that behaviorally appropriate trajectories are well-grooved. Clearly, we have much to learn about what this consists of, both at the behavioral and the neuronal levels. We do know, however, that if an infant has damage in some of the critical regions, such as the ventromedial cortex or amygdala, then typical acquisition of the right "Aristotelian" contours may be next to impossible, and more direct intervention may sometimes be necessary to obtain what normal children routinely achieve as they grow up.

The characterization of a choice or an action as "rational" caries a strongly normative component, implying, for example, that it was in one's long-range interest, or in the long-range interest of some relevantly specified group, or not inconsistent with other things one believes or what is believed by "reasonable" people. It is not sheerly descriptive, as when we describe an action as performed quickly or with a hammer. Claiming an action was rational often carries the implication that the choice was conducive in some significant way to the agent's interests or to those of his family, and that it properly took into account the consequences of the action, both long- and short-term (see also Johnson 1993); thus the evaluative component. Though a brief dictionary definition can capture some salient aspects of what it means to be rational and reasonable, it hardly does justice to the real complexity of the concept.

As children, we learn to evaluate actions as more or less rational by being exposed to prototypical examples, as well as to prototypical examples of foolish or unwise or irrational actions. Insofar as we learn by example, learning about rationality is like learning to recognize patterns in general, whether it be recognizing what is a dog, what is food, or when a person is embarrassed or weary. As Paul Churchland (1995) has argued, we also learn ethical concepts such as "fair" and "unfair," "kind" and "unkind," by being shown prototypical cases and generalizing to novel but relevantly similar situations.[10] Now, as we know, learning from examples is something networks do exceedingly well. Peer and parental feedback hone the pattern recognition network so that, over time, it comes closely to resemble the standard in the wider community. Nevertheless, as Socrates was fond of showing, articulating those standards is often a hopeless task, even when a person successfully uses the expression "rational," case by case. Making an algorithm for rational choice is almost certainly impossible. The systematic failure of artificial intelligence research to discover how to program computers to conform to common sense is an indication of the profoundly nonalgorithmic nature of common sense, rationality, and practical wisdom (see also Dreyfus 1972).

This is important because most philosophers regard the evaluative dimensions of ethical concepts to imply that their epistemology must be entirely different from that of descriptive concepts. What appears to be special about learning some concepts, such as "rational," "impractical," and "fair," is only that the basic wiring for feeling the appropriate emotions must be intact. That is, the prototypical situation of something being impractical or shortsighted typically arouses unpleasant feelings of dismay and concern; the prospect of something being dangerous arouses feelings of fear, and these feelings, along with perceptual features, are probably an integral part of what is learned in ethical "pattern recognition."

Simple dangerous situations—crossing a busy street, encountering a grizzly bear with cubs—can probably be learned as dangerous without the relevant feelings. At least that is suggested by the evidence of the Damasios from their patient S. M. who, you will recall, suffered amygdala destruction and lacks normal fear processing. Although she can identify which simple situations are dangerous, this seems for her to be a purely cognitive, nonaffective judgment. However, her recognition is poor when she needs to detect the menace or hostility or pathology in complex social situations, where no simple formula for identifying danger is available. As suggested earlier, the appropriate feelings may be necessary for skilled application of a concept, if not for the fairly routine applications. This is perhaps why we expect the fictional Mr. Spock, lacking emotions as he is, to be poor at predicting what will provoke strong sympathy or dread or embarrassment in humans.

Stories, both time-honored as well as those passing as local gossip, provide a basic core of scenarios where children imagine and feel, if only vicariously, the results of various choices, such as failing to prepare for future hard times (The Ant and the Grasshopper), or failing to heed warnings (The Boy Who Cried Wolf), of being conned by a smooth talker (Jack and the Beanstalk), of vanity in appearance (Narcissus). As children, we can vividly feel and imagine the foolishness of trying to please everybody (The Old Man and His Donkey), of not caring to please anybody (Scrooge in *A Christmas Carol*), and of pleasing the "wrong" people (the prodigal son). Many of the great and lasting stories, for example, by Shakespeare, Ibsen, Tolstoy, Balzac, are rife with moral ambiguity, reflecting the fact that real life is rife with conflicting feelings and emotions, and that simple foolishness is far easier to avoid than great tragedy. Buridan's dithering ass was just silly; Hamlet's ambivalence and hesitation were deeply tragic and all too understandable. In the great stories is also a reminder that our choices are always made amidst a deep and unavoidable ignorance of many of the details of the future, where coping with that very uncertainty is something about which one can be more or less wise. For all decisions save the trivial ones, there is no algorithm for making a wise choice (see again Johnson 1993; Flanagan 1991). As for matters such as choosing a career or a mate, having children or not, moving to a certain place or not, deciding the guilt or innocence of a person on trial, and so on, these are usually complex constraint-satisfaction problems.

As we deliberate about a choice, we are guided by—and guide others by—our reflection on past deeds, our recollection of pertinent stories, and our imagining of the sequence of effects that would be brought about by choosing one option or another. Antonio Damasio calls the feelings generated in the imagining-deliberating context "secondary emotions" (Damasio 1994, p. 134ff.) to indicate that they are a response not to external stimuli, but to internally generated representations and recollections. As we learn and grow up, we come to associate certain feelings with certain types of situation, and this combination can be reactivated when a similar set of conditions arises. Often a moral dilemma cannot be easily labeled, and instead we draw analogies between types of dilemmas: "This is like the time my father got lost in a blizzard and made a quinze." "This is like the time Clarence Darrow defended a teacher's right to teach evolutionary biology," and so forth. Recognition of a present situation as relevantly like a certain past case has, of course, a cognitive dimension, but it also evokes feelings that are similar to those evoked by the past case, and this is important in aiding the cortical network to relax into a solution concerning what to do next.

What Happens to the Concept of Responsibility?

We need now to return to the dominant background question motivating this essay. One very general conclusion is provoked by the foregoing discussion. On the whole, social groups work best when individuals are considered responsible agents, and hence, as a matter of practical policy, it is probably wisest to hold mature agents responsible for their behavior and for their habits. That is, it is probably in everyone's interests if the default assumption in place is that agents have control over their actions, and that, in general, agents are liable to punishment and praise for their actions. This is of course a highly complex and subtle issue, but the basic idea is that feeling the social consequences of one's choices is a critical part of socialization, of learning to be in the give-and-take of the group. (This pragmatic point of view, most closely associated with the ideas of Spinoza [1677], can also be found in the classic essays of Hobart [1934] and Schlick [1939].) Feeling those consequences is necessary for contouring the state-space landscape in the appropriate way, and that means feeling the approval and disapproval meted out. A child must learn about the physical world by interacting with it and bearing the consequences of his actions, or watching others engage the world, or hearing about others engage the world. As with social animals generally, learning about the social world involves cognitive-affective learning, directly or indirectly, about the nature of the social consequences of a choice. This must, of course, be consistent with reasonably protecting the developing child, and with compassion, kindness, and understanding. In short, I do not want the simplicity of the general conclusion to mask the tremendous subtleties of child-rearing. Underlying all the necessary subtlety, however, the basic pragmatist point is just this: If the only known way for "social decency" circuitry to develop requires that the subject generate the relevant feelings pursuant to social pattern recognition, and if that, in turn, requires experiences of praise (pleasure) and blame (pain) consequent upon his actions, then treating the agent as responsible for behavior is a pragmatically necessary operating assumption. That is, it is justified by its practical necessity.

This of course leaves it open that, under special circumstances, agents should be excused from responsibility or accorded diminished responsibility. In general, the law courts are struggling, case by case, to make reasonable judgments about what those circumstances are, and no simple rule really works. Neuropsychological data are clearly relevant here, as, for example, in cases where the subjects' brains show an anatomical resemblance to the brain of E. V. R. or S. M. Quite as obviously, however, the data do *not* show that no one is ever really responsible or deserving of punishment or praise. Nor do they show that, when life is hard, one is entitled to avoid responsibility.

Is direct intervention in the circuitry morally acceptable? This, too, is a hugely complex and infinitely ramifying issue. My personal bias is twofold: First, that in general, at any level, be it ecosystem or immune system, intervening in biology always requires great caution. When the target of the intervention is the nervous system, then caution by several more orders of magnitude is wanted. Still, not taking action is nonetheless doing something, and acts of omission can be every bit as consequential as acts of commission. Second, the movie, *A Clockwork Orange*, publicly associated with the very idea of direct neural intervention in criminal law, probably had a greater impact on our collective amygdaloid structures than it deserves to have. Certainly some kinds of direct intervention are morally objectionable. So much is easy. But all kinds? Even pharmacological? Is it possible that some forms of nervous system intervention might be more humane than lifelong incarceration or death? It seems to me likely that the general answer is yes. I do not know the detailed answers to these questions, but given what we now understand about the role of emotion in reason, perhaps the time has come to give them a careful, calm, and thorough reconsideration. Guided by

Aristotle, we may say that these are, au fond, pragmatic questions concerning the well-functioning of certain social animals, namely hominids.

Conclusions

I have considered three vintage philosophical theses in the context of new data from neuroscience: (1) feelings are an essential component of viable practical reasoning about what to do (David Hume); (2) moral agents come to be morally and practically wise not by dint of "pure cognition," but by developing through life experiences the appropriate cognitive-connate habits (Aristotle); and (3) agents need to acquire the cognitive-connate skills to evaluate the consequences of certain events and the price of taking risks, and hence must be treated, on the whole, as responsible agents (Hobart 1934; Schlick 1939). Each of the three theses has been controversial and remains so today; each has been the target of considerable philosophical criticism. Now, however, as the data come in from neuropsychology as well as experimental psychology and basic neuroscience, the empirical probability of each seems evident. One may interpret Damasio's book, *Descartes' Error*, as the beginning of a neurobiological perspective on the ideas of Aristotle and Hume. In this evolving scientific context, many important social policy questions must be considered afresh, including those concerned with the most efficacious means, consistent with other human values, for achieving civil harmony. Much, much more, of course, needs to be learned, for example, about the reward circuits in the brain, about pleasure and anxiety and fear. Philosophically, the emphasis with respect to civic, personal, and intellectual virtue has been focused almost exclusively on the cognitive domain, with the affective domain largely left out of the equation, as though the Kantian conception of reasoning and choice were in fact correct. In matters of educational and social policy, how best to factor in feeling and affect is something requiring a great deal of mulling, and practical wisdom. In any case, my hope is that understanding more about the empirical facts of decision making, both at the neuronal level and the behavioral level, may be useful as we aim for practical wisdom and ponder issues of social policy.

Acknowledgments

I am particularly indebted to Hanna Damasio and Antonio Damasio for extended discussions on these and related topics. I also thank Francis Crick, Paul Churchland, Rudolfo Llinás, David Brink, Deborah Forster, Jordan Hughes, Philip Kitcher, Laura Reider, and the members of the Experimental Philosophy Laboratory at University of California, San Diego.

III

The Philosophy of Science

15

A Deeper Unity: Some Feyerabendian Themes in Neurocomputational Form

Paul M. Churchland

I. Introduction

By the late '60s, every good materialist expected that epistemological theory would one day make explanatory contact, perhaps even a reductive contact, with a proper theory of brain function. Not even the most optimistic of us, however, expected this to happen in less than fifty years, and most would have guessed a great deal longer. And yet the time has arrived. Experimental neuroscience has revealed enough of the brain's microphysical organization, and mathematical analysis and computer simulation have revealed enough of its functional significance, that we can now address epistemological issues directly. Indeed, we are in a position to reconstruct, in neurocomputational terms, issues in the philosophy of science specifically. This is my aim in what follows.

A general accounting of the significance of neural network theory for the philosophy of science has been published elsewhere (P. M. Churchland 1989a, chapters 9 and 10). My aim here is to focus more particularly on five theses central to the philosophy of Paul Feyerabend. Those five theses are as follows.

1. Perceptual knowledge, without exception, is always an expression of some speculative framework, some *theory*: it is never ideologically neutral (Feyerabend 1958, 1962).

2. The commonsense (but still speculative) categorial framework with which we all understand our mental lives may not express the true nature of mind, nor capture its causally important aspects. This commonsense framework is in principle *displaceable* by a matured materialist framework, even as the vehicle of one's spontaneous, first-person psychological judgments (Feyerabend 1963a).

3. Competing theories can be, and occasionally are, *incommensurable*, in the double sense that (a) the terms and doctrines of the one theory find no adequate translation within the conceptual resources of the other theory, and (b) they have no logical connections to a common observational vocabulary whose accepted sentences might be used to make a reasoned empirical choice between them (Feyerabend 1962).

4. Scientific progress is at least occasionally contingent on the *proliferation* and exploration of mutually exclusive, large-scale conceptual alternatives to the dominant theory, and such alternative avenues of exploration are most needed precisely when the dominant theory has shown itself to be "empirically adequate" (Feyerabend 1963b).

5. The long-term best interests of intellectual progress require that we proliferate not only theories but research *methodologies* as well (Feyerabend 1970).

In my experience, most philosophers still find these claims to be individually repugnant and collectively confusing. This is not particularly surprising. Each claim is in conflict with common sense, and with a respectable epistemological tradition as well. Taken in isolation, and against that background, each one is bound to seem implausible, even reckless. But taken together, they form the nucleus of an alternative conception of knowledge, a serious and far-reaching conception with major virtues of its own.

Those virtues have been explored by a number of writers, most originally and most extensively by Feyerabend himself, but it is not my purpose here to review the existing arguments in support of these five themes. My purpose is to outline an entirely new line of argument, one drawn from computational neuroscience and connectionist artificial intelligence (AI). Research in these fields has recently made possible a novel conception of such notions as *mental representation, knowledge, learning, conceptual framework, perceptual recognition*, and *explanatory understanding*. Its portrayal of the kinematics and dynamics of cognitive activity differs sharply from the commonsense conception that underlies orthodox approaches to epistemology. The mere existence of such an alternative conception, one grounded in the brain's microanatomy, is sufficient to capture one's general interest. But this novel conception is of special interest in the present context, because it strongly supports all five of the Feyerabendian themes listed above. It provides a unitary explanation of why all five of them are jointly correct.

The claim being made here is a fairly strong one. Just as Newtonian mechanics successfully reduced Keplerian astronomy, so does a connectionist account of cognition reduce a Feyerabendian philosophy of science. Not everything in Kepler's account survived its Newtonian reduction, and not everything in Feyerabend's account survives its neurocomputational reduction. But in both examples the parallel of principle is sufficiently striking to make the claim of intertheoretic reduction and explanatory unification appropriate. And as with the case of Kepler and Newton, the cross-theoretic parallels serve to *vindicate* the principles reduced, at least in their rough outlines. I begin with a summary account of the kinematical and dynamical ideas that support this explanatory reduction.

II.   Neural Nets: An Elementary Account

A primary feature of neuronal organization is schematically depicted in the "neural network" of figure 15.1a. The circles in the bottom row of the network represent a population of sensory neurons, such as might be found in the retina. Each of these units projects a proprietary axonal fiber toward a second population of neuron-like units, such as might be found in the lateral geniculate nucleus (LGN), a midbrain structure that is the immediate target of the optic nerve. Each axon there divides into a fan of terminal branches, so as to make a synaptic connection with every unit in the second population. Real brains are not quite so exhaustive in their connectivity, but a typical axon can make many thousands or even hundreds of thousands of connections.

This arrangement allows any unit at the input layer to have an impact on the activation levels of all, or a great many, of the units at the second or "hidden" layer. An input stimulus such as light produces some activation level in a given input unit, which then conveys a signal of proportional strength along its axon and out the end branches to the many synaptic connections onto the hidden units. These connections stimulate or inhibit the hidden units, as a function of (a) the strength of the signal, (b) the size or "weight" of each synaptic connection, and (c) its polarity. A given hidden unit simply sums the effects incident from its many input synapses. The global effect is that a *pattern of activations* across the set of

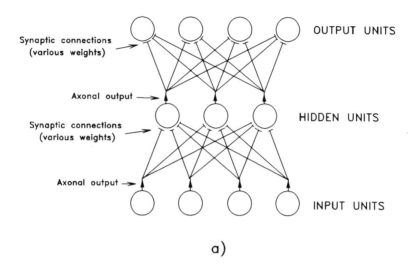

a)

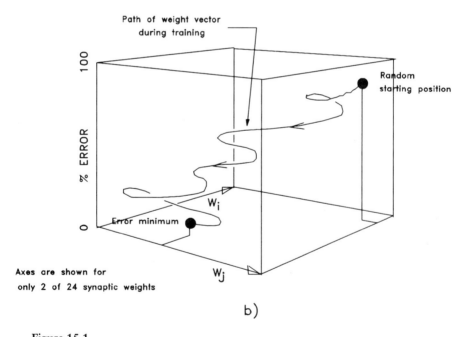

b)

Figure 15.1
(a) A simple feedforward network. (b) Weight-error space: the network's journey during learning.

input units produces a distinct *pattern of activations* across the set of hidden units. Which pattern gets produced, for a given input, is strictly determined by the configuration of synaptic weights meeting the hidden units.

The units in the second layer project in turn to a third population of units, such as might be found in the visual cortex at the back of the brain, there to make another set of synaptic connections. (In real brains this pattern typically branches, and is iterated through many layers—roughly, $5 < n < 50$—before the chain concludes in some population of motor or other "output" neurons. Real brains also display recurrent or "feedback" pathways not shown in figure 15.1a. But for purposes of illustration here, a nonbranching feedforward network of just three layers will suffice.) In this upper half of the network also, the global effect is that an activation pattern across the hidden units produces a distinct activation pattern across the output units. As before, exactly what pattern-to-pattern transformation takes place is fixed by the configuration of synaptic weights meeting the output units.

All told, this network is a device for transforming any one of a great many possible input vectors (i.e., activation patterns) into a uniquely corresponding output vector. It is a device for computing a specific function, and exactly which function it computes is fixed by the global configuration of its synaptic weights.

Now for the payoff. There are various procedures for adjusting the weights so as to yield a network that computes almost any function—that is, any general vector-to-vector transformation—that we might desire. In fact, we can even impose on it a function we are *unable to specify*, so long as we can supply a modestly large set of *examples* of the desired input-output pairs. This process is called "training up the network."

In artificial networks, training typically proceeds by entering a sample input vector at the lowest layer, letting it propagate upward through the network, noting the (usually erroneous) vector this produces at the topmost layer, calculating the difference between this actual output and the desired output, and then feeding this error measure into a special rule called the generalized delta rule (Rumelhart et al. 1986a, 1986b). That rule then dictates a small adjustment in the antecedent configuration of all of the synaptic weights in the network. This particular learning procedure is the popular "backpropagation" algorithm. Repeating this procedure many times, over the many input-output examples in the training set, forces the network to slide down an error gradient in the abstract space that represents its possible synaptic weights (figure 15.1b). The adjustments continue until the network has finally assumed a configuration of weights that does yield the appropriate outputs for all of the inputs in the training set.

To illustrate this technique with a real example, suppose we want the network to discriminate sonar echoes of large metallic objects, such as explosive mines, from sonar echoes of large submarine rocks. The discrimination of such echoes poses a serious problem because they are effectively indistinguishable by the human ear, and they vary widely in character even within each class. We begin by recording fifty different mine echoes and fifty different rock echoes, a fair sample of each. We then digitize the power profile of each echo with a frequency analyzer, and feed the resulting vector into the bank of input units (figure 15.2a). We want the output units to respond with appropriate activation levels (specifically, $\langle 1, 0 \rangle$ for a mine; $\langle 0, 1 \rangle$ for a rock) when fed an echo of either kind.

The network's initial verdicts are confused and meaningless, since its synaptic weights were set at random values. But under the pressure of the weight-nudging algorithm, it gradually learns to make the desired distinction among the initial examples. Its output behavior progressively approximates the correct output vectors. Most gratifyingly, after it has mastered the echoes in the training set, it will generalize: it will reliably identify mine and rock echoes from outside its training set, echoes it has never heard before. Mine echoes, it turns out, are indeed united by some subtle weave of features, to which weave the network has become tuned during the training process. The same is true for rock echoes. (See Gorman and Sejnowski 1988.)

Here we have a binary discrimination between a pair of diffuse and very hard-to-define acoustic properties. Indeed, *we never did define them*! It is the network that has generated an appropriate internal characterization of each type of sound, fueled only by examples. If we now examine the behavior of the hidden units during discriminatory acts in the trained network, we discover that the training process has partitioned the

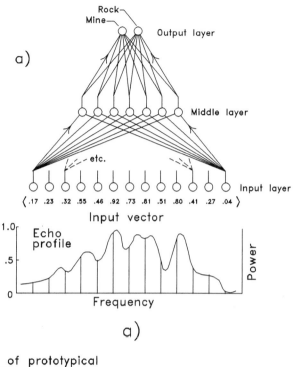

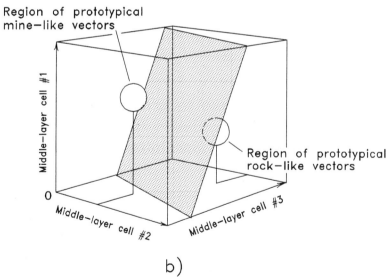

Figure 15.2
(a) Perceptual recognition with a larger network: presentation of the sonar echo.
(b) Learned partitions on the activation-vector space of the hidden units. Note the prototypical hot spots within each.

space of possible activation vectors across the hidden units (figure 15.2b). (Note that this space is not the space of figure 15.1b. Figure 15.1b depicts the space of possible synaptic weights. Figure 15.2b depicts the space of possible activation vectors across the middle layer.) The training process has generated a *similarity gradient* that culminates in two "hot spots"— two rough regions that represent the range of hidden-unit vector codings for a *prototypical* mine and a *prototypical* rock. The job of the top half of the network is then just the relatively simple one of discriminating these two subvolumes of that vector space.

Some salient features of such networks beg emphasis. First, the output verdict for any input is produced very swiftly, for the computation occurs in parallel. The global computation at each layer of units is distributed among many simultaneously active processing elements: the weighted synapses and the summative cell bodies. Hence the expression, "parallel distributed processing." Most strikingly, the speed of processing is entirely independent of both the number of units involved and the complexity of the function executed. Each layer could have ten units, or a hundred million; and its configuration of synaptic weights could be computing simple sums, or second-order differential equations. It would make no difference. Speed is determined solely by the number of distinct *layers* in the network. This makes for very swift processing indeed. In a living brain, where a typical information-processing pathway has something between five and fifty layers, and each pass through that hierarchy takes something between 10 and 20 ms per layer, we are looking at overall processing times, even for complex recognitional problems, of between 1/20th of a second and 1 second. As both experiment and common knowledge attest, this is the right range for living creatures.

Second, such networks are functionally persistent. They degrade gracefully under the scattered failure of synapses or even entire units. Since each synapse contributes such a tiny part to any computation, its demise makes an almost undetectable difference. In living creatures, the computational activity at any layer is essentially a case of multiplying an input vector by a very large matrix, where each synaptic weight represents one coefficient of that matrix (figure 15.3). Since the matrix is so large— typically in excess of $10^5 \times 10^3$ elements—it might have hundreds of thousands of positive and negative coefficients revert to zero and its

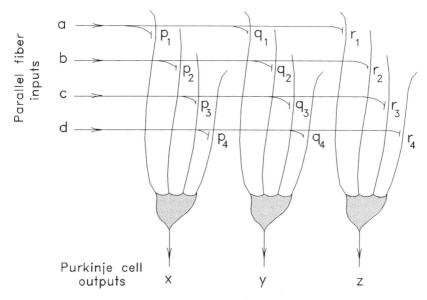

Figure 15.3
A schematic emphasizing the matrix-like array of synaptic connections between distinct cell populations. The input activation vector $\langle a, b, c, d \rangle$ is transformed into the output activation vector $\langle x, y, z \rangle$.

transformational character would change only slightly. That loss represents less than one tenth of one percent of its functional coefficients. Additionally, since networks learn, they can compensate for such minor losses by adjusting the weights of the surviving synapses.

Third, the network will regularly render correct verdicts given only a degraded version or a smallish part of a familiar input vector. This is because the degraded or partial vector is relevantly *similar* to a prototypical input, and the internal coding strategy generated in the course of training is exquisitely sensitive to such similarities among possible inputs.

And exactly which similarities are those? They are whichever similarities meet the joint condition that (a) they unite some significant portion of the examples in the training set, and (b) the network managed to become tuned to them in the course of training. The point is that there are often many overlapping dimensions of similarity being individually monitored by the trained network: individually they may be modest in their effects, but if several are detected together their impact can be decisive. Here we may recall Ludwig Wittgenstein's famous description of how humans can learn, by ostension, to detect "family resemblances" that defy easy definition. Artificial neural networks recreate exactly this phenomenon.

Finally, such networks can learn functions far more complex than the one illustrated, and make discriminations far beyond the binary example portrayed. In the course of learning to produce correctly pronounced speech (as output) in response to printed English text (as input), Rosenberg and Sejnowski's NETtalk (1987) partitioned its hidden-unit vector space into fully seventy-nine subspaces, one for each of the seventy-nine letter-to-phoneme transformations that characterize the phonetic significance of English spelling. Since there are seventy-nine distinct letter-to-phoneme associations in English writing, but only twenty-six letters in the alphabet, each letter clearly admits of several different phonetic interpretations, the correct one being determined by context. Despite this ambiguity, the network learned to detect which of several possible transforms is the appropriate one, by being sensitive to the contextual matter of which other letters flank the target letter inside the word. All of this is a notoriously irregular matter for English spelling, but a close approximation to the correct function was learned by the network even so.

As in the mine-rock network, an analysis of the behavior of the hidden units during each of the seventy-nine learned transformations reveals an important organization. For each letter-to-phoneme transformation, of course, the hidden layer displays a unique activation vector: a total of seventy-nine vectors in all. If one examines the similarity relations between these vectors in the trained network, as judged by their Euclidean proximity in the abstract activation vector space (see again figure 15.2b), one discovers that the learning process has produced a treelike hierarchy of types (figure 15.4). Similar sounds are grouped together and a global structure has emerged in which the deepest division is that between the consonants and the vowels. The network has spontaneously recovered, from the text on which it was trained, the phonetic structure of English speech!

Such revealing organization across the hidden-unit vector space is typical of trained networks in a great many contexts, and is a provocative feature of these machines. They partition that space into useful and

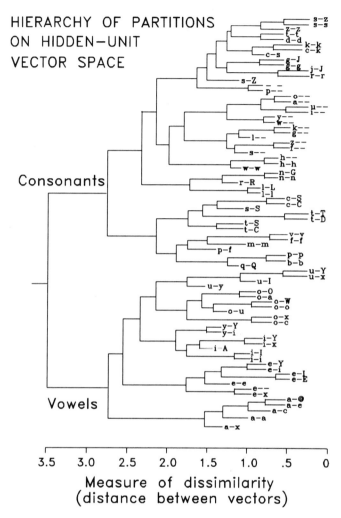

Figure 15.4
Root and branch representation of the phonetic similarity structure that develops across the activation-vector space of Rosenberg and Sejnowski's NETtalk during learning. (After Rosenberg and Sejnowski 1987.)

well-organized *categories* relative to the functional task that they are required to perform.

Other networks have learned to identify the three-dimensional configuration and orientation of curved surfaces, given only flat gray-scale pictures of those surfaces as input. That is, they solve a version of the classic shape-from-shading problem in visual psychology (Lehky and Sejnowski 1988a, 1988b). Still others learn to divine the grammatical elements of sentences fed as input, or to predict the molecular folding of proteins given amino acid sequences as input, or to categorize olfactory stimuli into a hierarchical taxonomy, or to guide a jointed limb to grasp perceived objects, or to predict payment behavior from loan-application profiles. These networks perform their surprising feats of learned categorization and perceptual discrimination with only the smallest of "neuronal" resources—usually much less than 10^3 units. This is less than one hundred millionth of the resources available in the human brain. With such powerful cognitive effects being displayed in such modest artificial models, it is plausible that they represent a major insight into the functional significance of our own brain's microstructure.

Let us briefly contrast this approach with the rule-governed symbol-manipulation approach of classical AI. Unlike standard serial-processing, programmable computers, neural nets typically have no representation of any rules, and they do not achieve their function-computing abilities by following any rules. They simply "embody" the desired function, as opposed to calculating it by recursive application of a set of rules listed in an externally imposed program. Moreover, since neural nets perform massively parallel processing, they can be many millions or even billions of times faster than serial machines on a wide range of problems, even though they are constructed of vastly slower physical components.

A further contrast concerns the manner of information storage. In neural networks, acquired knowledge is stored in a distributed fashion: specifically, in the intricate permutational structure of the global configuration of synaptic weights, which number at least 10^{14} in a human brain. The relevant aspects of that vast store are instantly accessed by the input vectors themselves, since the weights have been configured by the learning process precisely so as to produce the appropriate activation patterns in the layer receiving that input vector. This constitutes a form of "content-addressable" memory. Given the very high-dimensional representations employed by neural nets (namely, activation vectors across large cell populations), even smallish nets can be exquisitely sensitive to subtle and hard-to-express similarities among their perceptual inputs, and to the intricate contextual features that they may contain.

This welcome feature allows a network to activate the appropriate prototype vector at the hidden layer even when the input vector is only a partial or degraded version of a typical input. The prototypical "hot spots" in the activation space of the trained hidden layer function as "attractors" into which a wide variety of partial or degraded inputs will "fall." This phenomenon allows a well-trained network to recognize instances of its categorial system even in novel or noisy circumstances, and given only partial information. In the language of philosophical theory, this means that a trained network will regularly make an ampliative "inference" to the best available "explanation" of the input phenomena. And it will do so in milliseconds.

Finally, neural nets can learn a desired function and generate a categorial system adequate to compute it, even where its makers and trainers are ignorant of both. All it needs are sufficient examples of the relevant function. These are some of the more striking rewards we gain from our modest attention to the brain's empirical architecture.

III. Epistemological Issues in Neurocomputational Guise

Let us now turn away from smallish artificial networks and refocus our attention on a large-scale biological network: the human brain. The suggestion to be explored below is that cognitive activity in the brain follows the same pattern displayed in the artificial networks. Knowledge is stored in the global configuration of the brain's synaptic weights. Learning consists in the modification of those synaptic weights according to some adjustment procedure that is somehow sensitive to successful or erroneous performance by the network. Successful configuration of the weights yields a complex and hierarchically organized set of partitions across the various subpopulations of "hidden units" scattered throughout the brain. That is, it yields one of many possible categorial or conceptual frameworks. Conceptual change consists in reconfiguring the synaptic weights so as to produce a new set of partitions across the relevant population(s) of neurons.

In humans, such categorial frameworks can be clearly be of remarkable complexity, since the human brain boasts something like 10^3 neural subpopulations ("layers of hidden units") at a minimum, each of which has something like 10^8 distinct neurons. A coding vector with 10^8 elements in it can code the contents of a very large book, so we may expect the prototypes involved to characterize intricate things such as "stellar collapse" and "economic depression," as well as simple things like "raven" and "black."

Perceptual recognition consists in the activation of an appropriate prototype vector across some appropriate population of postsensory neurons. The achievement of explanatory understanding consists in exactly the same thing, although here the occasion that activates the vector need not always be sensory in character. Perceptual recognition is thus just a special case of explanatory understanding.

The preceding begins to evoke the range of epistemological material we can reconstruct in neurocomputational terms. (A more detailed and far-reaching account can be found in P. M. Churchland 1989a, chapters 9–11) We are now prepared to address the claim that motivated this paper, the claim that five salient themes of Paul Feyerabend's philosophy of science are a natural consequence of the neurocomputational perspective.

1.   On The Theory-Ladenness of All Perception
The argument here is about as brief and as decisive as it could be. Perception is of course more than mere peripheral transduction: it is a cognitive achievement. But on the model of cognition outlined above, no cognitive activity whatever takes place without the relevant input vectors passing through the complex filter of a large set of synaptic weights (see again figure 15.1a). Most important, any configuration of synaptic weights dictates a specific set of partitions on the activation space of the postsensory neurons to which they connect. And that set of partitions constitutes a specific conceptual framework or theory, one of many millions of alternative possible frameworks.

Any activation pattern produced across the relevant population of hidden units is thus a point in an antecedently existing space, a space with antecedently prepared similarity gradients and antecedently prepared partitions having an antecedently prepared significance for subsequent populations of neurons in the processing hierarchy. That antecedent framework and the configuration of weights that dictates it represent whatever "knowledge" the network has accumulated during past training. That framework may be well trained and finely tuned, or it may be uninstructed and inchoate. But whichever it is, no cognitive activity takes place save as the input vectors pass through that speculative configuration of synaptic connections, that *theory*. Theory-ladenness thus emerges not as an unwelcome and accidental blight on what would otherwise be a neutral cognitive achievement, but rather as that which makes processing activity genuinely *cognitive* in the first place.

From this perspective it is evident that the process of learning about the world is not just the process of learning which general beliefs to embrace, as guided by our neutral perceptual judgments. It is also a process of learning how most usefully and penetratingly to *perceive* the world, for there is just as much room for conceptual variation and conceptual exploration at the perceptual level as there is at any other level of knowledge.

The basic point to emphasize is that, since there are almost endlessly many different possible observational frameworks (that is, hidden-layer weight configurations), where the choice between *them* is *also* an epistemic decision, there can be no question of grounding all epistemic decisions in some neutral observation framework. There is no such framework, and epistemic decisions are not made by reference to its contents in any case. One can certainly regard the unprocessed activation vectors at the sensory input layer as theoretically neutral, but those sensory activation vectors are not themselves propositional attitudes, they are not truth-valuable, and they stand in no logical relations to anything. Their impact on subsequent activity is causal, not logical. Human knowledge thus has *causal* "foundations," but it has no *epistemic* foundations.

2. On Displacing Folk Psychology

Given the model of cognition outlined above, any conceptual framework whatever is a speculative attempt to process incoming vectors in a way that is useful to the network, and it is subject to modification or replacement as a function of whatever pressures are exerted by the network's learning algorithm. The system of partitions that constitutes one's "folk" conception of mental reality is no exception. It is a learned framework whose purpose is to render intelligible both the introspectable reality of one's own case and the continuing behavior of people in general. A suitable regime of training should be able to produce any one of a large variety of alternative conceptions (indeed, even the "folk" conception is nonuniform across cultures, and across individuals).

The idea of embracing an alternative to folk psychology was never very compelling so long as we could not even point toward a plausible alternative conception. But now we can. The neurocomputational framework of the preceding pages portrays cognitive representations as high-dimensional activation vectors, rather than as sentential or propositional attitudes. And it portrays cognitive activity as the synapse-driven transformation of vectors into other vectors, rather than as the rule-governed drawing of inferences from one proposition to another. It presents a fundamentally novel kinematics and dynamics of cognitive activity. It is not yet sufficiently developed for a general transfer of allegiance to take place. But it does hold promise of being descriptively and explanatorily superior to current folk psychology, by a wide margin, and it already presents real opportunities for first-person use.

One class of such opportunities concerns the various subjective sensory *qualia* which have so often been held up as paradigm examples of what materialism can never hope to explicate. A specific color quale emerges as a specific activation vector in a three (or four-)-dimensional space whose axes correspond to the three types of retinal cones (and perhaps also the rods). A taste quale emerges as a four-element activation vector in a 4-D space whose axes correspond to the four types of taste sensors in the mouth. Auditory qualia emerge as more variable vectors whose elements correspond to the places on the cochlea whose natural frequency corresponds to one element in the complex incoming sound. The dimensionality of these qualia is relatively low, and thus their internal structure is potentially learnable and reportable in detail, just as the structure of musical chords is learnable and reportable. As in the musical case, there is also an increased insight into the structure of and the relations within the apprehended domain. One has therefore mastered more than just an esoteric set of labels: one has increased one's understanding of the phenomena.

Qualia are peripheral phenomena, to be sure, and complexity goes up as we ascend the processing hierarchy. It remains to be seen how the story will go in the case of cognitive processing at the level of systematic linguistic activity. Perhaps the familiar propositional attitudes will be smoothly reduced by the computational structures we find there, and perhaps they will simply be eliminated from our scientific ontology because nothing of dynamical importance in the brain answers to them. But whichever is their fate—reduction by something superior, or elimination by something superior—the categories of folk psychology remain displace*able* in favor of some more penetrating categorial framework. The only real question is how large the doctrinal and ontological gap will turn out to be, between the triumphant new framework and its poorly informed historical predecessor.

3. On Incommensurable Alternatives

Consider a typical brain subpopulation of something like 10^8 neurons. Its abstract activation space will have 10^8 dimensions. Clearly a space of such high dimensionality can support an extraordinarily intricate hierarchical system of similarity gradients and partitions across that space. Equally clear is the commensurately great *variety* of such partitional configurations possible with such generous resources. Now the demand that all possible conceptual frameworks must be somehow translatable into our current conceptual framework is just the demand that each and every one of the billions of possible configurations just alluded to must stand in some equivalence relation to our current configuration. But there is not a reason in the world to think that there is any such relation that unites this vast diversity of frameworks: not in their internal structure, nor in their relations to the external world, nor in the input-output functions they sustain. On the contrary, they are all in competition with one another, in the sense that they are mutually exclusive configurations of the same activation-vector space.

The prospect of widespread incommensurability is unsettling to many philosophers because it threatens to make a reasoned empirical choice between competing theoretical frameworks impossible. The real threat, however, is not to the possibility of rational empirical choice, but to a deeply entrenched *theory* of what rational empirical choice consists in. That superannuated theory requires a relevantly neutral observation vocabulary among whose sentences the competing theories at issue have differential logical consequences. So long as one embraces that superannuated theory, one will perceive incommensurability as a threat to reason and objectivity. But once one puts that theory aside, one can get down to the serious business of exploring how empirical data *really* steer our theoretical commitments.

On the model of cognition here being explored, ongoing learning consists in the continual readjustment of the value-configuration of one's myriad synaptic weights. Exactly what factors drive such readjustments in the human brain is currently the focus of much research, but the familiar philosopher's stories about sets of sentences being accepted or rejected as a function of their logical relations with other sentences plays no detectable role in that research, and no detectable role in the brain's activity either. Instead, synaptic change appears to be driven by such factors as local increases in presynaptic or postsynaptic activity (post-tetanic potentiation), by temporal correlations or anticorrelations between the activity reaching a given synapse and the activity reaching other synaptic connections onto the same postsynaptic neuron (Hebbean learning), by the mutual accommodation of synaptic values under specific global constraints (Boltzmann learning), perhaps by the return distribution of conflict messages (backpropagation), and by other decidedly preconceptual or subconceptual processes.

None of this precludes the possible relevance of sentential and logical factors for *some* cases of learning at some high level of processing, but it does undermine the parochial view that all or even most of human learning must be captured in those terms. And it therefore frees us forever from the short-sighted objection that incommensurable alternatives would make objective learning impossible. Learning then proceeds, as it *usually* does, by other than "classical" means. This is good, because incommensurable alternatives are both possible and actual. They are also welcome, since "commensurability" is just a measure of the similarity between alternative frameworks, and sometimes what the epistemic situation requires is a profoundly different perspective on the world. Which brings us to the next theme.

4. On Proliferating Theories

Feyerabend's argument (1963b) for the wisdom of proliferating theories is a very striking one. He points out that important empirical facts can often be quite properly dismissed, as unrevealing noise or intractable chaos, when viewed from within one conceptual framework, while those "same" empirical facts appear as tractable, revealing, and as decisively incompatible with the first framework when they are viewed from within a second conceptual framework. His illustrative example is the empirical phenomenon of Brownian motion, which constitutes a perpetual motion machine of the second kind and is thus incompatible with the second law of classical thermodynamics. However, its status as such was not appreciated, and could not be fully appreciated, until the relevant details of Brownian motion were brought into clear focus by the new and very different *kinetic* theory of heat. What had been an exceedingly minor and opaque curiosity then emerged as a major and unusually revealing experimental phenomenon, one that refuted the classical second law.

Feyerabend has been criticized for overstating the case here. Laymon (1977) insists that Brownian motion could have been, and to some extent actually was, recognized as a problem for classical thermodynamics in advance of its successful analysis by the kinetic theory. Laymon may have a point, but I think his resistance here is a quibble (see also Couvalis 1988). Whatever minor worries might have been brewing in a few isolated breasts, the fact remains that the kinetic theory transformed our conception of Brownian motion, and made salient certain of its experimentally accessible features that otherwise might never have risen to consciousness. It is not true that all empirical facts are equally accessible, nor that their significance is equally evident, independently of the conceptual framework one brings to the experimental situation. This is all one needs to justify the proliferation of theories. And the case of Brownian motion remains a striking example of this important lesson.

From a neurocomputational perspective, this lesson is doubly clear. Anyone who has spent idle time watching a Hinton diagram evolve during the training of a neural network will have noticed that networks often persist in ignoring or in outright misinterpreting salient data until they have escaped the early and relatively benighted conceptual configuration into which the learning algorithm initially pushed them. They persist in such behavior until they have assumed a more penetrating conceptual configuration, one that responds properly to the ambiguous data. (A Hinton diagram is a raster-like display of all of the synaptic-weight values of the network being trained. These displayed values are updated after each presentation of a training example and consequent modification of the weights. Accordingly, one can watch the weights evolve under the steady pressure of the training examples.) If the proper final configuration of weights happens already to be known from prior training runs, one can even watch the "progress" of the weights as they collectively inch toward their optimal configuration.

What is striking is that for some problems (the exclusive OR function, for example), some specific weights regularly start off by evolving in exactly the *wrong* direction—they become more and more strongly negative, for example, when their proper final value should be strongly positive. One may find oneself yelling at the screen "No! This way! Over this way!," as the early network persists in giving erroneous outputs, and the wayward weights persist in evolving in the wrong direction. These frustrations abate only when the other weights in the network have evolved to a configuration that finally allows the network's learning algorithm to appreciate the various examples it has been "mishandling," and to pull the miscreant weights toward more useful values. The proper appreciation of some of the training data, to summarize the point, is sometimes impossible without a move to a different conceptual configuration.

This example illustrates that the moving point in weight-error space (see again figure 15.1b) is often obliged to take a highly circuitous path in following the local error gradient downward in hopes of finding a global error minimum. That path may well go through points that preclude both a decent output from the network and a proper lesson from the learning algorithm for at least some of the student weights. Only when the network reaches a subsequent point can these defects be repaired.

A more dramatic example of this empirical blindness occurs when, as occasionally happens, the evolving weight-space point gets caught in a purely "local minimum," that is, in a cul-de-sac in weight-error space in which the network is still producing somewhat erroneous outputs, but where every relatively small change in the synaptic weights produces an *increase* in the error measured at the network's output layer. For any learning algorithm that moves the weight-space point in small increments only, the network will be permanently stuck at that point. So far as it is concerned, it has achieved the "best possible" theory.

In order to escape such an epistemic predicament (and occasional entrapments are inevitable), we need a learning algorithm that at least occasionally requires the network to make a relatively *large* jump: a jump to a significantly different portion of synaptic weight space, to a significantly different conceptual configuration. From that new weight-space point, the network may then evolve quickly toward new achievements in error reduction.

It is evident that, for some global minima and some starting points, *you can't get there from here*, at least not by small increments of instruction. This is a clear argument for the wisdom of a learning strategy that at least occasionally exploits multiple starting points, or discontinuous shifts, in the attempt to find a descending path toward a genuinely global error minimum. It may be difficult to achieve such diversity in a single individual (but it is certainly not impossible; see P. M. Churchland 1989d). But it can readily be done with different individuals in the same scientific community. And of course it is done. That is the point of different "schools."

These considerations do not resolve the essentially political conflict between Feyerabend and Thomas Kuhn concerning how *much* of our resources to put into proliferation and how much into pursuing a single but highly progressive "paradigm." But it does mean that a wise research policy must recognize the need for striking, and endlessly restriking, a useful balance between these two opposing tensions. Proliferation is a desideratum that will never go away, because the prospect of a false but compelling local error minimum is a threat that will never go away, and because complacency is endemic to the human soul.

5.   On Proliferating Methodologies

The Feyerabend I have in mind here is of course the Feyerabend of "Against Method" (1970), in which he recommends an opportunistic anarchism, constrained only by the innate organization of the human nervous system, as a more promising policy in guiding our scientific behavior than is any of the methodological straitjackets so far articulated by scientists and philosophers of science. In a climate of methodological stories benighted by their formulation in logicolinguistic terms, this is certainly good advice. But it need not always be good advice: someday, perhaps, our acquired methodological wisdom may equal or surpass the innate wisdom of a healthy nervous system, because we have figured out how the nervous system works, and can see how to make it work even better.

This is not a vain hope. Guided by a variety of nonclassical learning algorithms, artificial neural networks have recently proved capable of some astonishing feats of knowledge acquisition, feats that represent a quantum leap over any of the classical logicolinguistic achievements. A new door has opened in normative epistemology, and it concerns the comparative virtues and capabilities of alternative learning algorithms, algorithms aimed not at adjusting sets of propositions so as to meet certain criteria of consistency or coherence, but aimed rather at adjusting iterated populations of synaptic weights so as to approximate certain input-output functions or certain dynamical behaviors. What is striking, even at this early stage of exploration, is that the *space of possible learning algorithms is enormous.* In the newly developed research program called "connectionist AI," almost as much research time is spent on critically exploring the diverse properties of various existing learning algorithms, and on devising and exploring new ones, as is spent on the properties of trained networks themselves (see Hinton 1989).

This is a healthy situation, and such proliferation should be encouraged. There are at least two major reasons for this. The first concerns the relatively limited aim of trying to understand how the human brain conducts its epistemic affairs. We need to explore the space of possible learning algorithms until we discover which specific place in it corresponds to the brain's mode of operation.

The second reason is deeper. Even supposing we succeed in identifying the brain's place in that space, there is no reason to suppose that our biologically innate learning algorithm is the best possible algorithm, or even that there *exists* a uniquely best learning algorithm. Perhaps they just get better and better, ad infinitum, which means that we must explore them indefinitely. Or perhaps they radiate along diverse dimensions of distinct virtue, to be explored as our changing needs dictate. The proliferation of learning algorithms is a virtuous policy of long-term science for much the same reasons that proliferation is a virtue in the case of theories. The alternatives are certainly there, and we will not appreciate their virtues unless we explore them.

This may place unreasonable demands on the human nervous system, since presumably it is insufficiently plastic to participate directly in this exploration. Its learning algorithms may be hopelessly hardwired into its structure. Methodological proliferation may therefore show itself only in artificially constructed brains designed specifically to do novel kinds of scientific exploration on our behalf. But this changes the philosophical point not at all.

The preceding defense of the proliferation of methodologies does not justify exactly the position that Feyerabend outlined in "Against Method". He is there reacting to the shortcomings of an old tradition in methodological research, rather than anticipating the possible virtues of a new tradition. But that is all right. The bottom line is that proliferating methodologies is a still a very good idea, and for reasons beyond those urged by Feyerabend.

Conclusion

Philosophers are not always so fortunate as Feyerabend appears to be, in respect of finding a systematic vindication of their ideas through an intertheoretic reduction by a later and more penetrating theoretical framework. One must be intrigued by the convergence of principle here, and one must be impressed by the insight that motivated Feyerabend's original articulation and defense of the five theses listed. It seems likely that each one of these important theses will live on, and grow, now in a neurocomputational guise.

16

Reply to Glymour

Paul M. Churchland

I think Glymour (1992) is right to be upset. The old epistemological ways are dying—cause enough for distress. Worse, their prospective replacements are still ragtag, unpolished, and strange. Moreover, there is an unsettling uncertainty or shift of focus as to which are the truly important problems to be addressed. But even so, the objective theoretical situation holds more promise than at any time since the '40s, and in his frustration Glymour misrepresents it rather badly. And sometimes carelessly. My aim in this note is to address and correct some of his complaints. Several of them are welcome, in that they represent questions that any intelligent observer would pose. These will receive the bulk of my attention.

Glymour opens his critique by referring to my "recent connectionist crush." This phrase implies volumes, but unfairly. I have been arguing publicly for some kind of nonsentential brain-based kinematics for cognition since 1971, and have been defending in particular a vector-coding, matrix-processing approach to animal cognition since 1982, before the term "connectionism" was ever coined. For me, the appeal of this vector-matrix approach derived from its virtues within empirical and theoretical *neuroscience*, not artificial intelligence (AI) or philosophy. It embodied a powerful account of motor control, sensory processing, and sensorimotor coordination, an account that was both inspired by and explanatory of the brain's microorganization in terrestrial animals generally (see, e.g., P. M. Churchland 1986a, reprinted as chapter 5 of P. M. Churchland 1989a).

By contrast, the true virtues of a vector-matrix approach to *AI* became publicly apparent only after the backpropagation algorithm found widespread use, after 1986, as an efficient means of *configuring* the weights (= the matrix coefficients) of artificial multilayered networks. This allowed networks to be quickly trained to various cognitive capacities, which then allowed us to analyze in detail the computational basis of these acquired capacities. By then, some of us saw this (wholly welcome) development as a case of the AI community finally catching up, conceptually, with long-standing themes in the empirical and theoretical neurosciences.

In sum, my own approach to these issues is neither recent nor narrowly connectionist in character. Neither is it a crush, in the sense that implies a only a shallow and fleeting commitment. Having taxed the patience of my generous but skeptical colleagues for two decades now, I am sure that they will recognize a long and determined commitment to the kinematical themes that appear in *A Neurocomputational Perspective* (hereinafter *NCP*).

What about those themes? At the end of his third paragraph, Glymour expresses disappointment that they do not include any "new formal or computational results of any kind." Here I am inclined to some surprise, since four modest results occur immediately to me. The first concerns the unexpected size of the human *conceptual space*, as roughly calculated in *NCP*, and the explorational difficulties that this superastronomical volume entails (pp. 249–53). A second result concerns the character of *conceptual simplicity*, as neurocomputationally construed, and the reason why creatures blessed with it will generalize more successfully than others when confronted with novel sensory situations (pp. 179–81). A third result concerns the necessity for acknowledging at least two quite distinct processes of *learning* in highly developed creatures: a more basic process that is relatively slow, continuous, and inevitably destructive of prior concepts; and a secondary process possible only in recurrent networks, a process that is fast, discontinuous, and largely conservative of prior concepts (pp. 236–41). A fourth result concerns the presumptive *computational identity* of three phenomena counted as quite distinct from within common sense, namely, perceptual recognition, explanatory understanding, and inference to the best explanation (chapter 10 of *NCP*). These results may yet prove to be flawed in some way, but it is wrong to imply their nonexistence.

Perhaps Glymour meant something more restrictively a priori by the phrase, "formal or computational results," sufficiently restrictive to exclude the examples just cited. If so, then his original complaint is misconceived. For I take pains to emphasize at several places that my aims are those of an empirical scientist, not those of a logician or of any other presumptively a priori discipline (see, e.g., *NCP*, p. 198). In effect, Glymour is complaining that *NCP* does not approach the philosophy of science the way that he and others have traditionally approached it. But it is that very tradition whose methodological assumptions are now in question.

Let us turn to some of Glymour's specific criticisms. He asks after my account of a *specific* theory—electrodynamics, or thermodynamics, say—as opposed to a person's global theory of the world-in-general. My considered view of the *latter* is that it consists of the intricate set of partitions that learning has produced across a person's high-dimensional neuronal activation space. (This is outlined explicitly on pp. 232–4 of *NCP*, where the alternative explication in terms of a global set of synaptic weights is rejected on grounds that it puts impossible demands on the sameness of global theories across individuals.) From that perspective, a specific theory such as electrodynamics is naturally construed as a specific prototypical *subvolume* of that global activation space, a subvolume with its own partitional substructure, perhaps.

This account does put single concepts and entire theories on the same footing: a theory is just a highly structured prototype. However odd, this is indeed part of the story. (It should not seem *so* odd. The "semantic" view of theories [van Fraassen 1980] makes a similar move when it construes an entire theory as a single complex predicate.) In any case, this is the account that emerges on p. 236, where I refer to the phenomenon of multiple conceptual competence. The account is then put to systematic work in my subsequent discussion of mere conceptual redeployment vs. outright conceptual change.

Glymour shows some comprehension of this shift in emphasis—from points in weight space to partitions across activation space—but he gets it garbled. He ascribes to me the view that a concept or theory is "a partition of *weight* space" (italics mine). This is nonsense. There are no relevant partitions in weight space, only positions and learning trajectories.

It is the *activation* space that accumulates an intricate set of useful partitions in the course of learning.

Glymour complains that I leave entirely unaddressed the question of how two people share the same theory. He will find explicit discussions on pp. 171 and 234 of *NCP* (see also chapter 7 of this book). My long discussion of conceptual redeployment (pp. 237–41) includes a further account of how two people can share a theory—the theory of waves, for example–while differing in the domains where they count it true. Huygens, for example, thought this theory true of light, while Newton did not. Huygens and Newton share the theory because they have a relevantly similar set of partitions across their activation spaces (i.e., they possess closely similar prototypes), which produce relevantly similar cognitive, verbal, and manipulative behavior when the shared prototype is activated. But they differ in their respective commitments to the theory because in Huygens the prototype is typically activated when he confronts water waves, sound waves, *and* light waves, while in Newton it is typically activated only in the first two cases. When Newton confronts optical phenomena, in the appropriate cognitive context, it is rather a *ballistic particle* prototype that typically gets activated.

As with duck/rabbit figures, one can choose, or learn, to apprehend some part of the world in quite different ways. One can systematically apprehend optical phenomena as wave phenomena, or as particle phenomena. And one can explore at length the subsequent rewards or disappointments that each mode of apprehension brings with it. In this way are theories "tested," whether one is a juvenile mouse or an aging human scientist.

This sketch leaves open all of the details of learning, to be sure. But that is deliberate. Just what theory of learning we should embrace as descriptive of normal, healthy brains is still a profoundly open question, as I emphasized on p. 187 in closing a survey discussion of the existing neurocomputational wisdom on the topic. Closing that question requires a great deal more empirical research into the functional plasticity of the nervous system. I cannot close that question a priori. And neither can Glymour. But one can draw a provisional lesson at this point about the kinematical framework within which any comprehensive theory of human and animal learning must function: it will be a kinematics of synaptic weight configurations and of prototype activations across vast populations of neurons. The familiar kinematics of sentences will come in only derivatively and peripherally, if it comes in at all.

I am puzzled to find Glymour claiming that none of the preceding questions is even addressed in chapters 9 through 11 of *NCP*. They are all addressed, repeatedly and in depth. And my answers are not hard to find. The index at the back of *NCP* will lead one to all of the page references cited above, and more.

On the issue of theory-ladenness I shall here say little. My paper on the philosophy of Paul Feyerabend (chapter 15) contains a detailed discussion of the matter as reconstructed in neurocomputational terms. It will support the following brief response to Glymour's criticisms. The fact of many configurational alternatives is only one part of the story, which is why Glymour has trouble seeing the connection. The second part concerns the fact that no cognitive activity occurs save as information is processed through some one of those many possible configurations of synaptic weights. And the third part is that any weight configuration represents or realizes a speculative framework or theory as to the structure of some part of the world. It follows that any cognitive activity—perception included—presupposes a speculative theory.

This account does indeed portray unmodulated coding at the absolute sensory periphery as being free of theory, as Glymour and I both remark (*NCP*, p. 189; Glymour, *MSPS*, p. 355). But it also leaves it outside the domain of cognitive activity. Peripheral transduction is just that: transduction of one form of energy into another. Cognitive activity does not begin until the coded input vector hits the first bank of weighted connections. From that point onward, the input is (not just energetically but informationally) transformed into the speculative framework of the creature's acquired theories; it is represented as a point in the speculatively partitioned and antecedently structured space of possible neuronal activation patterns. In short, it is theory-laden.

Glymour concludes by remarking on the lack of any substantial methodological or normative contributions in *NCP*. There is some point to his complaint. My concerns are indeed primarily descriptive and explanatory. Yet I am again puzzled to hear him make the strong claim that normative questions are not even recognized, especially if he has in mind, as he says, the evaluation of *explanations*, and the matter of how good ones fit into a reliable empirical method. For I have discussed precisely this question at length, and proposed an explicit answer. It is cataloged in my index, under "Explanation, evaluation of, 220–223."

I there explore four dimensions in which explanatory understanding, construed as prototype activation, can be evaluated within a neuro-computational framework. The most important of these, in the present context, is the dimension of *simplicity. Ceteris paribus*, an activated prototype is better if it is a part of the most *unified* conceptual con-figuration. What simplicity and unity amount to is discussed in *NCP*, chapter 9, pp. 179–81, where it is observed that networks that have formed the simplest or most unified partitions across their activation spaces are networks that do much better at generalizing their knowledge to novel cases. Very briefly, they do better at recognizing novel situations for what they are, because they have generated a relevantly unified similarity gradient that will catch novel cases in the same subvolume that catches the training cases.

The account thus proposes a novel account of what simplicity or unity is, and of why it is an epistemic virtue. This result seemed especially en-couraging to me, since it constitutes an unexpected success on the *normative* front, and at a specific place, moreover, where the traditional approaches have proved a chronic failure. Be that as it may, the question was certainly addressed, and I would have been interested in Glymour's criticisms of the answer proposed.

As I see it, our normative and methodological insights are very likely to flourish as our explanatory insight into neural function and neural plasticity increases. But as I remark on p. 220, we are too early in the latter game to draw very much from it yet. Glymour complains that I have drawn too little. My concern is that I may have tried to draw too much.

I conclude by pointing to an important background difference between Glymour and me, one that peeks out at two or three points in his paper, a difference that may do something to explain the divergent evaluations we display elsewhere. Glymour evidently regards as unproblematic the "elementary [distinction] between a theory, or a system of claims, and the physical/computational states someone is in when he has a system of beliefs." (I, in any case, am charged with missing it.) And to judge from his remarks in paragraphs 4 and 7, Glymour also regards the kinematics of beliefs and other propositional attitudes as unproblematic.

People familiar with my earlier work in the philosophy of mind will recall that I find both of these things to be problematic in the extreme, and for reasons quite independent of traditional issues in the philosophy of science. For reasons outlined in many places, including chapter 1 of *NCP*, I am strongly inclined toward a revisionary or eliminative materialism concerning the mind. From such a perspective one is more or less compelled to seek an epistemology and a philosophy of science of the character at issue. From Glymour's more conservative perspective, that approach is bound to seem mad. I quite understand this. But my answer is simple. Glymour is mistaken in both areas.

17

To Transform the Phenomena: Feyerabend, Proliferation, and Recurrent Neural Networks

Paul M. Churchland

Paul Feyerabend recommended the methodological policy of proliferating competing theories as a means of uncovering new empirical data, and thus as a means of increasing the empirical constraints that all theories must confront. Feyerabend's policy is here defended as a clear consequence of connectionist models of explanatory understanding and learning. An earlier connectionist "vindication" is criticized, and a more realistic and penetrating account is offered in terms of the computationally plastic cognitive profile displayed by neural networks with a recurrent architecture.

1. Introduction

Some years ago, I picked out five salient epistemological theses in the writings of Paul Feyerabend, and I attempted to show that those same five theses flowed naturally, and independently, from the emerging discipline of computational neuroscience (see chapter 15). In short, the claim was that a "connectionist" model of cognitive activity successfully reduces a Feyerabendian philosophy of science. Specifically, the inevitable theory-ladenness of perception, the displaceability of folk psychology, the incommensurability of many theoretical alternatives, the permanent need for proliferating theoretical alternatives, and the need even for proliferating methodologies—all of these modestly radical theses emerge as presumptive lessons of cognitive neurobiology, or so I then claimed. This convergence of principle was arresting to me for all of the obvious reasons, but also because the five theses at issue no longer seemed radical at all, once they were assembled in neurocomputational dress. They seemed harmless and benign, almost reassuring.

I take up the topic again partly because of the occasion of this symposium, but also because the case now seems to me importantly stronger than it did then. In particular, an additional argument has emerged for the fourth of the five Feyerabendian theses, namely, the methodological virtue of proliferating large-scale theoretical or conceptual *alternatives* to currently dominant theories, even when (especially when) those dominant theories are "empirically adequate." The new argument derives from our increased understanding of the computational capacities and the cognitive profile of what are called *recurrent* neural networks. To outline that argument and explore that profile is the main task of this brief essay.

2.   Proliferation: The Original Argument

Feyerabend's argument for the desirability of proliferating competing theories went substantially beyond the widely acknowledged fact that data always underdetermine theory. Given that there is always an infinity of possible explanations for any finite set of data, it remains a permanent possibility that one's current explanatory hypothesis, no matter how successful, is inferior to some alternative hypothesis yet to be articulated. To this much, all may agree. And all may agree that this provides at least some rationale for the proliferation of theories.

But Feyerabend made a further claim. Alternative theories, he argued, have the capacity not just to offer competing and potentially superior explanations of one and the same set of data; they have the unique potential for *transforming* the available data itself, in welcome and revealing ways, and for finding *additional* data where before there seemed nothing but intractable chaos or meaningless noise.

This position is already voiced in Feyerabend's earliest papers. It is a consequence of the fully *theoretical* character of all so-called "observation reports": different theories brought to the very same experimental situation will fund interestingly different families of observation reports (Feyerabend 1958). It is also a consequence of the fact that one's own sense organs, no less than any other physical instruments of measurement or detection, always require some conceptual *interpretation* of the significance of their inevitably complex behavior: distinct theories will not only fund distinct interpretations—they will also select out, as informationally significant in the first place, different elements of that complex behavioral profile (Feyerabend 1962).

Both of these arguments, however, were a fairly hard sell at the time. The first required dumping an entire epistemological theory: classical foundational empiricism. And the second required the adoption of a radically naturalist interpretation of human cognition. Few were moved.

Fortunately, Feyerabend found an arresting way to make the desired point without requiring from his readers a prior commitment to these radical premises. In "How to Be a Good Empiricist—A Plea for Tolerance in Matters Epistemological" (1963b), he cited the case of Brownian motion as a telling illustration of the transformation of intractable chaos and meaningless noise into systematic and revealing empirical data. Brownian motion, you will recall, is the ceaseless zigzag jittering motion of, for example, microscopic pollen grains suspended in water, or smoke particles suspended in air. Its initial discovery in 1827 had no impact on anything, but there was a small puzzle concerning the cause of that ceaseless motion. Robert Brown himself, a gentleman naturalist skilled with the microscope, guessed first that he was seeing the locomotor behavior of tiny animals. But this could not account for the motion of the (clearly nonbiological) smoke particles. Something else was going on, but it was unclear what it might be. The motion of a Brownian particle was an unpredictable rotational and translational meander in three-dimensional space. And it was far from clear that its evidently random dance had any significance at all, even for biology, let alone for physics. It sat more or less quietly, without an agreed-upon explanation, for the better part of a century.

As we now understand it, however, the motion of a Brownian particle is one of the most direct experimental manifestations available of both the molecular constitution of matter and the kinetic character of heat. The smoke particles' motion is caused by the individual impacts of the millions of fast-moving air molecules that surround it. The smoke particle is just large enough to be seen in the microscope, yet still small enough to show the effects of the erratic hail of submicroscopic ballistic particles rattling it from every side. Individually, those molecules have motion in that, collectively, they have a temperature above absolute zero. And they continue moving, *ceaselessly*, because they interact with one another in a series of perfectly elastic collisions.

Such a system, remarks Feyerabend, constitutes a perpetual motion machine of the second kind—a system of mechanical interactions in which no kinetic energy is dissipated as heat. The phenomenon of Brownian motion is thus a standing refutation of the classical second law of thermodynamics, then one of the best-confirmed "empirical laws" of classical physics. And yet it is far from clear, just from looking at it, that Brownian motion has this giant-killing character. It does not look like much of anything but empty noise. So long as one approaches a Brownian particle with classical thermodynamics in hand, its motion remains an intractable chaos with no clear relevance to anything.

If, however, one approaches the Brownian smoke particle with the quite different assumptions of the kinetic-corpuscular theory of heat, its behavioral profile suddenly teems with potential significance. The permanence of that puzzling motion is only the first of many giveaways. For example, if heat truly is nothing more than molecular motion, then increasing the temperature of the gas should increase that motion, and thus should increase the violence of the smoke particles' jittering dance. Correlatively, lowering the gas's temperature should reduce the violence of that dance. And so it does.

Further, raising (or lowering) the pressure of the gas will raise (or lower) the number of molecules colliding with the smoke particle each second, thus smoothing (or aggravating) the observable character of its motion. And if we hold both temperature and pressure constant, but vary the elemental gas in which the particle is suspended, we should get slightly different Brownian motions for each gas: in hydrogen at standard temperature and pressure (STP), a Brownian particle will receive many more (but much gentler) impacts per second than it will receive in oxygen at STP, because a hydrogen molecule is only one-sixteenth as massive as an oxygen molecule. Brownian motion should thus be more jagged in oxygen than in hydrogen, and progressively more jagged still in carbon dioxide, krypton, and xenon.

Finally—and most important, historically—if the volume of gas is placed in a gravitational field, then the (much more massive) smoke particles suspended within it will collectively behave like a miniature "atmosphere." On average, each particle will have a translational energy of $3kT/2$, but in fact there will be a statistical distribution around that mean value. This means that some of the smoke particles will have more energy than others, and will thus be found at higher altitudes than others, although the density of such high flyers will fall off exponentially with increasing altitude, just as with the Earth's atmosphere itself. The experiments of Jean Perrin in 1908, with gum resin particles suspended in a liquid, revealed just such an exponentially fading vertical distribution of those Brownian particles. And from the details of that distribution, he was even able to deduce a credible value for Avogadro's number, a value that cohered well with the values reached by wholly unrelated methods.

Thus the early positive case for the corpuscular-kinetic theory. But let us not forget that all of this novel or reinterpreted data was at the same time a devastating critique of the classical theories of heat, which could not begin to account for any of it; and of the classical second law, which asserted the impossibility of the perfectly elastic mechanical interactions that the new theory required, and that the ceaseless jittering of the Brownian particles seemed to reflect.

The point Feyerabend wished to make in recalling all of this was that, without the organizing perspective of the kinetic-corpuscular theory of heat, the subtle information implicit in the broad range of Brownian behaviors would never have emerged from the shadows in which it was buried. Brownian motion, of course, *is* noise. But it is noise with a well-behaved and interestingly variable profile. Brownian motion is a clear historical case where our appreciation of the significance, and even the existence, of robustly repeatable experimental data depended decisively on our approaching the empirical world with a specific theory in mind.

Thus the virtue of proliferating candidate theories in any domain: it occasionally enables us to find a new significance in old data, and to uncover and appreciate new empirical data, data which can then serve to constrain our theoretical beliefs more tightly and more responsibly than would otherwise have been possible. In the end, then, it is not the counsel of a romantic and uncritical pluralism. It is just the reverse: it is a reasoned strategy for enhancing the range of *empirical* criticisms that any theory must face. (Sections 5 and 9 of Feyerabend's 1963b paper make this interpretation perfectly clear.)

3. Proliferation: An Old Neurocomputational Argument

My 1991 paper (chapter 15) attempted to construct a neurocomputational rationale for the virtue of the Feyerabendian policy of proliferation.

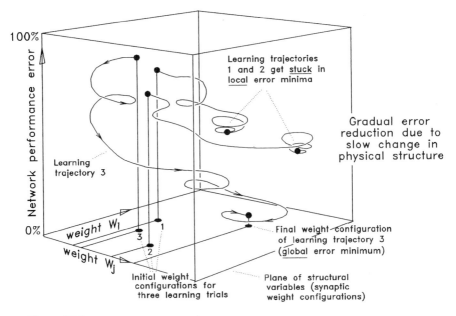

100% — Network performance error — 0%

Learning trajectories
1 and 2 get <u>stuck</u> in
local error minima

Gradual error
reduction due to
slow change in
physical structure

Learning
trajectory 3

weight W_i

weight W_j

Final weight configuration
of learning trajectory 3
(global error minimum)

Initial weight
configurations for
three learning trials

Plane of structural
variables (synaptic
weight configurations)

Figure 17.1

If we assume that humans are multilayered neural networks that learn, under the continuing pressure of experience, by the gradual modification of the strengths or "weights" of their myriad synaptic connections, then we should be aware of a common wrinkle in their learning behavior that is evident in even the simplest of artificial models. Specifically, how well a given network manages to learn a certain task (a complex discrimination task, for example) is quite sensitive to the initial configuration of the network's synaptic weights. The same network, subjected to the same training examples, and guided by the same learning algorithm, will often "bottom out," at very different levels of performance, depending on the particular structural/cognitive state it happened to occupy when the training began. As illustrated in figure 17.1, the amount of learning (= error reduction) that takes place is *path sensitive*: from some regions in synaptic weight space, the network is doomed to slide into a merely local minimum in the overall error landscape, a minimum from which no series of training examples will ever dislodge it. That is to say, a network can quite properly learn its way into a cognitive configuration that yields nontrivial performance, but then be utterly unable to profit further from continued exposure to the data. The network gets "stuck" in a merely local error minimum. It gets captured, as it were, by a "false paradigm."

To maximize the likelihood that we find the weight configuration that yields the *global* error minimum (that is, *maximal* performance), it is therefore wise to submit our network to the same training regime several times, starting with a different *initial* configuration each time. In this way we can escape the blinkers inevitably imposed by each of a large range of (unfortunate) initial cognitive states. The lesson for humans, I then suggested, was that we should encourage the proliferation of different intellectual schools, theoretical perspectives, or research programs, in order to achieve the same goal in ourselves.

The point is legitimate, but I now think the analogy is strained. For one thing, a single human individual cannot hope to modify his synaptic weight configuration with the ease with which a computer modeler can manipulate an artificial neural network. An adult human's synaptic weights are not open to casual change of the kind required. In adults, they mostly do not change at all. Hopping briskly around in weight space, thence to explore different learning trajectories, is impossible advice to an individual human. My original advice, therefore, can be realistic only for *groups* of humans, where distinct persons pursue distinct paths.

Second, I doubt it is true, as the analogy implies, that theoretical progress consists in the gradual modification of the synaptic weight configurations of the world's scientists, either individually or collectively. The initial *training* of those scientists presumably does consist in such a drawn-out process. But the occasional and dramatic post-training cognitive achievements that we prize seem to involve a different kinematics, and a different dynamics. Most obviously, the time scales are wrong. Major scientific discoveries, from Archimedes' "Eureka!" through Newton's falling apple/moon at Woolsthorp to Röntgen's identification of x-rays, regularly take place on a time scale ranging from a critical few seconds to a critical several days, whereas major synaptic reorganization in the brain takes place on a time scale of months to years. Evidently, humans command a mechanism for conceptual change that is much swifter than the structural reconfigurations that synaptic change involves.

Third, the process of synaptic reconfiguration—to achieve new modes of data processing—entails the simultaneous destruction and abandonment of *old* modes of data processing, the ones embodied in the old synaptic configuration. But we humans are quite able to reconceive data without thereby losing competence in the application of old conceptual frameworks.

These difficulties, and others, would seem to demand a quite different account of the sort of interpretational plasticity displayed in Feyerabend's Brownian motion example, and in other historical examples of the reconceptualization of experimental data. Fortunately, multilayer neural networks with "descending" or "recurrent" axonal pathways provide the elements of such an account. This possibility was scouted very briefly (and rather timorously) in my 1989b. Let me here try to do better.

4.   Proliferation: A New Neurocomputational Argument

The contrast between purely feedforward networks and recurrent networks is schematically displayed in figure 17.2. For our purposes, perhaps

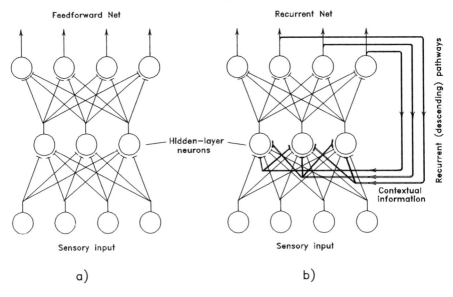

Figure 17.2

the most important difference is as follows. In the purely feedforward case in figure 17.2a, the network's activation-pattern response, across the "hidden"-layer neurons, to any pattern of activation levels across the input layer, is dictated entirely by the configuration of synaptic weights that connect those two layers. So long as those weights remain fixed, the same input will always produce the same response (= pattern of activations) at the hidden layer.

In the recurrent case in figure 17.2b, however, the hidden-layer neurons receive axonal input from *two* sources rather than just one. As before, the initial "sensory" layer is one of those sources. But there is also a secondary source of information, a source located higher up in the network's data-processing hierarchy. The cartoon sketch in figure 17.2b portrays a recurrent loop that reaches back a single layer, but in multi-layer networks such as the human brain, such descending pathways often reach back two, three, or even many layers. (At this point, take a quick look at the puzzling and degraded graphical items shown in figure 17.3, and then return to the next paragraph.)

Such recurrent information serves to *modulate* the activational behavior of the neurons at the first hidden layer. It can provide a temporary perceptual or interpretational *bias* above and beyond the discriminational biases permanently embodied in the network as a result of its prior training and its relatively fixed configuration of synaptic weights. The recurrent information can slightly "preactivate" the hidden-layer neurons in the direction of a specific, already learned, discriminational category. The result can be that a severely degraded or partial input at the sensory layer will, thanks to the specific character of that recurrent priming, successfully produce the usual or canonical activation pattern (across the hidden-layer neurons) for that learned category. A discrimination that might have been difficult or impossible, in the absence of the recurrent modulation, can be a quick and easy discrimination in its presence. Trained networks tend presumptively to "fill in" missing information in any case—the phenomenon is called *vector completion*—but recurrent modulation can make a decisive difference between success and failure in any given case.

The graphical items you observed in figure 17.3 will serve to illustrate the principle. Quite likely, neither one of them made much sense to you.

a)

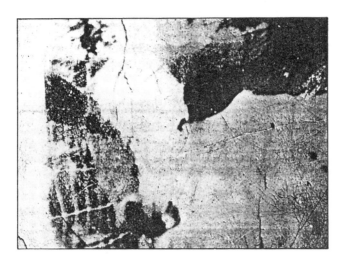

b)

Figure 17.3

But observe them again with the following information in mind. Figure 17.3a is a portly floor washer with bucket, seen from behind. Figure 17.3b is a close-up of a cow, with its face taking up most of the left half of the picture. A rectangular-grid wire fence can be seen at the lower left, behind the cow, whose shoulder and back lie at the upper-middle right. If you did not see these figures before, you will almost certainly see them now. And seeing them puts you in a position to anticipate the specific ways in which they are likely to behave over time, or in response to changing circumstances. Such behavior, therefore, will display a significance to the prepared observer that would otherwise be absent.

The cognitive activity of a recurrent network, plainly, is a function not just of its physical structure and its current sensory input. It is also a function of the prior *dynamical* state of the entire system. It is a function of the network's prior frame of mind, of the "concerns" it was then addressing, of the "take" it already had on its sensory environment, of the direction of the "attention" it happened then to be paying. We have here a *dynamical* mechanism whereby a network can display, on a very short time scale, quite different cognitive responses to one and the same sensory input. Depending on the contextual information possessed by the network, what gets categorized as chaos or noise in one condition gets recognized as something familiar in another.

A third example will bring out a related point. Observe the scarf-shrouded old woman in figure 17.4, with her large bony nose, her chin buried in her woolly shawl, her vacant gaze and toothless mouth. This is an easy figure and probably you would have come to the same recognition without any help from me. But now that your visual system is firmly captured by one dynamical attractor or prototypical category, consider the possibility that you have completely misinterpreted the figure before you, that there is an alternative and much more realistic take on it. Specifically, it is a *young* woman that you are looking at. She is facing away from you, the tip of her nose barely visible beyond her left cheek. What you took to be the left nostril of a large nose is in fact the left jawbone of an entire face, and what you took to be a glazed eye is in fact a perfectly normal ear. Very likely you now see a different organization within figure 17.4, and you can probably say what the horizontal slash of the old woman's "mouth" really is.[1]

Figure 17.4

Once again, recurrent modulation of the activity of your visual system results in a transformation of the scene before you. And in this third case, it represents an escape not just from chaos and confusion, but from a highly compelling alternative conceptualization, one that might have held you captive indefinitely had you been denied the cognitive assistance of an explicit alternative account.

Elsewhere (1989c) I have argued that perceptual recognition is just one species of explanatory understanding, and that explanatory understanding consists in the activation of one of one's antecedently learned prototype vectors. I call this the *prototype-activation* or P-A model of explanatory understanding, and I commend its sundry virtues for your critical evaluation. On this occasion, I wish only to repeat the following claim. Large-scale theoretical or explanatory advances in our scientific understanding typically consist in the fairly swift redeployment and sub-sequent exploitation, in domains both familiar and novel, of prototypes already learned from prior experience. To cite some familiar examples: planetary motion turns out to be an instance of *projectile motion*, though

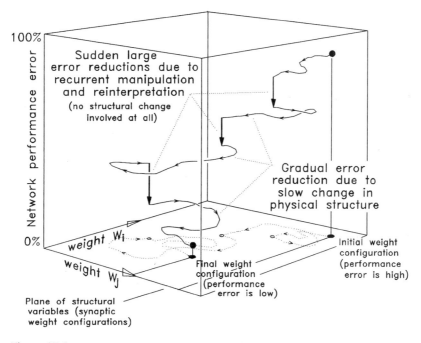

Figure 17.5

on an unexpectedly large scale; light turns out to be *transverse waves* of some sort, though of an unprecedentedly high frequency; and heat turns out to be just the *energy of motion*, although on an unexpectedly small scale.

With recurrent-network models of cognition, we can account for both the initial acquisition of such prototypical categories (by slow learning at the hands of repeated experience and gradual synaptic change), and their occasional and highly profitable redeployment (at the hands of recurrent modulation of our perceptual activity) in domains *outside* the domain of their original acquisition. This two-process model of cognitive activity is represented in figure 17.5. In contrast to figure 17.1, the learning trajectories here display an occasional discontinuous drop in the error dimension, a drop in performance error that is not owed to any structural (synaptic) changes whatever. The sudden achievement of new levels of performance is owed entirely to *dynamical* factors that go unrepresented in a typical weight-error diagram. Those dynamical factors consist of the ongoing activational states of the entire network. What is evident from the diagrams, and from the preceding discussion, is that the dynamical system of the human brain can occasionally wander into a new region of its vast activational space, a region in which its existing cognitive capacities are put to entirely novel uses, a region in which at least some of its perceptual activities are systematically transformed, thanks to a new regime of recurrent modulation of those activities. Once that regime is in place, one's perceptual exploration of the world can find structure and organization that would otherwise have remained invisible.

If this is even roughly how human cognition works, then there is a clear and powerful argument for a policy of trying to bring new and unorthodox theories to bear on any domain where we prize increased understanding: we will not gain the occasional benefits of a systematically transformed and potentially augmented experience if we do not explore the vehicles most likely to provide it, namely alternative theories.

5. Concluding Remarks

Feyerabend, I think, was clearly right in recommending proliferation as a virtuous policy. I hope I have (finally) provided an adequate account, in neurocomputational terms, of why he was right to do so. The politics of administrating such a policy, to be sure, remain to be discussed. Thomas Kuhn *shared* Paul Feyerabend's "radical" views on the plasticity and theory-laden character of our perceptual experience, and yet Kuhn recommended a very conservative policy that focuses most of our research resources on the currently dominant paradigm. Kuhn had arguments of his own. For example, a "transformed experience" on the part of a few scattered individuals will not serve to move our collective understanding forward unless there exists a widely shared framework of understanding and evaluation to which such novel "results" can be brought for responsible examination and subsequent dissemination. A shared framework of this kind is of such immense value to the learning process that it must be positively protected from the casual predations of unorthodox enthusiasms, which will always be with us.

I am unable to arbitrate these competing tensions here, and will not try to do so. I confess that my political impulse inclines to Kuhn: it is a chaotic world out there and we must prize the monumental achievements of our institutions of scientific research and education. But my epistemological impulses, and my heart, incline to Feyerabend. Modern science is easily tough enough to tolerate, and even to encourage, the permanent proliferation of competing theories. We need only keep our standards high for evaluating their success. Maximizing the severity of those standards, it is arguable, was Feyerabend's ultimate aim.

18

How Parapsychology Could Become a Science

Paul M. Churchland

An important methodological argument is outlined in support of general theoretical challenges to the dominant materialist paradigm. The idea is that the empirical inadequacies of a dominant theory can be hidden from view by various factors, and will emerge from the shadows only when viewed from the perspective of a systematic conceptual alternative. The question then posed is whether parapsychology provides a conceptual alternative adequate to this task. The provisional conclusion drawn is that it does not. Some further consequences are drawn from this concerning the experimental side of the parapsychological tradition.

My title gives me away, but not entirely. Parapsychology, as currently practiced, does not seem to me to be a genuine science. Or more accurately, since these things are a matter of degree, parapsychology seems to me to display an exceedingly low grade of scientific activity, worthy of most of the skepticism and the indifference it engenders in the rest of the scientific community. On the other hand, I think it could become a respectable science. What I wish to explore is how it might do so.

I. An Argument for Tolerance

My initial approach to these issues is from the standpoint of a materialist. That is to say, I am profoundly moved by the extraordinary empirical success of the various physical sciences, from subatomic physics up through biochemistry, evolutionary biology, the neurosciences, astronomy, cosmology, and natural history. The systematic and interlocking success of these sciences requires us to take very seriously the hypothesis that all phenomena in the universe, without exception, arise from the intricate articulation of a relatively small variety of purely physical elements acting in accordance with a relatively small variety of purely physical laws.

In particular, it seems overwhelmingly likely to me that all of the phenomena displayed in sentient creatures are likewise just a further instance and articulation of the properties of law-governed physical matter. We are evidently made of matter. We evolved, by a complex but purely physical process, from earlier and simpler organisms, also made of matter, whose lineage leads us back to a purely chemical primordial soup. And our sensory, cognitive, and motor activities, to the extent that we understand them, are just a further mix of chemical, electrical, and mechanical goings on. The appeal of this broadly grounded conceptual framework is one of the principal reasons why the vast majority of scientists find claims of "psychic" phenomena to be so implausible, for these claims are incompatible with the materialist's well-grounded conception of the universe and our place in it.

On the other hand, I am sensible that this standpoint may be mistaken. Its explanatory success to date, no matter how broadly based, does not guarantee its truth. Other frameworks, at other points in history, have enjoyed a similar dominion over the range of human experience, yet have proved in the end to be quite wrong. The organismic Aristotelian hegemony comes to mind here. In that case, it was the very comprehensiveness of the overall world-view that tended to blind us to the many failures that became apparent under close focus. Perhaps the modern materialist is similarly blinkered. And perhaps the research carried out under the banner of parapsychology is just the sort we need to set us free.

How likely this is, we shall discuss in due course. We shall have to weigh the systematic success of the physical sciences against the claims of the parapsychologists, who will insist that there are a variety of experimental results that cannot be explained in terms of existing physical science. I am going to avoid this empirical issue for a few more pages, however, since there is a purely *methodological* argument that can be raised in support of the rationality of pursuing parapsychological research, however strong might be the substantive evidential position enjoyed by materialism.

The argument derives from Paul Feyerabend (1963b), and has nothing essential to do with the virtues or vices of parapsychology. Feyerabend points out that sometimes the only way to discover the truly significant empirical inadequacies in an old and deeply entrenched theory is to construct alternative theories with which to provide entirely *new* interpretations of the old and familiar experimental data. Any successful theory quite properly ignores or suppresses a good deal of faintly troublesome empirical evidence as irrelevant and inevitable "noise." No theory ever fits all of the experimental data perfectly, if for no other reason than that the experimental situations that test them always embody a horizon of subtle detail beyond which we have neither knowledge nor control. Over that horizon lie the inevitable elements that are too minor, too complex, and too inaccessible to be worth trying to unravel or control. Small discrepancies between the favored theory and the results of experiment can therefore often be ascribed to the noisy activity of factors just over the horizon of controllable detail.

There is no essential vice in this. The alternative is to try to control the position and character of every particle in the universe. Instead, we control as much as we think it is necessary and prudent to control, and let the rest go. And those experimental areas where we cannot hope to control the details we do believe to be relevant, we simply avoid as intractable and unrevealing. The favored theory may not illuminate them, but its current "failure" to do so is not regarded as any strike against it.

It remains possible, however, that the important empirical facts that reflect the falsehood of the favored and so far "successful" theory are to be found in precisely those experimental areas thought to be intractable, or are to be found just over the horizon of controlled detail in areas that are tractable. In such cases the favored theory enjoys a safety from refutation that it does not deserve. The refuting facts are there, but for complex reasons they are difficult or impossible to see, at least while we continue to interpret the situation in terms of the favored theory. For it is that same theory that helps us decide which details are relevant and which are irrelevant, and which situations are tractable and which are intractable.

The best way to escape from such a predicament, suggests Feyerabend, is to construct a comparably general *alternative* theory with which to generate entirely new interpretations of the experimental data, of which details are and are not relevant, and of which situations are and are not tractable. This can have the effect of highlighting certain details hitherto suppressed, of pulling new signal out of old noise, and of discovering important order where before we saw only chaos. In particular, such a reconfigured vision can reveal dramatic failures in the old theory, failures that were invisible, as failures, from within the old framework.

Feyerabend provides a striking example of this phenomenon, which is worth a brief summary. The reader will forgive me if I oversimplify the physics somewhat in order to highlight the methodological point.

The "old entrenched theory" of this story is the classical theory of heat and energy, which contained as one of its central elements the principle that all mechanical interactions involve at least some conversion of the mechanical energy involved into heat. This means that any isolated system of bodies in motion must eventually "run down," in the way that the balls on a billiard table, after bouncing off the cushion and each other for a time, come eventually to rest, their kinetic (mechanical) energy having been dissipated throughout the system in the form of heat. They, and the cushions, and the surrounding air, have a slightly higher temperature than they did before being set in motion.

The important point here is the generality of the principle—called the second law of Classical Thermodynamics. According to this principle, *any* system of mechanical interactions closed to the entry of outside energy— a turning flywheel, an oscillating pendulum, a swarm of Ping-Pong balls bouncing in a box—must eventually run down and come to rest.

The "important falsifying phenomenon" of this story is Brownian motion, discovered by the botanist Robert Brown in the early nineteenth century. Brownian motion is the ceaseless agitation of microscopic particles suspended in water or air, such as plant spores or smoke particles. The chaotic and apparently undiminished motion of such particles can be seen, and often was seen, through a microscope, but it was not seen to have anything crucial to do with classical thermodynamics and the second law. Brown's initial guess as to the nature of this barely detectable motion appealed to biology: the spores after all, were alive. The equally active but lifeless smoke particles scotched that hypothesis, but there was still no significant threat to the second law. Who could be sure whether or not new energy was constantly being supplied from some microscopic source, and who could possibly compile an accurate energy budget for such fantastically small particles or the diffuse medium in which they were suspended, in order to see whether or not it all squared with the demands of the classical theory? Such things were beyond experimental determination. And so Brownian motion remained at most a minor puzzle to the classical theorist, if it was noticed at all, which for the most part it wasn't. The classical theory strode the landscape like an unchallenged giant.

But not for long. An alternative and comparably general theory of heat was eventually developed, from motives that had nothing to do with Brownian motion. This theory—the modern kinetic theory of heat—proposed that heat energy is nothing but a special case of mechanical (kinetic) energy, to wit, the mechanical energy of the *molecules* of which common solids, liquids, and gases are composed. They too have motion, bouncing around chaotically or oscillating busily away down at the submicroscopic level. The temperature of any body was claimed to be nothing but a measure of how vigorously its constituent molecules are knocking about. And the inevitable "conversion" of macrolevel kinetic energy into heat, so insisted upon by the classical second law, turns out to be nothing but the redistribution of kinetic energy from the macro- to the microlevel. A bouncing ball eventually comes to rest, but only because its chaotically bustling molecules, and those of the air and the floor, each take on a tiny part of the motion that used to be so coherently lodged in the unified motion of the ball as a whole. The ball is now still, but faintly warmer, as is the floor and the surrounding air. The ball's original energy lives on as an increase in the activity of its bustling molecules, and of the molecules of the floor and the surrounding air.

But what of the bouncing molecules themselves? Will they not dissipate *their* kinetic energy as they bounce off each other, just as the ball does? Will they not come finally to rest also—still, but faintly warmer? No, said the kinetic theory. Molecular interactions are *perfectly elastic*—which is just another way of saying that no energy is lost in any such interaction—and so the particles go on bouncing happily away forever. Molecules cannot dissipate their kinetic energy away into heat, because their motion is already what constitutes heat. A closed system of bouncing molecules, therefore, will *never run down*.

This theory was not well received by the majority, and understandably so. For one thing, it postulated entities of a size that specifically precluded their ever being observed by humans. And for another, these constitutionally "shy" particles were supposed to be perfectly (*perfectly*) elastic in their mutual collisions, in direct contradiction to the well-founded classical second law. On the face of things, it was both methodologically suspect and factually improbable.

How to test this startling new theory concerning the nature of heat? There were many ways, but only one of them need concern us here. Molecules were too small to be seen, even with a microscope, so there was clearly no hope of seeing directly whether a warm gas consists of molecules in ceaseless motion. However, if we suspend particles in the gas, particles small enough to be knocked around by the bustling gas molecules on every side, but large enough to be seen, at least with a microscope, then the ceaseless motion of the molecules will be reflected in a ceaseless dance on the part of the suspended particles. That is to say, if the kinetic theory of heat is true, then Brownian motion ought to exist! Futhermore, the violence of that motion should be directly proportional to the absolute temperature of the gas (the faster the molecules are moving, the more the smoke particles will be bounced around); and the violence of that motion should be inversely proportional to the size of the suspended smoke particles (the smaller the smoke particles, the more easily they will be shoved around). Further still, the kinetic theory made predictions about the gravitational distribution of smoke particles as a function of temperature, and it yielded a nice derivation of the classical gas law as well. But we need not go into these here. Suffice it to say that all of these predictions were experimentally accessible, and all of them were corroborated in detail.

In this way did a minor curiosity, of dubious relevance to anything, emerge as a major phenomenon. It revealed the hidden character of both matter and heat, and it constituted a standing refutation of the classical second law. But it did so only because a new theory showed us a new way to make sense of it. Had we stuck to the categories and vision of the classical theory, the significance of Brownian motion might never have been appreciated.

The moral of the story is that we should always be tolerant of the proliferation of theoretical viewpoints. Indeed, we should actively encourage it, even if our current theories suffer no obvious empirical shortcomings. This does not mean that we should put aside successful

theories and productive research programs in order to pursue every cock-
amamy idea that comes down the pike. That would be uncritical, irre-
sponsible, and monstrously inefficient. But it does mean that we should
be wary of conceptual monopoly, however well earned. And it means we
should always be solicitous of genuine attempts to articulate and explore
interesting conceptual alternatives.

II. Parapsychology: The Theoretical Side

Can we properly apply this moral to the case of parapsychology? I believe we can. But it has not been my aim to conjure up a limp apologia
for "psychic" explorations, and then walk away. What I have in mind,
rather, is this. The kinetic theory of heat is a clear example of a scientific
success won against great odds. What general features of that theory,
and/or what features of the methodology of its proponents, made it such
a success? If we can answer this question, then we can confront the next
logical question. Do the theories proposed and the methodology displayed by the proponents of parapsychology have anything like the same
virtuous features displayed in our benchmark case? Let us see.

The first advantage possessed by the kinetic theorists was a systematic
and detailed alternative *theory* concerning the phenomena in question.
The new theory specified that any gas, for example, was constituted by
a large number of perfectly elastic particles having mass, volume, and
velocity. It told us that the steady pressure exerted by the gas on the walls
of any container is just the effect of the particles repeatedly bouncing off
it. It stated that the total heat in any system is the sum of the kinetic energy of all its molecules. It told us that the global temperature of the
system is just the kinetic energy level of one of its average molecules. And
since the notions of mass, velocity, and kinetic energy were quite well
understood by then, the whole range of submicroscopic activity could be
addressed with the language and the laws of classical Newtonian mechanics. Kinetic theorists could address the phenomena confronting them
with an impressive array of theoretical resources.

Of course there were many things that remained to be unraveled—the
mass and velocity of the proposed corpuscles, the different heat capacities
displayed by different substances, and the disappearance of latent heat

during melting and boiling. But the theory itself suggested very definite theoretical and experimental approaches to these problems, approaches that bore fruit in surprisingly short order. In the absence of such a specific, powerful, and highly detailed theory, such progress could not have been made.

Does parapsychology possess any significant body of theory concerning what the nonmaterial mind is like, a theory of what nonphysical elements compose it, and what nonphysical laws govern their interactions with each other and with the various aspects of the material world? Let me emphasize that this question concerns only the *existence* of relevant theory, not its verification. Does parapsychology have any significant body of generally shared theory with which to even address the empirical phenomena? The embarrassing fact is that it does not. A search through the pages of the *Journal of Parapsychology*, one of the more respectable organs of parapsychological communication, will discover many experiments designed to reveal some surprising capacity on the part of humans or animals. But the reader will find almost nothing in the way of positive, systematic, and well-defined theory concerning the nature of mental substance or mental properties and the quantitative or formal laws that govern their interaction and behavior.

Such theory as one does find is vague, impressionistic, and nonquantitative; it is usually aimed at a very narrow range of phenomena; and it is almost always idiosyncratic to the author. There is no settled core of theory whose past successes have unified the community behind it, whose current form has been shaped in response to past experimental failures, and whose experimental agenda drives the assembled discipline forward. These elements, so central to established sciences, are poignantly missing in the case at issue. To a philosopher or historian of science, parapsychology appears as a strikingly *atheoretical* discipline. Beyond the vague assumption that conscious agents have a nonphysical aspect of some kind, which gets somehow expressed in occasional displays of paranormal perception or paranormal manipulation, there is simply no accepted core of general theory to be found.

What one does find is a great deal of predominantly *experimental* research, aimed at isolating and demonstrating effects that transcend explanation in terms of physical science. Characteristically, such experiments are concerned to identify cases of successful perception of some kind or other, where perception is thought to be physically impossible (e.g., remote viewing, telepathy, clairvoyance); or they are concerned to identify cases of successful control or manipulation of some kind, where control is thought to be physically impossible (e.g., psychokinesis, telepathy). These experiments are often very elaborate, exploiting the same range of high-tech electronic equipment found in established branches of science, and they exploit the very same techniques of statistical evaluation approved elsewhere. In fact, the experimental drill is so well-oiled that it can be directed at any arbitrary set of variables among which one might suspect a statistically significant relationship.

As a result, parapsychological research has the collective character of a mass fishing expedition. Lacking any general theory with which to discriminate one part of the lake from another, one drops one's experimental line wherever local impulse suggests that one do so. The collective result is a jumble of ill-motivated results that move the discipline in no particular direction, because they motivate no widely accepted modifications to the core of guiding theory. For there is no such core.

There are further problems with the methodology of looking for some effect, any effect, that cannot be accounted for in normal physical terms. For when such results are achieved (or rather, are alleged to be achieved), the results may indeed be mysterious from a physical point of view, but they remain equally mysterious from the nonphysical point of view. The reason is that the parapsychologists are no better able to provide an explanation than are the physicists, for parapsychology has no significant theoretical resources with which to construct any explanations. If someone predicts the results of a long series of coin tosses with 100 percent accuracy, it is no *explanation* of this surprising result simply to say that the subject "has precognition." As well explain why sodium amytal puts you to sleep by saying it "has a dormative virtue." A real explanation would cite the nonphysical mechanisms involved, identify the empirical facts that reflect them, appeal to the laws that govern them, and then deduce exactly the surprising effect observed. Parapsychology does none of these things.

Contrast all of this with the case of the kinetic theory of heat. The experimental research conducted by the kinetic theorists was not aimed at finding experimental results that could not be accounted for by the classical theory. It was aimed at testing the specific provisions of the kinetic theory. When experimental successes were achieved, they were successes not principally or even usually because they defied any classical explanation, but because they yielded even more accurately to explanation and prediction in terms of the kinetic-corpuscular theory. The kinetic theory did not shine by reflected failure; it shone by its own light.

In contrast, parapsychology shines only by the reflected failures of materialism, if it shines at all. Parapsychology has no explanatory successes it can call its own, because it has no substantial theory it can call its own. If there is no detailed theory, there can be no detailed explanations. And if there are no detailed explanations, then parapsychology cannot shine with its own light.

The want of significant theory, therefore, is a very serious deficit. But even more serious, I believe, is the lack of any movement on the part of the parapsychological community, throughout its entire history, to attempt to repair this yawning deficit. Rather, professional concern has always been centered on anecdotes about past or current psychic marvels, and/or on experiments designed to uncover a clearly paraphysical effect. But no effect, no matter how startling, can be confidently identified as "paraphysical" unless the effect finds a uniquely successful explanation in terms of some detailed paraphysical theory. In the absence of such an explanatory success, the surprising effect will be no more than that. It will be just another surprising and currently unexplained effect. There need be nothing remotely "paraphysical" about it.

Accordingly, the dogged experimental pursuit of paraphysical results within a vacuum of genuine paraphysical theory seems to me to be methodologically barren, even if the experiments are performed with meticulous care, and even if they produce some genuinely puzzling results. Brownian motion was also a deeply puzzling result, and it too was found by respectable researchers using respectable techniques. But it did not count a fig against classical thermodynamics, nor would it ever have done so, save that the new kinetic theory finally gave intelligible form to its significance. What parapsychology needs more than anything else, therefore, is some specific and substantial theory, to give form to its vague aspirations, and systematic guidance to its experimental activity.

So long as it lacks such theory, it will never be a science, no matter how many experiments it accumulates.

There is a methodological vice with which all of us are familiar. Philosophers are especially familiar with it, since they have so often been (justly) accused of displaying it. The vice consists in the attempt to make large-scale theoretical progress in the absence of any systematic experimental input to control the ongoing development of theory. The result is "castles in the air." Those who proceed in this fashion will protest that they are theorists. And so they are. They will protest that their theories are coherent and imaginative. And so they may be. But the overall procedure falls well short of being science.

That vice has a converse, less commonly seen, but just as barren in its output. This second vice consists in the attempt to make large-scale experimental progress in the absence of any systematic theory to guide the experimental tradition, and to be modified in light of the outcomes. The result is a bin of meaningless correlations among parameters of questionable significance. Those whose proceed in this fashion will protest that they are genuine experimentalists. And so they are. They will protest that the experiments are honestly and accurately performed. And so they may be. But the overall procedure falls well short of being science. Like the preceding aspirants, such people are just playing at being scientists.

In advance of examining the parapsychological tradition, as represented in the pages of its own journal, one might have guessed that it suffers primarily from the first defect. But of these two maladies, it is not the first, I assert, but the second, that most closely characterizes the weakness of parapsychology.

III. Parapsychology: The Experimental Side

I have already leveled my major criticism of the experimental tradition of parapsychology. It is a methodological criticism, and it implies nothing untoward about the honesty or the critical care of those who conduct the relevant experiments. The discussion to this point has been deliberately uncritical in its representation of the reliability of the experimental results of parapsychology. That is because the validity of the methodological criticism I have been concerned to make is quite independent of how reliable those results might be. But it would be misleading of me to leave the reader with the impression that there are any generally accepted results in this area. Certainly there are none that are widely accepted outside the relatively small parapsychological community. There is as yet no experimental analog to Brownian motion on which they, and we, might chew.

In fact, it is not clear that they have any interesting and repeatable positive results at all. The history of the subject is full of major and minor scandals, ranging from the engineered seances of the '20s and '30s, to the deliberate manufacture of false data by the renowned S.G. Soal in the '40s, to the gizmo-aided "psychophotography" of T. Serios in the '60s, to the hopelessly ill-controlled experiments of R. Targ and H. Puthoff centered on Uri Geller (an undeclared but highly skilled magician) in the '70s. These comic operas, and others, have been discussed at length elsewhere (Randi, 1982), and so I shall not pursue them here. But they are worth mentioning, and not just because they were scandals. These cases are a sobering lesson because each was widely held in its time to constitute the best evidence of paranormal phenomena ever advanced. And they are further worth mentioning because the frailties they record are endemic to the human soul.

On the other hand, we cannot tar everyone with the brush of fools, nor even the majority. Parapsychologists quite often report wholly negative results, and what better testament to honesty than this? What we want to know is, what should we make of those few studies, apparently conducted with scrupulous care and integrity, which show statistically significant deviations from what we think is physically explicable?

There is no completely general answer that is adequate to this question. Each case should be dealt with on its own merits. But one thing we can demand, before we get too excited about any given case, is that the result be replicated, preferably by an independent laboratory. The reasons for this have nothing particular to do with either mendacity or stupidity. If, during five years of parapsychological research, 1000 statistical experiments are performed with perfect care and honesty, we are bound to get a very small percentage of cases that nudge or exceed the level of "significance," on statistical grounds alone. That is to say, there will be a small handful of "positive" results, even if there is nothing to parapsychology, and even if the investigators are scrupulous and the experimental protocols faultless.

This handful, we may assume, gets published. But consider. If 500 of the original 1000 experiments are forgotten because their disappointed investigators decide to pursue career development in other directions; and if 400 of the remaining 500 experiments are forgotten because they also were negative, and their investigators undertake further experiments which constitute the remaining 100; and if 80 of these, though honestly submitted, are never published because the editors are impatient with yet more negative parapsychological results; then the "accidentally significant" handful of positive results—say, 3 or 4 of the original 1000 experiments—will be published against an apparent sample of only 20 published experiments. They will thus appear to have a significance they have not earned.

The way to unmask such statistical accidents (and real cases, to repeat, are inevitable) is just to repeat the handful of standout experiments and see if the original results are replicated. To my knowledge, no genuinely anomalous result has ever survived this test. There are of course many surprising results that have and continue to be replicated, often in the media or in other public forums. But while impressive, these turn out not to be parapsychological.

Fire-walking is a good example. It has been performed many thousands of times in many different cultures, and is it often associated with paranormal claims. There is a "self-realization institute" here in my own community which occasionally holds fire-walking sessions down on the beach in the wee hours of the morning. Such sessions are put on as the culmination of a five-hour self-realization seminar, and the purpose of having the paying customers walk (briskly) across a carefully prepared bed of coals is to demonstrate to them the powers they have acquired at the hands of their psychic advisors. A few walkers acquire blisters from the experience, but most do not, and they are understandably amazed at the entire spectacle. The explanation, they are told, is that they have learned to enhance the "biomagnetic field" surrounding their feet, which field serves to shield them from the heat.

This is utter nonsense, of course, but the coals are indeed at a fairly high temperature. Though old and dying, they are still glowing red, at least in the dark. The trick is that there is no trick. At that stage of advanced combustion, the coals have the density of styrofoam and a very low specific heat capacity. Though high in temperature, the coals simply do not contain enough heat energy, and cannot conduct it into the foot quickly enough, to cause significant burns in the roughly 1.6 seconds of total contact each foot touches the coals (four steps per foot × 0.4 second). People expect to be burned by anything that is even faintly incandescent, but it is not always so. The bed of coals must be very carefully and knowledgeably prepared, however, so I strongly urge against ever trying this yourself, especially with standard charcoal briquets, the material most likely to be at hand. These are hotter than most wood coals, and they crumble underfoot, releasing extra heat. Do not ever step on them.

What I do recommend trying is the following. In the dark, so that you may better judge the radiant state of the coals, pick up a dying coal with some barbeque tongs, and touch it very briefly to the sole of your foot, or the heel of your hand. This mode of experimentation allows for greater control, and is markedly safer. You will be surprised at how benign is the effect of such a coal, at least for contact exposures of *less* than half a second. Fire-walking is both real and replicable, but it is not paranormal (see Leikind and McCarthy) 1985; P. M. Churchland 1986b).

Another common spectacle is some form of mind-reading or clairvoyance displayed by a media magician, professed or unprofessed. Here I can convey no general summary of how the tricks are performed: magicians have endless ways of fooling us. But I can give you the flavor of the class by relating one of its typical instances.

My wife and colleague, Patricia Churchland, once amazed her freshman philosophy class by reading aloud, with eyes closed, the phrases concealed in a pile of sealed manila envelopes that the students had severally submitted to her at the beginning of class. At each "psychic reading" of a still-sealed envelope, she would ask if any student had indeed submitted the announced phrase. While the relevant student expressed amazed acknowledgment, she would then open the envelope to casually check the accuracy of her reading, and then move on to the next envelope, and to the psychic divination of its contents.

She gets every one right. The trick is impressive, and it requires only one confidant among the students, someone to falsely acknowledge success on the very first envelope "read." In fact, she simply makes up her first reading, and counts on the voiced agreement of the one confidant. While opening the envelope to "check the accuracy" of this first and wholly confabulatory reading, she is in fact discovering what some other perfectly honest student has written inside the first envelope. This becomes the basis for the second "reading." While holding the second envelope mysteriously to her forehead, she voices the contents of the now-discarded first envelope. The author of that envelope's contents acknowledges this "success," usually with further expressions of amazement, and the envelope is simultaneously opened and "checked" by the psychic for accuracy. This supplies the basis for the third reading. And so on through the entire pile. The classroom result is a delicious pandemonium. Psychic powers, evidently, are easier to come by than you might have thought.

These two examples, psychic reading and fire-walking, do not bear directly on academic parapsychology. But they do help us to see how ostensibly paranormal phenomena can be conjured from the normal and the ordinary. And they do help to arm us against the predators in this general area, of which there are many. We must have a certain sympathy for those attempting to do responsible paranormal research against the background of media nonsense, cultish practices, and the financial exploitation of gullible suckers. It is rather like trying to conduct a legitimate escort service in the midst of a booming red-light district. Any passing constable can be forgiven his initial suspicion. And his second and third.

I began this paper by asking how parapsychology could become a science. My answer is that it needs some organizing theory. And it needs an experimental tradition that is aimed at the positive task of testing and refining that alternative general theory of mind, rather than at the negative task of finding some unpatchable hole in materialism. Parapsychologists have not provided the raw conceptual materials with which to construct a coherent and well-motivated research program, even if materialism is *in fact* false. That is why parapsychology remains a pseudoscience.

Notes

Chapter 1

This chapter first appeared in a slightly different version in Guttenplan, S., ed., *Companion to the Mind*. London: Blackwell, 1996, 306–14.

Chapter 2

This chapter first appeared in Edgington, D. W., ed., *Proceedings of the Aristotelian Society* 63(suppl.):313–19. John Haldane's "Understanding Folk" appears there also.

Chapter 3

This chapter first appeared in *Mind and Language* 8, no. 2 (1993):211–22, as part of a symposium on an essay by Barbara Hannan entitled, "Don't Stop Believing: The Case Against Eliminative Materialism."

Chapter 4

This chapter first appeared in *Philosophy and Phenomenological Research* 52 (1992), as part of a symposium on Hilary Putnam's book, *Representation and Reality* (Cambridge, Mass.: The MIT Press).

Chapter 5

This chapter first appeared in *Scientific American* (January 1990):26–31, as part of a symposium with John Searle, whose contribution to that issue was entitled "Is the Brain's Mind a Computer Program?," 26–31.

Chapter 6

This chapter first appeared in *Seminars in the Neurosciences*, 2, no. 4 (1990): 249–56.

Chapter 7

This chapter first appeared in *The Journal of Philosophy*, 95, no. 1 (1998): 5–32.

1. Paul Churchland, "Fodor and Lepore: State-space semantics and meaning Holism." *Philosophy and Phenomenological Research* 53 (1993):667–72. Jerry Fodor and Ernest Lepore, "Reply to Churchland." *Philosophy and Phenomenological Research* 53 (1993):679–82. Paul Churchland, "Second Reply to Fodor and Lepore. In *The Churchlands and their critics*, edited by R. McCauley. Oxford: Blackwell, 1996b:278–83. But for their original chapter, the entire exchange appears in McCauley, *The Churchlands and Their Critics*.

2. Cf. Churchland 1996b, *op cit.*, 282.

3. Paul Churchland, *A Neurocomputational Perspective: The Nature of Mind and the Structure of Science*, Cambridge, Mass.: The MIT Press, 1989a, chapters 10 and 11. Also Churchland 1996b, *op cit.*

4. Paul Churchland, *A Neurocomputational Perspective*, chapter 11.

5. See, for example, the short critiques of Quine, Davidson, and Putnam in P. M. Churchland; *Scientific Realism and the Plasticity of Mind*, 1979, section 9; and the longer critique of Fodor in Paul Churchland, "Perceptual Plasticity and Theoretical Neutrality: A Reply to Jerry Fodor," *Philosophy of Science* 55 (1988):167–87, reprinted in P. M. Churchland, *Scientific Realism*, 255–79.

Chapter 8

This chapter first appeared in *London Review of Books*, 16, no. 9 (1994), as a review of Searle, J. R. 1992. *The Rediscovery of the Mind*. Cambridge, Mass: The MIT Press.

Chapter 9

This chapter first appeared in *Journal of Philosophy*, 93 (May 1996):211–28.

1. Cf. John Searle, "Intrinsic Intentionality: Reply to Criticisms of Minds, Brains, and Programs, *Behavioral and Brain Sciences* 3 (1980):450–6; also *The Rediscovery of the Mind*. Cambridge, Mass.: The MIT Press, 1992:78–82.

2. Cf. Searle, Is the Brain's Mind a Computer Program? *Scientific American*, 262, no. 1 (1990):26–31, here pp. 26–7; also *The Rediscovery of Mind*, 93–5.

3. Cf. Searle, "Intrinsic Intentionality," 417–57; also "Is the Brain's Mind a Computer Program?," 26–31. This analogy was earlier deployed in Paul Churchland and Churchand, Patricia, "Could a Machine Think?" *Scientific American* 262, no. 1 (1990):32–7. We did not then appreciate that the analogy was a member of a systematic and much larger family.

4. Cf. Searle, *The Rediscovery of Mind*, 122; also Searle, "The Mystery of Consciousness: Part II," *The New York Review of Books*, 42, no. 18 (1995):54–61, here p. 58.

5. Cf. Searle, *The Rediscovery of Mind*, 117–8.

6. Cf. Searle, *The Rediscovery of Mind*, 132, 151–6.

7. Cf. Searle, *The Rediscovery of Mind*, 1, 89–93, 124–6; also Searle, "The Mystery of Consciousness: Part II," 55–6.

8. Cf. David Chalmers, "The Puzzle of Conscious Experience," *Scientific American* 273, no. 6 (1995): pp. 81–2.

9. Cf. Frank Jackson, "Epiphenomenal Qualia" *Philosophical Quarterly*, 32, no. 127 (1982):127–36, here p. 130; also Chalmers, "The Puzzle of Conscious Experience," 81–2.

10. Cf. Chalmers, "The Puzzle of Conscious Experience," 82–3; also Searle, "The Mystery of Consciousness: Part II": 55–6.

11. Cf. Thomas Nagel, "What Is It Like to Be a Bat?" *Philosophical Review* 83, no. 4: 437; also Searle, *The Rediscovery of Mind*, 116–24.

12. Cf. Searle, *The Rediscovery of Mind*, 124, 112–6. Though here is not the place to mount a systematic criticism of it, it must be said that Searle's 1992 sketch of the nature and varieties of reduction muddies far more than it clarifies. First, it wrongly assimilates ontological reduction to ontological elimination. Second, there is no further category or "halfway house"—Searle's so-called "causal reduction"—distinct from ontological reduction. And third, as we just saw, the account attempts to stipulate the closure of certain empirically open questions. To a neutral philosopher of science, Searle's account will appear more as a reflection of his peculiar intuitions in the philosophy of mind rather than as an independently motivated attempt to account for the full range of cases throughout the history of science.

13. See Mary Hesse, "Is There an Independent Observation Language?" In *The Nature and Function of Scientific Theories*, edited by R. Colodny, Pittsburgh: Pittsburgh University Press, 1970, 35–77.

Chapter 10

This is an expanded version of a paper first published in Churchland, P. M. 1989c. *A Neurocomputational Perspective*. Cambridge, Mass.: The MIT Press, 67–76.

Chapter 11

This chapter first appeared in *Seminars in Neurology*, 17, no. 2 (1997):101–8.

Chapter 12

This chapter first appeared in B. Dahlbom, ed., *Dennett and His Critics*. Oxford: Blackwells, 1993, 13–27.

Chapter 13

This chapter first appeared in *Journal of Consciousness Studies*, 2 (1995):10–29. We thank the following persons for valuable discussions, advice, and insights: Oron Shagrir, David Chalmers, Paul Churchland, Francis Crick, Mark Ellisman, Andrew Hibbs, Brian Keeley, Christof Koch, Steve Quartz, Terry Sejnowski, Chuck Stevens, Timothy van Gelder, Hal White, Robin Zagone, the participants of EPL (Experimental Philosophy Laboratory, University of California, San Diego), and three helpful anonymous reviewers.

1. Although Dennett's book title, *Consciousness Explained* (Dennett, 1990) rather misleadingly suggests otherwise.

2. Cf. the classic by Bray (1992); Hall (1992); Sossin, Fisher, and Scheller (1989).

3. "Quantal release" at the synapse means either that a vesicle of transmitter is released or it is not. It means that when there is release, the whole vesicle opens and all its transmitter is released into the synaptic cleft. This is in no sense a quantum-mechanical effect. Also, by "explanatorily significant" we mean any effect which is not capturable by a classical biochemical explanation.

4. There is a very simple—and fallacious—argument sometimes tugging at the physicist's intuitions. Its clearest formulation is, to our knowledge, owed to the philosopher of science and mathematics, Itamar Pitowski, in honor of whom we call this the *Pitowski syllogism*: (1) we really do not understand the nature of consciousness; (2) the only things in the physical world we really do not understand are quantum-level phenomena; therefore, these are probably the same mystery. As Pitowski is quick to point out, however, premise 2 is clearly false.

5. At least this is our best, most sympathetic, and long-pondered shot at it. We do acknowledge that the presentation of the argument in *Shadows* is complex, the issues are complex, and that the compact account is a simplification. We have no interest in merely setting up a straw man, but there is value in having the crux of the argument clear.

6. For purposes of this paper, soundness is a property of procedures or mechanisms or the exercise of capacities. Soundness can be taken to be roughly equivalent to "truth-producing," meaning that, given true premises, when the normal functioning of the procedure or mechanism or capacity produces conclusions,

they are true ones, not false ones. Soundness should thus not be thought of as necessarily tied to algorithmic or syntactic procedures, though these too might be sound. More generally: statements can be true or false, arguments can be valid or invalid, procedures, etc. can be sound or not. Though our expression, "truth-producing," is less conventional than "truth-preserving" in this context, it is called for in order to accommodate Penrose's very interesting idea that things other than algorithms, formal systems, and the like, might be sound.

7. Penrose does argue that chaotic processes are themselves algorithmic (Penrose, 1994b, pp. 177–9), in that they can be simulated to any desired degree of accuracy by digital computational mechanisms. While some may feel this subsumption of chaotic systems to algorithmic ones is unjustified, we propose to grant this premise.

8. For a brief but powerful criticism of Penrose on the Gödel result, see Putnam (1994).

9. Thus we will follow Penrose in using the term "nonalgorithmic" only for those processes which cannot even be approximated with an algorithm. This will contrast with "weakly nonalgorithmic," which just means not following explicit rules.

10. See note 21, below.

11. In brief, what Gödel showed was that for any sufficiently powerful consistent formal axiomatic system F, there will be true statements, expressible in F, yet not provable in F. In particular, the statement that F is consistent, call this G(F), will not be provable in F, provided that F is in fact consistent. Curiously, G(F) will be provable in F if F is in fact inconsistent, that is, if G(F) is false. In a nutshell, the argument for A1a is that since humans are sound (hence consistent), and since we can know that we are sound, we cannot be relying on any formal system for our knowledge. This is because if we were exclusively using some sound formal system, we could never know (prove) our own soundness. Penrose's treatment of this argument is much more complete (Penrose, 1994b).

12. As Penrose himself notes, this seems to be what Turing thought was the real moral of the Gödel result. Turing (1986) is worth quoting at length.

It might be argued that there is a fundamental contradiction in the idea of a machine with intelligence. It is certainly true that "acting like a machine" has come to be synonymous with lack of adaptability ... It has for instance been shown that with certain logical systems there can be no machine which will distinguish provable formulae of the system from unprovable ... Thus if a machine is made for this purpose it must in some cases fail to give an answer. On the other hand, if a mathematician is confronted with such a problem he would search around and find new methods of proof, so that he ought to be able to reach a decision about any given formula. Against it I would say that fair play must be given to the machine. Instead of it sometimes giving no answer we could arrange it so that it gives occasional wrong answers. But the human mathematician would likewise make blunders when trying out new techniques. It is easy for us to regard these blunders as not counting, and give him another chance, but the machine would probably be allowed no mercy. In other words then, if a machine is expected to be infallible, it cannot also be intelligent. There are several mathematical theorems which say almost exactly that. But these theorems say nothing about how much intelligence may be displayed if a machine makes no pretense at infallibility.

13. See note 15, below.

14. *Modus ponens* has the form: if P then Q, P; so Q. *Modus tollens* has the form: if P then Q, not Q; so not P.

15. Note that the emphasis here is on *soundness*, and not just consistency. While it of course has been proved that the axiom of choice (and hence its denial) are independent of ZF, and thus consistent with it, it does not follow that both are *sound* when added to ZF. In fact, on any reasonable account of what soundness means, they cannot both be so.

16. A particularly striking example of the tenuousness of the Penrose assumption concerning mathematical intuitions was encountered when one of us (R. G.) was discussing these issues with a mathematics graduate who admitted, in good faith, the following: "I firmly believe that Zorn's lemma is true, and I'm convinced that Zorn's lemma is equivalent to the axiom of choice, and yet I am certain that the axiom of choice must be false."

17. For a lucid and compelling discussion of a non-Platonist approach to mathematics, see Kitcher (1984b).

18. Penrose might object that our argument relies on the variable or dicey mathematical competence of individual mathematicians, while his argument is couched in terms of the competence of the mathematical community as a whole (see discussion in Penrose, 1994b, pp. 97–101). This move would be rhetorically awkward, since presumably consciousness, in all its putative nonalgorithmic glory, is supported by brains, and brains are supported by individuals.

19. Cf. Stich (1990) for an excellent critical discussion of the link between evolutionary pressures and truth.

20. This is a point which we understand G. Kreisel to have made in correspondence with Francis Crick.

21. These are pp. 132–8 and 434–9. Fixing an adequate interpretation of these sections is difficult, as it is unclear if Penrose takes quasicrystals to be evidence for nonalgorithmic processes, or simply nonlocal but algorithmic ones. The paragraph bridging pp. 438–9 in *Emperor* seems to favor the reading where nonalgorithmicity is at issue. Curiously, there is no mention of quasicrystals in *Shadows*, perhaps because Penrose does not (any longer?) take them to provide evidence of such physical actions. If this be the case, then perhaps he would agree with the discussion in this section.

22. In the context of the present discussion, superradiance is a quantum-mechanical effect in which water molecules within the microtubule might act in ways roughly analogous to a laser. Specifically, these molecules, because they have dipole moments, could coherently emit radiation by shifting between angular momentum states. This effect, if it exists, would depend crucially on the purity of the water within the tubule, as well as on the properties of the tubule

itself, such as its diameter and minute details of its electric field. See Jibu et al. (1994); Hameroff (1994).

23. Franks and Lieb (1994); for further discussion, see Bowdle, Horita and Kharasch (1994).

24. In this paragraph, as well as in (1) above, we are in the awkward situation of merely stating that there is no direct evidence of such and such. This is not because we are simply discounting Hameroff's evidence, but because, so far as we can see, he does not offer any. His arguments take more the form of demonstrating how certain phenomena might be possible, not of providing direct evidence for them.

25. Gilman, Goodman, and Gilman (1990). This was brought to our attention by Chuck Stevens. For evidence that small though "effective" amounts of colchicine do pass the blood-brain barrier, see Bennett, Alberti, and Flood (1981). A number of studies (e.g., Kolasa et al. 1992; Emerich and Walsh 1991) injected colchicine directly into the brain of rats and then ran various behavioral tests on them. No such studies we have seen mention any problems associated with consciousness, including Bensimon and Chermat (1991) who injected rat brains directly with colchicine every day for ten days, Conner and Varon (1992) who directly injected the brain at several different locations, and Ceccaldi, Ermine, and Tsiang (1990) who pumped colchicine continuously into rat brains over extended periods of time with an osmotic pump. Note that all these studies used colchicine *specifically because it depolymerizes microtubules*, disrupting their transport function. It is revealing to note that many of these studies mention that the rats were anesthetized before being sacrificed, which implies that the microtubule disruption *did not* render them unconscious, and that the normal anesthetic *did* render them unconscious (presumably in some manner other than affecting the already-depolymerized microtubules, *contra* Penrose and Hammeroff).

26. And probably any other putative quantum-mechanical effect supported by microtubules as well. In fact, it seems also to be a problem for other accounts of the importance of microtubular computation (quantum-mechanical or otherwise) as supporting consciousness or cognition, for example, Hameroff (1994); Hameroff and Watt (1982).

27. Of course, depending on the story told about exactly what kinds of quantum coherence are important and how they are maintained in spatially separate regions, the presence of transmitter molecules and electric fields may not be a problem. The problem is that these details are not provided.

28. Ions in close proximity to the tubulin dimers would affect their electrical properties and hence their capacity to engage in or support these sorts of quantum phenomena. See Jibu et al. (1994); Hameroff (1994).

Chapter 14

First published in A. R. Damasio et al. eds., *The Neurobiology of Decision-Making*. Berlin: Springer-Verlag, 1996, 181–99.

1. This is, needless to say, somewhat oversimplified.

2. Kant actually says, "The rule and direction for knowing how you go about *sharing in happiness* ..." (my italics) because the matter arises in the context of a teacher-student dialogue about a particular case, namely, how to help others and whether to give them what they want. Pretty clearly Kant intends the point to be general, and hence my more general interpolation.

3. Or as Marge Piercy remarks in *Braided Lives* (1982) "... treats his emotions like mice that infest our basement or rats in the garage, as vermin to be crushed in traps and poisoned with bait."

4. This was originally broadcast in the '60s. More recently, its successor, *Star Trek: The Next Generation*, has also been wildly popular. Spock has been replaced by the android, Data, who is largely without emotion, while Whorf, an alien who is "animalistic" and highly emotional, has also been included.

5. Spock does not, however, resemble EVR (see below) in his decision making.

6. For an excellent discussion of faculty psychology, see Wittrup (1994).

7. The GSR measures change in conductivity of the skin as a function of increased sweat on the skin, which is an effect produced by the sympathetic system of the nervous system.

8. Benjamin Libet, using a very different experimental paradigm (Libet 1985), came to a similar conclusion concerning nonconscious processes underlying decisions.

9. An earlier hypothesis related to this view was suggested by Paul MacLean (1949, 1952). He said, "As a working hypothesis, it can be inferred that the limbic system is for the 'body viscous,' a visceral brain that interprets and gives expression to its incoming information in terms of feeling ..." (1952). See also Papez (1937) and Kluver and Bucy (1937, 1938).

10. In his splendid book, *Moral Imagination* (1993), Mark Johnson argues for a similar view. See also Owen Flanagan's excellent book, *Varieties of Moral Personality: Ethics and Psychological Realism* (1991).

Chapter 15

This chapter first appeared in G. Munevar, ed., *Beyond Reason: Essays in Honor of Paul Feyerabend*. Netherlands: Kluwer, 1991, 1–23. Reprinted in R. Giere, ed., *Cognitive Models of Science*. Vol. 15 of *Minnesota Studies in the Philosophy of Science*. Minneapolis: University of Minnesota Press, 1992, 341–63.

Chapter 16

This chapter first appeared in R. Giere, ed., *Cognitive Models of Science*, Vol. 15 of *Minnesota Studies in the Philosophy of Science*. Minneapolis: University of Minnesota Press, 1992, 475–80.

Chapter 17

This chapter first appeared in *Philosophy of Science* I (suppl.) (1997), as part of a symposium honoring the late Paul Feyerabend.

1. It is a black velvet "choker" necklace around a slender neck.

Chapter 18

This chapter first appeared in *Inquiry*, 30, no. 3, 1987, 227–39.

References

Adolphs, R., D. Tranel, A. Bechara, H. Damasio, and A. R. Damasio. 1996. Neuropsychological approaches to reasoning and decision making. In *The neurobiology of decision-making*, edited by A. R. Damasio, et al. Berlin: Springer-Verlag, 157–80.

Anderson, J. A., and E. Rosenfeld, eds. 1988. *Neurocomputing: Foundations of research*. Cambridge, Mass.: The MIT Press.

Aristotle. 1995. *The Nichomachean ethics*. Translated by J. A. K. Thompson. Harmondsworth, U.K.: Penguin Books.

Baars, B. J. 1988. *A cognitive theory of consciousness*. Cambridge, U.K.: Cambridge University Press.

Baker, L. R. 1987. *Saving belief*. Princeton: Princeton University Press.

Bartoshuk, L. M. 1978. Gustatory system. In *Handbook of behavioral neurobiology*. Vol. 1, *Sensory integration*, edited by R. B. Masterson. New York: Plenum Press, 503–67.

Bates, E., and B. MacWhinney. 1989. Functionalism and the competition model. In *The crosslinguistic study of sentence processing*, edited by E. Bates and B. MacWhinney. Cambridge, U.K.: Cambridge University Press.

Bechara, A., A. Damasio, H. Damasio, and S. W. Anderson. 1994. Insensitivity to future consequences following damage to human prefrontal cortex. *Cognition* 50:7–15.

Beghossian, P. 1990. The status of content. *Philosophical Review* 99:157–84.

Benacerraf, P., and H. Putnam, eds. 1983. *Philosophy of mathematics: Selected readings*. Englewood Cliffs, N.J.: Prentice-Hall.

Bennett, B. M., D. D. Hoffman, and C. Prakash. 1989. *Observer mechanics*. San Diego: Academic Press.

Bennett, E., M. H. Alberti, and J. Flood. 1981. Uptake of [^{3}H]colchicine into brain and liver of mouse, rat, and chick. *Pharmacology, Biochemistry and Behavior* 14:863–9.

Bensimon, G. and R. Chermat. 1991. Microtubule disruption and cognitive defects: Effect of colchicine on learning behavior in rats. *Pharmacology, Biochemistry and Behavior* 38:141–5.

Block, N. 1980. *Readings in the philosophy of psychology* Vol. 1. Cambridge, Mass.: Harvard University Press.

Bloor, D. 1976. *Knowledge and social imagery*. Chicago: University of Chicago Press.

Bogen, J. E. 1995. On the neurophysiology of consciousness: I. An overview. *Consciousness and Cognition* 4:52–62.

Boyer, C. 1959. *The history of the calculus and its conceptual development*. New York: Dover Publications.

Bowdle, T. A., A. Horita, and E. D. Kharasch. 1994. *The pharmacological basis of anesthesiology*. New York: Churchill Livingstone.

Bray, D. 1992. *Cell movements*. New York: Garland.

Campbell, C. A. 1957. *On selfhood and godhood*. London: George Allen.

Ceccaldi, P. E., A. Ermine, and H. Tsiang. 1990. Continuous delivery of colchicine in the rat brain with osmotic pumps for inhibition of rabies virus transport. *Journal of Virological Methods* 28:79–83.

Chalmers, D. 1995. The puzzle of conscious experience. *Scientific American*, 273, no. 6:80–6.

Chalmers, D. 1996. *The conscious mind*. Oxford: Oxford University Press.

Cheney, D. L., and R. M. Seyfarth. 1990. *How monkeys see the world*. Chicago: University of Chicago Press.

Churchland, P. M. 1970. The logical character of action explanations. *Philosophical Review* 79:214–36.

Churchland, P. M. 1979. *Scientific realism and the plasticity of mind*. Cambridge, U.K.: Cambridge University Press.

Churchland, P. M. 1981. Eliminative materialism and the propositional attitudes. *Journal of Philosophy* 78, no. 2:67–90.

Churchland, P. M. 1982. The anti-realist epistemology of van Fraassen's *The scientific image*. *Pacific Philosophical Quarterly* 63:226–35. An expanded version of this paper is reprinted under the title, The ontological status of observables: In praise of the superempirical virtues. In *Images of science*, edited by P. M. Churchland and C. A. Hooker. Chicago: University of Chicago Press, 1985; also in Churchland 1989a, 139–52.

Churchland, P. M. 1984. *Matter and consciousness*. Cambridge, Mass.: The MIT Press.

Churchland, P. M. 1985a. Reduction, qualia, and the direct introspection of brain states. *Journal of Philosophy* 82, no. 1:8–28.

Churchland, P. M. 1985b. Conceptual progress and word/world relations: In search of the essence of natural kinds. *Canadian Journal of Philosophy* 15, no. 1:1–17.

Churchland, P. M. 1986a. Some reductive strategies in cognitive neurobiology. *Mind* 95:279–309.

Churchland, P. M. 1986b. Firewalking and physics. *The Skeptical Inquirer* 10, no. 3:284–5.

Churchland, P. M. 1988a. Folk psychology and the explanation of human behaviour. *Proceedings of the Aristotelian Society* (suppl.) 62:209–21. Reprinted in Churchland, P. M. 1989a, 111–27.

Churchland, P. M. 1988b. Perceptual plasticity and theoretical neutrality: A reply to Jerry Fodor. *Philosophy of Science* 55:167–487. Reprinted in Churchland, P. M. 1989a, 255–79.

Churchland, P. M. 1989a. *A neurocomputational perspective: The nature of mind and the structure of science.* Cambridge, Mass.: The MIT Press.

Churchland, P. M. 1989b. On the nature of theories: A neurocomputational perspective. *Scientific theories: Minnesota studies in the philosophy of science,* 14, edited by W. Savage. Minneapolis: University of Minnesota Press, 59–101.

Churchland, P. M. 1989c. On the nature of explanation: A PDP approach. Chap. 10 in *A neurocomputational perspective: The Nature of Mind and the Structure of Science.* Cambridge, Mass.: The MIT Press, 1989. Reprinted in Misiek, J., ed. *Rationality.* Vol. 175 of *Boston Studies in the Philosophy of Science.* Dordrecht, Netherlands: Kluwer, 1995.

Churchland, P. M. 1989d. Learning and conceptual change. Chap. 11 in *A Neurocomputational Perspective: The Nature of Mind and the Structure of Science.* Cambridge, Mass.: The MIT Press, 1989.

Churchland, P. M. 1992. Activation vectors versus propositional attitudes: How the *brain* represents reality. *Philosophy and Phenomenological Research* 52.

Churchland, P. M. 1993. State-space semantics and meaning holism. *Philosophy and Phenomenological Research* 53:667–72.

Churchland, P. M. 1995. *The engine of reason, the seat of the soul: A philosophical journey into the brain.* Cambridge, Mass.: The MIT Press.

Churchland, P. M. 1996a. The rediscovery of light. *Journal of Philosophy* 93, no. 5:211–28.

Churchland, P. M. 1996b. Second reply to Fodor and Lepore. In *The Churchlands and their critics,* edited by R. McCauley. Oxford: Blackwell, 278–83.

Churchland, P. M. 1997. Recent work on consciousness: Philosophical, theoretical, and empirical. *Seminars in Neurology* 17, no. 2:179–86.

Churchland, P. M., and P. S. Churchland. 1990a. Could a machine think? *Scientific American* 262, no. 1:32–7.

Churchland, P. M., and P. S. Churchland. 1990b. Intertheoretic reduction: A neuroscientist's field guide. *Seminars in the Neurosciences* 2:249–56.

Churchland, P. M., and C. A. Hooker, eds. 1985. *Images of science: scientific realism versus constructive empiricism,* Foundations of Science Series (Chicago, University of Chicago Press).

Churchland, P. S. 1986. *Neurophilosophy: Toward a unified understanding of the mind-brain*. Cambridge, Mass.: The MIT Press.

Churchland, P. S. 1988. Reduction and the neurobiological basis of consciousness. In *Consciousness in contemporary science*, edited by A. J. Marcel and E. Bisiach. Oxford: Oxford University Press. 273–304.

Churchland, P. S., and T. Sejnowski. 1992. *The computational brain*. Cambridge, Mass.: The MIT Press.

Clark, Andy 1989. *Microcognition*. Cambridge, Mass.: The MIT Press.

Clark, Austen 1993. *Sensory Qualities*. Oxford: Oxford University Press.

Clutton-Brock, T. H., and G. A. Parker. 1995. Punishment in animal societies. *Nature* 373:209–16.

Conner, J. M., and S. Varon. 1992. Distribution of nerve growth factor–like immunoreactive neurons in the adult rat brain following colchicine treatment. *Journal of Comparative Neurology* 326:347–62.

Couvalis, S. G. 1988. Feyerabend and Laymon on brownian motion. *Philosophy of Science* 55:415–21.

Crane, H. D., and T. P. Piantanida. 1983. On seeing reddish-green and yellowish-blue. *Science* 221:1078–9.

Crick, F. 1994. *The astonishing hypothesis*. New York: Scribners.

Crick, F., and C. Koch. 1990. Towards a neurobiological theory of consciousness. *Seminars in the Neurosciences* 2:263–76.

Damasio, A. R. 1994. *Descartes' error*. New York: Putnam & Sons.

Damasio, A. R., and H. Damasio. 1996. Images and subjectivity: Neurobiological trials and tribulations. In *The Churchlands and their critics*, edited by R. McCauley. Oxford: Blackwell, 163–75.

Damasio, A. R., D. Tranel, and H. Damasio. 1991. Somatic markers and the guidance of behavior. In *Frontal lobe function and dysfunction*, edited by H. Levin. New York: Oxford University Press.

Davidson, D. 1970. Mental events. In *Experience and Theory*, edited by L. Foster and J. Swanson. Amherst: University of Massachusetts Press.

Dennett, D. C. 1969. *Content and consciousness*. London: Routledge & Kegan Paul.

Dennett, D. C. 1978. *Brainstorms*. Cambridge, Mass.: The MIT Press.

Dennett, D. C. 1981. Three kinds of intentional psychology. In *Reduction, time and reality*, edited by R. Healey. Cambridge, U.K.: Cambridge University Press, 37–61. Reprinted in Dennett, D. C. 1987. *The intentional stance*. Cambridge, Mass.: The MIT Press.

Dennett, D. C. 1984. *Elbow room*. Cambridge, Mass.: The MIT Press.

Dennett, D. C. 1987a. Fast thinking. In Dennett, D. C. 1987. *The intentional stance*. Cambridge, Mass: The MIT Press, 323–38.

Dennett, D. C. 1987b. *The intentional stance*. Cambridge, Mass: The MIT Press.

Dennett, D. C. 1991. *Consciousness explained*. Boston: Little, Brown.

DeSousa, R. 1990. *The rationality of emotion*. Cambridge, Mass.: The MIT Press.

Devitt, M. 1990. Transcendentalism about content. *Pacific Philosophical Quarterly* 71, no. 4:247–63.

Donagan, A. 1977. *The theory of morality*, Chicago: Chicago University Press.

Dreyfus, H. L. 1972. *What computers can't do: A critique of artificial reason*. New York: Harper & Row.

Dummett, M. 1991. *The logical basis of metaphysics*, Cambridge, Mass.: Harvard University Press.

Elman, J. 1992. Grammatical structure and distributed representations. In *Connectionism: Theory and Practice*, edited by S. Davis. Vol. 3 of *Vancouver studies in cognitive science*. Oxford: Oxford University Press, 138–94.

Edelman, G. E. 1989. *The remembered present: A biological theory of consciousness*. New York: Basic Books.

Emerich, D. F., and T. J. Walsh. 1991. Ganglioside AGF2 prevents the cognitive impairments and cholinergic cell loss following intraventricular colchicine. *Experimental Neurology* 112:328–37.

Feyerabend, P. K. 1958. An attempt at a realistic interpretation of experience. *Proceedings of the Aristotelian Society* 58:143. Reprinted in Feyerabend, P. K. 1981. *Realism, rationalism, and scientific method: Philosophical papers*. Vol. 1. Cambridge, U.K.: Cambridge University Press, 17–43.

Feyerabend, P. K. 1962. Explanation, reduction, and empiricism. In *Scientific explanation, space and time*, edited by H. Feigl and G. Maxwell. Vol. 3 of *Minnesota studies in the philosophy of science*. Minneapolis: University of Minnesota Press, 28–97.

Feyerabend, P. K. 1963a. Materialism and the mind-body problem. *Review of Metaphysics* 17:49–66. Reprinted in *The Mind-Brain Identity Theory*, edited by C. V. Borst. Toronto: Macmillan, 1970, 142–56. Also in Feyerabend, P. K. 1981. *Realism, rationalism, and scientific method: Philosophical papers*. Vol. 1. Cambridge, U.K.: Cambridge University Press.

Feyerabend, P. K. 1963b. How to be a good empiricist—A plea for tolerance in matters epistemological. In *Philosophy of science: The Delaware seminar*. Vol. 2, edited by B. Baumrin. New York: Interscience Publications, 3–19. Reprinted in Brody B., ed. 1970, *Readings in the philosophy of science*. Englewood Cliffs, N.J.: Prentice Hall, 319–42. Also in Morick H., ed. 1972, *Challenges to empiricism*. Belmont, Calif.: Wadsworth, 164–93.

Feyerabend, P. K. 1970. Against method: Outline of an anarchistic theory of knowledge. In *Analyses of Theories and Methods of Physics and Psychology*, edited by Radner and Winokur. Vol. 4 of *Minnesota studies in the philosophy of science*. Minneapolis: University of Minnesota Press, 27ff.

Fiorani, M., R. Gattass, M. P. G. Rosa, and C. E. Rocha-Miranda. 1990. Changes in receptive field (RF) size of single cells in primate V1 as a correlate of perceptual completion. *Society for Neuroscience Abstracts* 16:1219.

Fiorani, M., M. P. G. Rosa, R. Gattass, and C. E. Rocha-Miranda. 1992. Visual responses outside the "classical" receptive field in primate striate cortex: A possible correlate of perceptual completion. *Proceedings of the National Academy of Sciences* 89:8547–51.

Flanagan, O. 1991. *Varieties of moral personality: Ethics and psychological realism.* Cambridge, Mass.: Harvard University Press.

Flanagan, O. 1996. Self-expression in sleep: Neuroscience and dreams. In *Self-expressions: Minds, morals, and the meaning of life.* Cambridge, Mass.: MIT Press, 32–52.

Flanagan, O. (forthcoming) Prospects for a unified theory of consciousness, or, What dreams are made of. In *Scientific approaches to the question of consciousness: The 25th Carnegie symposium on cognition,* edited by J. Cohen and J. Schooler. Hillsdale, N.J.: Erllbaum,

Fodor, J. A. 1968. *Psychological explanation.* New York: Random House.

Fodor, J. A. 1975. *The language of thought.* New York: Crowell.

Fodor, J. A. 1991. *A theory of content and other essays.* Cambridge, Mass.: The MIT Press.

Fodor, J. A., and E. Lepore. 1992. *Holism: A shopper's guide.* Oxford: Blackwell.

Fodor, J. A., and E. Lepore. 1993. Reply to Churchland. *Philosophy and Phenomenological Research* 53:679–82.

Franks, N. P., and W. R. Lieb. 1994. Molecular and cellular mechanisms of general anaesthesia. *Nature* 367:607–14.

Gattass, R., Fiorani, et al. 1992. Changes in receptive field size in V1 and its relation to perceptual completion. In *The visual system from genesis to maturity,* edited by R. Lent. Boston: Birkhäuser.

Gewirth, A. 1978. *Reason and morality.* Chicago: Chicago University Press.

Gilbert, C. D., and T. N. Wiesel. 1992. Receptive field dynamics in adult primary visual cortex. *Nature* 356:150–2.

Gilman, A. G., LS. Goodman, and A. Gilman, eds. 1990. Goodman and Gilman's *The pharmacological basis of therapeutics,* 8th ed. New York: Pergamon Press.

Glymour, C. 1992. Invasion of the mind snatchers. In *Cognitive models of science,* Minnnesota Studies in the Philosophy of Science, Vol. XV, edited by R. N. Giere. Minneapolis: University of Minnesota Press, 465–71.

Goldman, A. 1992. The Psychology of Folk Psychology. *Behavioral and Brain Sciences.*

Gordon, R. 1986. Folk psychology as simulation. *Mind & Language* 1, no. 2:

Gorman, R. P., and T. J. Sejnowski. 1988. Learned classification of sonar targets using a massively-parallel network. *IEEE Transactions: Acoustics, Speech, and Signal Processing* 36:1135–40.

Grice, H. P. 1957. Meaning. *Philosophical Review* 66:377–88.

Grush, R., and P. S. Churchland. 1995. Gaps in Penrose's toilings. *Journal of Consciousness Studies*, 2 (1995):10–29.

Haldane, J. 1988. Understanding folk. *Proceedings of the Aristotelian Society* 62(suppl.):223–54.

Hall, Z. D., ed. 1992. *An introduction to molecular biology*. Sunderland, Mass.: Sinauer.

Hameroff, S. R. 1994. Quantum coherence in microtubules: A neural basis for emergent consciousness? *Journal of Consciousness Studies* 1:98–118.

Hameroff, S. R., J. E. Dayhoff, R. Lahoz-Beltra, A. Samsonovich, and S. Rasmussen. 1992. Models for molecular computation: Conformational automata in the cytoskeleton. *IEEE Computer* (special issue on molecular computing):30–9.

Hameroff, S. R., S. Rasmussen, and B. Mansson. 1989. Molecular automata in microtubules: Basic computational logic for the living state? In *Artificial life: SFI studies in the sciences of complexity*, edited by C. Langton. New York: Addison-Wesley.

Hameroff, S. R., and R. C. Watt. 1982. Information processing in microtubules. *Journal of Theoretical Biology* 98:549–61.

Hannan, B. 1993. Don't stop believing: The case against eliminative materialism. *Mind & Language* 8:165–79.

Hanson, N. R. 1958. *Patterns of discovery*. Cambridge, U.K.: Cambridge University Press.

Hardin, C. L. 1988. *Color for philosophers: Unweaving the rainbow*. Indianapolis: Hackett.

Hesse, M. 1970. Is there an independent observation language? In *The nature and function of scientific theories*, edited by R. Colodny. Pittsburgh: Pittsburgh University Press.

Heyting, A. 1956. *Intuitionism: An introduction*. Amsterdam: North-Holland.

Hinton, G. E. 1989. Connectionist learning procedures. *Artificial Intelligence* 40:185–234.

Hobart, R. E. 1934. Free will as involving determinism and inconceivable without it. *Mind* 43:1–27.

Horgan, T., and J. Woodward. 1985. Folk psychology is here to stay. *Philosophical Review* 94:197–220.

Hornik, K., M. Stinchcombe, and H. White. 1989. Multi-layer feedforward networks are universal approximators. *Neural Networks* 2, no. 5:359–66.

Hubel, D. H., and M. S. Livingstone. 1987. Segregation of form, color, and stereopsis in primate area 18. *Journal of Neuroscience* 7:3378–415.

Hume, D. 1739/1888. *A Treatise of Human Nature*, edited by L. A. Selby-Bigge. Oxford: Oxford University Press.

Hurvich, L. M. 1981. *Color vision*. Sunderland, Mass.: Sinauer, 132.

Jackson, F. 1982. Epiphenomenal qualia. *Philosophical quarterly* 32, no. 127: 127–36.

Jackson, F. 1986. What Mary didn't know. *Journal of Philosophy* 83:291–5.

Jibu, M., S. Hagen, S. R. Hameroff, K. H. Pribram, and K. Yasue. 1994. Quantum optical coherence in cytoskeletal microtubules: Implications for brain function. *BioSystems* 32:195–209.

Johnson, M. 1993. *Moral imagination*. Chicago: Chicago University Press.

Jordan, M. I. 1989. Serial order: A parallel distributed processing approach. In *Advances in Connectionist Theory*, edited by J. Elman and D. Rumelhart. Hillsdale, N.J.: Erllbaum.

Kagan, J. 1994. *Galen's prophecy: Temperament in human nature*. New York: Basic Books.

Kant, I. 1797/1964. Fragments of a moral catechism. In *The metaphysical principles of virtue*. Translated by James Ellington. New York: Bobbs-Merrill, 148–53.

Kenny, A. J. P. 1989. *The metaphysics of mind*. Oxford: Clarendon Press.

Kitcher, P. W. 1984a. In defense of intentional psychology. *Journal of Philosophy* 71:89–106.

Kitcher, P. 1984b. *The nature of mathematical knowledge*. Oxford: Oxford University Press.

Kluver, H., and P. C. Bucy. 1937. "Psychic blindness" and other symptoms following bilateral temporal lobectomy in rhesus monkeys. *American Journal of Physiology* 119:352–7.

Kluver, H., and P. C. Bucy. 1938. An analysis of certain effects of bilateral temporal lobectomy in the rhesus monkey, with special reference to "psychic blindness." *Journal of Psychology* 5:33–54.

Kolasa, K., R. S. Jope, M. S. Baird, and G. V. Johnson. 1992. Alterations of choline acetyltransferase, phosphoinositide hydrolysis, and cytoskeletal proteins in rat brain in response to colchicine administration. *Experimental Brain Research* 89:496–500.

Krauskopf, J. 1963. Effect of the retinal image stabilization on the appearance of heterochromatic targets. *Journal of the Optical Society of America* 53:741.

Kuhn, T. S. 1962. *The structure of scientific revolutions*. Chicago: University of Chicago Press.

Laakso, A., and G. Cottrell. 1998. Qualia and cluster analysis: Assessing representational similarity between neural systems. Under review.

Lakatos, I. 1976. *Proofs and refutations*. Cambridge, U.K.: Cambridge University Press.

Land, E. 1977. The retinex theory of color vision. *Scientific American* (December):108–28.

Laymon, R. 1977. Feyerabend, Brownian motion, and the hiddenness of refuting facts. *Philosophy of Science* 44:225–47.

Lehky, S., and T. J. Sejnowski. 1988a. Computing shape from shading with a neural network model. In *Computational neuroscience*, edited by E. Schwartz. Cambridge, Mass.: The MIT Press.

Lehky, S., and T. J. Sejnowski. 1988b. Network model of shape-from-shading: Neural function arises from both receptive and projective fields. *Nature* 333: 452–4.

Leikind, B. J., and W. J. McCarthy. 1985. An investigation of firewalking. *The Skeptical Inquirer*, 10, no. 1:23–35.

Lewis, D. 1972. psychophysical and theoretical identifications. *Australasian Journal of Philosophy*, 50. Reprinted in Block, N., ed. 1980. *Readings in the philosophy of psychology*. Vol. 1. Cambridge, Mass.: Harvard University Press, 249–58.

Lewis, D. 1983. Postscript to "mad pain and Martian pain." In *Philosophical papers*. Vol. 1. Oxford: Oxford University Press.

Libet, B. 1985. Unconscious cerebral initiative and the role of conscious will in voluntary action. *The Behavioral and Brain Sciences* 8:529–66.

Lindsay, P. H., and D. A. Norman. 1972. *Human information processing*. New York: Academic Press.

Llinás, R., and D. Pare. 1993. Of dreaming and wakefulness. *Neuroscience* 44:521–35.

Llinás, R., and U. Ribary. 1993. Coherent 40-Hz oscillation characterizes dream state in humans. *Proceedings of the National Academy of Sciences* 90:2078–81.

Llinás, R., U. Ribary, M. Joliot, and X. J. Wang. 1994. Content and context in temporal thalamocortical binding. In *Temporal coding in the brain*, edited by G. Buzsaki. Berlin: Springer-Verlag,

Logothetis, N., and J. D. Schall. 1989. Neural correlates of subjective visual perception. *Science* 245:753–61.

MacLean, P. D. 1949. Psychosomatic disease and the "visceral brain." Recent developments on the Papez theory of emotion. *Psychosomatic Medicine* 11:338–53.

MacLean, P. D. 1952. Some psychiatric implications of physiological studies on frontotemporal portion of limbic system (visceral brain). *Electrophysiological and Clinical Neurophysiology* 4:407–18.

McCauley, R. N. 1993. Why the blind can't lead the blind: Dennett on the blind spot, blind sight, and sensory qualia. *Consciousness and Cognition* 2, no. 2:155–64.

McGinn, C. 1982. *The subjective view: Secondary qualities and indexical thoughts.* Oxford: Oxford University Press.

Mead, C. 1989. *Analog VLSI and neural systems.* Reading, Mass.: Addison-Wesley.

Mead, C., and M. Mahowald. 1991. The silicon retina. *Scientific American* 258.

Nagel, T. 1970. *The possibility of altruism.* Princeton, N.J.: Princeton University Press.

Nagel, T. 1974. What is it like to be a bat? *Philosophical Review* 83, no. 4:435–50.

Nemirow, L. 1980. Review of Thomas Nagel's *Mortal questions. Philosophical Review* 89:473–7.

Nicholls, J. G., A. R. Martin, and B. G. Wallace. 1992. *From neuron to brain.* Sunderland, Mass.: Sinauer.

Onada, G. Y., P. J. Steinhardt, D. P. DiVincenzo, and J. E. S. Socolar. 1988. Growing perfect quasicrystals. *Physical Review Letters* 60:2688.

Papez, J. W. 1937. A proposed mechanism of emotion. *Archives of Neurology and Psychiatry* 38:725–44.

Penrose, R. 1989. *The emperor's new mind.* Oxford: Oxford University Press.

Penrose, R. 1994a. Interview with Jane Clark. *Journal of Consciousness Studies* 1:17–24.

Penrose, R. 1994b. *Shadows of the mind.* Oxford: Oxford University Press.

Peters, A., S. L. Palay, and H. Webster. 1978. *The fine structure of the nervous system.* Philadelphia: W.B. Saunders.

Pettet, M. W., and C. D. Gilbert. 1991. Contextual stimuli influence receptive field size of single neurons in cat primary visual cortex. *Neuroscience Abstracts* 431:12.

Piantanida, T. P. 1985. Temporal modulation sensitivity of the blue mechanism: Measurements made with extraretinal chromatic adaptation. *Vision Research* 25:1439–44.

Piantanida, T. P., and J. Larimer. 1989. The impact of boundaries on color: Stabilized image studies. *Journal of Imaging Technology* 15:58–63.

Piercy, M. 1982. *Braided lives.* New York: Knopf.

Popper, K., and J. Eccles. 1978. *The self and its brain.* New York: Springer Verlag.

Putnam, H. 1960. Minds and machines. In *Dimensions of Mind,* edited by S. Hook. New York: New York University Press.

Putnam, H. 1988. *Representation and reality.* Cambridge, Mass.: The MIT Press.

Putnam, H. 1994. The best of all possible brains? Review of *Shadows of the mind, New York Times Book Review* November.

Quine, W. V. O. 1970. *Philosophy of logic*. Englewoods Cliffs, N.J.: Prentice-Hall.

Ramachandran, V. S. 1992. Blind spots. *Scientific American* 266:86–91.

Ramachandran, V. S. 1992. Filling in gaps in perception: Part I. *Current Directions in Psychological Science*. 2:199–205

Ramachandran, V. S. 1993. Filling in gaps in perception: Part II. *Current Directions in Psychological Science*. 3:56–65.

Ramachandran, V. S., and R. L. Gregory. 1991. Perceptual filling in of artificially induced scotomas in human vision. *Nature* 350:699–702.

Ramachandran, V. S., D. Rogers-Ramachandran, and H. Damasio. (forthcoming). Perceptual "filling in" of scotomas of cortical origin.

Randi, J. 1982. *Flim-flam! Psychics, ESP, unicorns, and other delusions*. Buffalo, N.Y.: Prometheus Books.

Rawls, J. 1971. *A theory of justice*. Cambridge, Mass.: Harvard University Press.

Rorty, R. 1965. Mind-body identity, privacy, and categories. *Review of Metaphysics* 1:

Rosenberg, C. R., and T. J. Sejnowski. 1987. Parallel networks that learn to pronounce English text. *Complex Systems* 1:145–68.

Rudder-Baker, L. 1987. *Saving belief: A critique of physicalism*. Princeton, N.J.: Princeton University Press.

Rumelhart, D. E., G. E. Hinton, and R. J. Williams. 1986a. Learning internal representations by error propagation. In *Parallel Distributed Processing: Explorations in the Microstructure of Cognition*. Vol. 1, edited by D. E. Rumelhart, J. L. McClelland, and the PDP Research Group. Cambridge, Mass.: The MIT Press, 318–62.

Rumelhart, D. E., G. E. Hinton, and R. J. Williams. 1986b. Learning representations by back-propagating errors. *Nature* 323.

Ryle, G. 1949. *The concept of mind*. New York: Barnes & Noble.

Sasajima, Y., K. Adachi, H. Tanaka, M. Ichimura, et al. 1994. Computer simulation of the growth process of binary quasicrystals. *Japanese Journal of Applied Physics* 33:2673–4.

Saver, J. L., and A. R. Damasio. 1991. Preserved access and processing of social knowledge in a patient with acquired sociopathy due to ventromedial frontal damage. *Neuropsychologia* 29:1241–9.

Schlick, M. 1939. When is a man responsible? In *Problems of Ethics*. Translated by D. Rynin. New York: Prentice-Hall, 143–56.

Searle, J. R. 1980a. Minds, brains, and programs. *Behavioral and Brain Sciences* 3:417–57.

Searle, J. R. 1980b. Intrinsic intentionality: Reply to criticisms of minds, brains, and programs. *Behavioral and Brain Sciences* 3:450–7.

Searle, J. R. 1983. *Intentionality: An essay in the philosophy of mind*. Cambridge, U.K.: Cambridge University Press.

Searle, J. R. 1990. Is the brain's mind a computer program? *Scientific American* 262, no. 1:26–7.

Searle, J. R. 1992. *The rediscovery of the mind*. Cambridge, Mass.: The MIT Press.

Searle, J. R. 1995. Review of Dennett, Edelman, and Rosenfield. *The New York Review of Books* 62, no. 18: 58.

Sellars, W. 1956. Empiricism and the philosophy of mind, edited by H. Feigl and M. Scriven. Vol. I of *Minnesota Studies in the Philosophy of Science*. Minneapolis, University of Minnesota Press. Reprinted in Sellars, W. 1963. *Science, perception and reality*. London: Routledge & Kegan Paul.

Sejnowski, T. J., P. K. Kienker, and G. E. Hinton. 1986. Learning symmetry groups with hidden units: Beyond the perceptron. *Physica D*, 22D:260–75.

Sossin, W. S., J. M. Fisher, and R. H. Scheller. 1989. Cellular and molecular biology of neuropeptide processing and packaging. *Neuron* 2:1407–17.

Spinoza, B. 1677. *Ethics*. In *The Collected Works of Spinoza*, edited by E. Curley. Princeton, N.J.: Princeton University Press.

Steriade, M., D. A. McCormick, and T. J. Sejnowski. 1993. Thalamicocortical oscillations in the sleeping and aroused brain. *Science* 262:679–85.

Stevens, C. F., and Y. Y. Wang. 1994. Changes in reliability of synaptic function as a mechanism for plasticity. *Nature* 371:704–7.

Stich, S. 1990. *The fragmentation of reason*. Cambridge, Mass.: The MIT Press.

Strawson, P. F. 1958. Persons. In *Concepts, theories, and the mind-body problem*, edited by H. Feigl, M. Scriven, and G. Maxwell. Vol. 2 of *Minnesota Studies in the Philosophy of Science*. Minneapolis: University of Minnesota Press, 330–5.

Taylor, C. 1970. Mind-body identity: A side issue? In *The Mind/Brain Identity Theory*, edited by C. V. Borst. Toronto: Macmillan, 231–41.

Taylor, C. 1987. Overcoming epistemology. In *After philosophy: End or transformation?*, edited by K. Baynes, J. Bohman, and T. McCarthy. Cambridge, Mass.: The MIT Press, 464–88.

Taylor, R. 1974. *Metaphysics*. Englewood Cliffs, N.J.: Prentice-Hall.

Turing, A. 1986. Lecture to the London Mathematical Society on 20 February 1947. In *A. M. Turing's ACE report of 1946 and other papers*, edited by B. E. Carpenter and R. W. Doran. Vol. 10 of the *Charles Babbage Institute Reprint Series for the History of Computing*. Cambridge, Mass.: The MIT Press.

Turing, A. M. 1950. Computing machinery and intelligence. *Mind* 59:433–60.

Van Essen, D. C., and C. H. Anderson. 1990. Information processing in primate vision. In *An Introduction to Neural and Electronic Networks*, edited by S. Zornetzer. San Diego: Academic Press.

Van Essen, D. C., and J. Maunsell. 1983. Hierarchical organization and functional streams in the visual cortex. *Trends in Neuroscience* 6:370–5.

Van Fraassen, B. 1980. *The scientific image.* Oxford: Oxford University Press.

de Waal, F. B. M. 1982. *Chimpanzee politics.* London: Allen & Unwin.

de Waal, F. B. M. 1989. Dominance "style" and primate social organization. *Comparative socioecology: The behavioral ecology of humans and other mammals,* edited by V. Standen and R. Foley. Oxford: Blackwell.

Wilkes, K. 1981. Functionalism, psychology, and the philosophy of mind. *Philosophical Topics* 12, no. 1:

Wilkes, K. 1984. Pragmatics in science and theory in common sense. *Inquiry* 27:339–61.

Wittrup, E. 1994. A mind with a heart of its own. Ph.D. diss. University of California, San Diego.

Zeki, S. 1980. The representation of colours in the cerebral cortex. *Nature* 284:412–8.

Index